D1631362

hlbc

7227

THE HIDDEN LIFE OF
THE BODY OF CHRIST

THE HIDDEN LIFE
OF THE
BODY OF CHRIST

BY

ERIC HAYMAN

THE FAITH PRESS
7 TUFTON STREET LONDON SW1

FIRST PUBLISHED IN 1963

© *Eric Hayman, 1963*

ST. AUGUSTINE'S COLLEGE

LIBRARY

CANTERBURY

PRINTED IN GREAT BRITAIN
in 10 point Garamond type
BY THE FAITH PRESS LTD.
LEIGHTON BUZZARD

FOR
1889   I.M.H.   1932

CONTENTS

INTRODUCTION

THIS book is about the Contemplative Way in Christian spiritual life. That statement excludes many aspects of Christian faith and practice—notably those for which the Church is usually best known by those outside her fellowship—those for which she is commended or even admired, so long as the admirer can remain quite uncommitted to any action. 'Contemplative,' however, is a word that is hedged by suspicion and misunderstanding. By the world, knowing little or nothing of that which it judges, contemplation is held to be a waste of time, of energy, or of potentiality. The Church is always liable to come under judgment from the 'good pagan.' Her acts of charity and compassion may be held to her credit. The outsider will think of St. Francis and of St. Vincent de Paul. The great contemplatives are by comparison unknown, or are suspect as emotional hysterics. Where it is allowed, even with regret, that a special religious vocation is often given to those who must take their religion seriously, it is preferred that they should show their fervour by intense activity. The contemplative way, and the element of withdrawal and enclosure which accompanies it, is despised as self-regarding escape.

Despite this fact, however, it is still a common phenomenon, in a world torn apart by wars and by social revolution, that remedies are presented to assist an escape from the realm of turmoil, or as a means of mastery. To the exponents of these remedies Christian tradition is merely pathetic. 'Everything you can do the East can do better.' They are convinced, for example, in their enthusiasm for the Vedantist revival, that the Mahayana school of Buddhism, and particularly the Zen-Buddhist form of mind-training, offers a spiritual way far superior to Christian doctrine or practice. Such ideas are dangerous, and by no means at their end, but this book is concerned with the realities of the Contemplative Way and not with its imitations. It is not here our purpose to analyse or criticize substitutes for religion. We are concerned to trace and to show forth the insistent trend to 'mean God and none of His goods' which appears as a hidden life-stream over centuries of spiritual history both before and after the Incarnation.

A third line of attack upon the contemplative comes from within the family of the Church, within the Catholic obedience, and often within the formal Religious Life itself. The life of the Christian, it is rightly urged, is inseparable from the Body of Christ. Christian devotion has its own language and its own means of expression. The liturgical, and above all the sacramental, path has been clearly sign-posted. Prayer and worship are inseparable from the Catholic dogma which has surrounded them from the earliest days. The prayer of the Contemplative is feared as an unpredictable thing, uncontrollable by authority. Above all it is suspect of the dreadful nightmare of 'Mysticism.' That term has only to enter discussion in some Church circles to raise the darkest fears. 'What is this thing? What does it do and what does it mean? We do not know, and it is safer not to inquire. Let it be anathema.'

This fear seems strange when one considers the long roll of contemplatives who have been beatified or canonized by the Church over many centuries. It might surely be assumed that the company of St. Teresa of Jesus and St. John of the Cross—of St. Bernard of Clairvaux and St. Bruno—of St. Anthony and St. Romuald—was sufficient passport to orthodoxy. The fact that St. Benedict established the liturgical office in choir as the main occupation and purpose of his Order, and found in that absorbing work the true *Opus Dei,* offers no possible criticism of the Contemplative Way. His successors rightly claim their holy father as a true contemplative; and the same valuation of the Divine Office is made by the Cistercian Order, as well as in Charterhouse and Carmel.

But the problem may be taken out of the specialized setting of the Religious Life and found in the secular Church, where it is not confined to the Catholic tradition. An illuminating instance arose during the preparation for the Third World Conference on Faith and Order at Lund in 1952. A liturgical commission, largely composed of Lutheran and Reformed scholars, had taken keen interest in the liturgical revival which was beginning to restore the traditional worship of the Catholic world to Lutheran Germany. At a later stage the same Commission had also accepted a new approach to ecumenical discussion by interchange of experience and practice in the field of devotion and of ascetic theology. These matters are still largely unknown to Continental Protestantism, and some German liturgists were deeply troubled by what they imagined to be a threat to their newly-ordered worship from any emphasis on devotional practice. There is in fact no reason for the liturgist to fear the contemplative; still less may the contemplative ever undervalue the Church's liturgy; it is in fact impossible for him to do so while his spiritual life is nurtured so largely on the Psalter. But reason for such fears has been freely imagined even where it cannot exist.

It is specially interesting to see a parallel objection to Jewish mysticism common in Jewish liturgical circles. In the history of Jewish spirituality there are living contacts with the main stream of Christian experience in prayer, and these will be studied in later chapters. For the moment it is sufficient to note that Jewish tradition and Jewish liturgiology have often been more acutely suspicious of Jewish mysticism than have Christians regarding their own similar fears. It is of course obvious that the legalistic stresses inherent in Judaism might be expected to react more violently from the rise of the contemplative way in their midst. Some of the aberrations of Jewish mysticism, moreover, have been far more dangerous in their Gnostic emphasis than almost anything in Christian history. They have erred in precisely the same seemingly perennial direction which marks the pseudo-religious experimenting of the neo-Vedantist. They deserve condemnation as heresy, not merely in Christian terms, but in terms of the doctrine of the Eternal God which is common alike to Judaism and to its Christian fulfilment. At certain periods Jewish mysticism has undoubtedly presented a greater danger to Jewish Orthodoxy than Christianity has itself suffered from similar causes. A passing historical observation may record that Sabbatai Zevi, whose erratic Messianism will be noted later, was a contemporary of the Quaker James Nayler in England. The parallel is suggestive, since both cases illustrate the perils of an unbalanced mysticism. Both fall into the widespread confusion between a true *contact* with God and the illusion of *identity*. Both these men created or permitted a veneration for themselves as beings far nearer than others to the divine sphere. It will be seen in the course of this study how deeply the excesses of such pseudo-Messianism hindered true valuation of the finest elements in Hasidic spirituality in later years.

What was termed 'the truth of the contemplative way' must be seen in Jewish as well as in Christian terms, and in so doing we are reminded of a long Catholic tradition which traces the Church's birth to the obedience of Abraham, and to the consequent promised destiny of the holy people.

'There is one Church and only one—the Church of Abraham and his seed —there never has been and never will be any other. . . . The Jewish Church and the Christian Church are one; the Jewish Church was ever intended to become Catholic, and the Catholic Church is nothing but the Jewish Church come to its full stature.' [1]

These brief references to three lines of initial difficulty raised by the presentation of the Contemplative Way have been made solely in order to reassure those who might distrust the book from the outset because it deals with an outlook and a way of life from which they are averse by instinctive prejudice. The book is the work of an Anglican contemplative who, though he is not bound to seek an *imprimatur*, would still reject willingly any approach to the subject which was not rooted in Catholic faith and practice; or any consequent life which was not in accord with the discipline and authority of Holy Church. Doubtless this avowal will merely prove a strong deterrent to another type of reader—those for whom the hope of 'mysticism' sugars the pill of discipline. The book was written within an Anglican Contemplative Community, but it is in no way limited to the Religious life, and may be of some small use to people in the world, if they discover in it some of the less familiar ways by which God has drawn others to Himself.

E.H.

The Monastery of C.S.W.G.
Crawley Down
Sussex
  August 1958

St. Gregory's Priory
Three Rivers
Michigan, U.S.A.
  June 1961

ACKNOWLEDGMENTS

THANKS are due to the following for permission to make quotations : to Burns, Oates Ltd for extracts from *The Complete Works of St. John of the Cross,* edited by Allison Peers; to Sheed and Ward Ltd, for extracts from *The Complete Works of St. Teresa of Jesus,* edited by Allison Peers; and to Schocken Books Inc., New York, for extracts from *Major Trends in Jewish Mysticism* by Gershom G. Scholem; and from *Tales of the Hasidim,* by Martin Buber; also to Peter Davis Ltd for extracts from *The Psalter and the Life of Prayer* by Annie H. Small. These and all other quotations are specifically acknowledged on pp. 219–23 of this book. I hope that the authors concerned will accept thanks for their help, and forgive any unwitting breach of copyright.

E.H.

PART I

CHAPTER ONE

THE PURPOSE OF GOD
IN A PERFECTED HUMANITY

THE foundation of the Christian faith rests on the Church's belief in one God, Father, Son and Holy Spirit. As she stands always on the outskirts of the mystery of the Blessed Trinity, the Church finds herself contemplating it in two aspects—a perfection of Being and a perfection of Unity. These are concepts shared, in part at least and with varying understanding, by two other great religious families. Christianity derives directly from the heritage of Judaism. Judaism suffered in turn a drastic Reformation seven centuries later from Islam. There is one essential common to all. They reverence the reality of the Divine Being, and assert (if in different tones of faith) the perfection of the Unity. For them all there is a profound faith and an exaltation of worship. 'Hear, O Israel, the Lord our God is one Lord; and thou shalt love the Lord thy God with all thy soul and with all thy might.' Against the background of the *Shema* is heard a sterner note in the daily cry of the Muezzin. 'Allah is One: there is no God but Allah.' No memory of a cruel story of persecution and war can ignore the intense and daily discipline of devotion from men who may not hear the call with their outward ears.

So far the ways might appear to coincide. But the Christian is enabled through Revelation to see in that Unity a wealth of meaning which neither his predecessors in Judaism nor his successors in Islam have realized. The reality of Being itself is enriched : the wholeness of Unity remains in a far greater wonder. To the mystery of Being there is added the mystery and pattern of Relationship. For the Christian as for his forbears in the desert the burden of life on earth could be eased, and his path lightened by reflecting upon Supreme being. He could share with them the disclosure of the Divine Compassion. 'I will make all my goodness pass before thee.' The thought of a Divine regard for the creature : the knowledge that he was not a cypher in a dark world, but the object of an everlasting mercy—all this is a treasure shared with centuries of Judaism. But now the Unity has disclosed itself fully, though our understanding of the mystery remains but partial. He begins to know its richness because of its diversity—never losing sight of the undivided Godhead nor blurring the clear outlines of separateness. Alike in the ascended Lord and in the companionship of the Holy Spirit he learns the glory of the Father. In each Divine Person he learns to see the wholeness of the Divine Society. This conviction comes slowly through varying and simple personal experience, without necessarily being founded on the technicalities of 'circumincession.' For the Christian this last wonder is perhaps the most compelling, the most adorable truth. For all his problems in the human world are problems of relationship, and human relationships too often lack the binding mystery of Unity. Where it is known, it is too often at the cost of true relationship. Separateness overwhelms him. His relationships are precarious, subject to change of mood or of potential, if not indeed to rivalry and intrigue. He longs deeply for a living unity, yet in sheer frustration and disappointment is driven back to separateness. Such imperfections of human society show by sheer contrast the inherent unity of relationship within the Divine Society of the Blessed Trinity. Man's separateness must for ever baffle him. The longing to preserve himself—to safeguard his own privacy—foredooms him to miss the truly personal corporate life in which alone his fulfilment is intended. The one condition upon which his human life can make sense is out of his reach. It can only be given to him—never attained by him. And that—just that—is God's meaning. To the Lady Julian of Norwich in her solitude it was made clear that 'Love is His meaning.' *Agape*—the fullness of the relationships within the Divine Society—is also the completeness of the relationship between man and God. It is further the basis of all relationships within the Body of Christ, where we 'know one another in that which is Eternal.' It can be commanded against the impulses of natural desire or natural aversion, because its motive is always in the dedicated life. It is that coinherence through which man's personal fulfilment is found only in the corporate personality of the Church.

We ask in this opening chapter concerning God's purpose in a perfected humanity. We look behind the purpose of Redemption to the purpose of Creation itself. In so doing there is no stopping-place between the silence of unknowing, and a child's attempt to speak of something it can never know. But the attempt must be made. It will be justified not by its achievement, but by learning something more of the hidden wholeness for which man has sought and ever seeks. For as we come to see, through the mystery of the Divine Being, the added mystery of relationship within the Blessed Trinity, there is a sense of utter completeness. The Divine necessity which binds each Person to the other Persons, each holding in Himself the fullness of the whole, each receiving everything while needing nothing—each utterly complete and yet longing for completion in each Other—that

Divine necessity can need no added good. Any heretical separation of the Three Persons, clouding the Unity as if for a logical dissection of the fullness of one, leads at once to absurdity—to the paradox of one Person longing with Divine envy for enjoyment of the gifts which mark another not Himself. Those who are deeply concerned in the furtherance of the union of Christendom may reflect that at this point some fall into the cold chill of Unitarianism; others lose their balance in excessive Christo-centric devotion; or others again adopt a conception of the Holy Spirit which makes of the Holy Name of God a synonym for the arrogance of subjective private judgment. This whole gamut of heresy may stem from so simple, and common, an error of well-intentioned Christian judgment. The basic loneliness which colours the journals of 'Mark Rutherford': the poetic enthusiasm of Charles Wesley's hymns, and the confident independence in which George Fox can write 'Ask not what Peter and Paul say—what can *thou* say'— all these have qualities which might enrich the whole, but can only lead to the decay of the sectarian part. Just as this nightmare would be rejected before it could be dreamed, so we look also at the familiar notion that Creation was demanded by the loneliness of God. A Celtic poet has used words of great beauty here:

> 'Like God, who in divine distress,
> Grew tired of awful loneliness;
> And flung His arm o'er vibrant space,
> And pluck'd the strings of time and place,
> And broke His uttermost repose
> With song that through Creation goes;
> The song of sweet imperfect things,
> That murmurs through my seven strings.' [2]

Yet in the Divine Will of the Blessed Trinity the act of self-expression was contained. We can conceive it only from the conditions of Time and Succession. Yet it must be true before Time had been ordained— before succession could, in consequence, be experienced by men. 'Whatsoever the Lord pleased, that did he' (Ps. 135 : 6). Our Creation was surely inherent in the perfect being of God. It could not have been a passing idea within an unchanging Being. And so we affirm that He who in Himself was possessed of all, and who found His perfect joy in the interplay of Wisdom, Love and Power within His all-sufficient Divine Society, gave expression to the Will which is Himself. He caused Time to be; within its framework He established His spiritual and His physical creation—the angelic world and the material world—and in the setting so prepared He made man, who Himself in the fullness of Time would be made Man. In token of the

17

supernatural perfection in which he was made, man is established in a relationship—in a coinherence. 'It is not good that the man should be alone' (Gen. 2 : 18). He is to share, according to his measure, in the mystery of relationship. The intended perfection of the relationship of Man and Woman, becoming in one another one flesh, has an infinite range of possibility for human understanding of the unity within the Divine Being in the Divine Will. Likewise, in another aspect of the same truth, the perfect unity of Will between the Incarnate Lord and the Father is the archetype of the spiritual union with Himself which the Lord commands to those who love Him. Though man be made after the likeness of God and in His Image, he cannot receive the mystery of the Divine Being. That mystery is complete and incommunicable. Creation may be conceived as an extension of the Divine Being, though never as an addition to its perfection. But the mystery of relationship—the inner life of the Divine Society—is the intended pattern. It is not the goal of an evolutionary process—something into which an embryo humanity is destined to expand. It is the pattern of man's making—the clue to his being. And in the communication of that mystery the perfection of Godhead is extended to the creation. The perfection is neither diminished within the Divine Society, nor is it increased. The coinherence of the Divine Persons in their unity is eternal and changeless. But the Wisdom, the Love and the Power which so move within the Blessed Trinity are extended into the new order of relationship—an order which once did not exist save in the Divine Mind, but now is made to be—an order dependent wholly and continually upon the Divine Will.

Such a self-expression of the Godhead could never be cut off from its origin by the Will of God. The gift is not unconditional. It is conditioned by freedom. The knowledge of relationship conveyed to the Adam has no meaning save as it is a permitted participation in the Divine Unity. The gift depends on the acknowledgment—as in the physical world the flow of electrical energy depends on its return to the source through an unbroken circuit. The gift depends upon the fitting response, which is in fact the exercise of the gift. It depends upon complete correspondence in grace. The Adam are not God. The work committed to them remains His work, conditioned likewise by their freedom of response. In their being and their doing one thing only can make sense—a correspondence of wills in perfect obedience. Such a correspondence of wills implies a perfect knowledge of the pattern Will, and this implies a perfect contemplation of God, on which alone sure knowledge can rest. When we have looked at Him for ever, we may begin to touch the outskirts of His ways, and to interpret 'the whisper that we hear of him' (Job 26 : 14). 'But then face to face. Then shall I understand as all along I have been understood' (1 Cor. 13 : 12). This longing

'is something that all men who desire to please God ought to desire for ever. It is in these souls that peace is established in the world. They are the strength of the world, because they are the tabernacles of God in the world. They are the ones who keep the universe from being destroyed.' [3]

The gift could have no meaning apart from a response of this precise quality. The gift was of God, and so was good in all its bearings. On no other assumption could the overflow of the Divine mystery have been conceived. But on that assumption and with that obedience the pattern was complete, and God saw that it was very good. In that precise assumption we find the hidden secret of the Contemplative Way. There rests the whole purpose of this study, and any significance it may be judged to possess. This prayer of the Contemplative is just the opening of his entire being in the stillness of utter obedience—a stillness which is supreme action.

The fact of obedience involves the acceptance of this limitation. There is no loss of freedom in such acceptance, for there is no freedom, but only the chaos of anarchy, when men traverse the accepted limits of their own holding and covet their neighbour's estate. If that be obviously so in human affairs, it is more so by far when the limits of man's estate guard him from trespass into a different order of being. A law of coinherence, given and defined, held man within his given estate. He shared the mystery of relationship, but he could not share the mystery of Being. One measure of the Divine joy was allowed to him, because it was fitting to his creaturely condition. He was allowed the perfect Law of Fellowship, which must yet be exercised 'in the pattern of the Mount' (Heb. 8 : 5) if it is to be known as joy, and not as a seed-bed of strife and jealousy. In that exercise, wide knowledge was opened to him—a knowledge which could expand in the course of its proper use, and could develop and adapt itself to all his proper need. It was knowledge measured to his own being, and to his function in the Mind of the Creator. But the picture of revelation shows that there was, at any rate, one field of knowledge proper to God alone. This knowledge is presented as being the knowledge of good and evil, which knowledge might lead not merely to a choice of evil, but to a choice of the forbidden good.

A modern analogy may be interposed here without breaking the sequence, for it lies heavily on all Christian minds to-day. In the distant but ever-present light of man's primal choice one is disposed to question seriously whether the invasion of the atomic structure, and the consequent ever-expanding vistas of power, may not likewise be a choice of the forbidden good. What is disclosed is what God has made, and it is therefore good. But God uses what He has made in His own way, which is not the wrecking and obliteration of human beings made in His special image. If men still claim that the good achieved is justified by the achievement, it would mean that they also claim to be as God, knowing good and evil. Let them first reflect that the Divinity they covet has also the quality of discriminating between good and evil. The knowledge is forbidden to those incapable of such discrimination.

'The Adam had been created and were existing in a state of knowledge of good and nothing but good. They knew that there was some kind of alternative, and they knew that the rejection of that alternative was part of their relation to the Omnipotence that created them. That relation was part of the good they enjoyed.' 4

The accepted limit was violated. The primal trespass from the estate of a given perfection was deliberately willed against the known will of God. The first loss of obedience shattered the stillness of the union through which as in a mirror man might contemplate the flawless perfection of the Mind of God. It was but the reflection that he could see, even as the astronomer observes only the reflection from his vast telescope, unable to look directly upon the brightness it receives. It was never the actuality. But in the stillness of contemplative obedience nothing could enter to distort the image. By the withdrawal of that guardian obedience, the joy for which man had been made was brought to an end. The remote descendants of the Adam in modern times choose to pretend that they had lost only some super-added quality—some *tour de force* in their being, doubtless good to have received, but not indispensable to a full human development, since the race had manifestly survived, much had been accomplished, and much more awaited accomplishment. Only in Pelagian complacency can that device be sustained. We do not need a morbid exaggeration of St. Augustine's teaching to reject entirely the thought of a temporary and local lapse— the frustration of an experiment which had shown promise. The purpose of the Adam's making no longer existed. The human race they were still destined to found—for perverted powers were still realities— could not of itself regain its course in joyful union with the Creator. The Adam were driven from the Paradise of the Divine joy, and became the cause of the Divine regret. The disobedience shattered the stillness of their intended life, and its clanging echoes still disturb the earth which is our home. The one act of the Adam—so careless of their deed —so convinced that the enhancement of their glory was self-sufficient, and needed no external stay—has meant that all who succeed them inherit the resultant confusion, and come to assume that their own efforts to restore and reorder that confusion are all-important. From the stillness of obedience we have passed to the clamour of programmes. The passage is swift and desperate from the contemplation of Eternal Spirit to the urge which would evolve more and more complex transient Matter. The process develops its own automatism. The dulled sensitivity of mankind can no longer be offended. We do not understand, and have no longer a criterion from which to learn, what we have lost.

There is in this primal disobedience no simple mistake which can be observed, isolated, neutralized, and in future avoided by experience. Something irreplaceable by any will of man has been destroyed. It was unique, though it should and could have appeared in countless exemplars. The principle of the total acceptance and instinctive adoration of all which the majesty of God has presented as the setting of our lives—that inevitability of joy has been discarded. In one of Charles Williams' most searching parables a modern Lilith tries to lure a modern Eve from her given joy.

> 'Every one wants something—tell me what you want.' . . . 'But I don't. You can't think how I don't. How could I want anything but what is?' [5]

In that moment when obedience was thrown away for the sake of an imagined good beyond the known Will of God, the Body of Christ which was to be, and which existed already in its fullness in the mind of God, was robbed of the wholeness of its hidden life. It was made the victim of a choice of externality—of curious change and shifting desires. It is not difficult to see that false choice as single, as personal, as unique—and as eternal. And we who read, and we who write that fact know that it is true—'most native and our own.' Prof. C. S. Lewis has shown the same pattern in a tale of present day marital relationship :

> 'You do not fail in obedience through lack of love, but have lost love because you never attempted obedience. . . . No one has ever told you that obedience—humility—is an erotic necessity. You are putting equality just where it ought not to be.' [6]

To the Christian intercessor, bearing as he does the weight of what was so done, it must seem that any desire for equality with God is unthinkable. But he has watched the self-emptying of his Incarnate Lord. He has seen the very God subject of his own perfect will to his own perfect obedience. He has watched, in later generations of the blessed, those who have dared to speak even of the spiritual marriage of the soul and the Bridegroom, and whose one cry has always been :

'Have humility, and again humility. It is by humility that the Lord allows Himself to be conquered, so that He will do all that we ask of Him.' [7]

Again, those whose mind and soul have been preoccupied by the miracle of Love into which they are being brought, can never forget the same consummate example :

'Fix your eyes on the Crucified, and nothing else will be of much importance to you. . . . Do you know when people really become spiritual? It is when they become the slaves of God and are branded with His sign. . . . Then He can sell them as slaves to the whole world, as He Himself was sold.' [8]

There is here no deprivation of the powers of the soul. All are enhanced, so that the soul is brought into an increasing realization of God's purposes and of His present wish. It is the knowledge of activity, of the present work of the Body of Christ in the world. Thus it should be unthinkable that the soul could desire any state other than that to which God has brought it. The gift of Paradise was indeed the perfection of relationship. Its echo sounds in the Eternal promise that 'where I am there shall also my servant be' (John 12 : 26). Therefore is obedience the secret of the hidden life of the Body.

CHAPTER TWO

THE PREPARING OF THE REDEMPTION

IN the moment of Man's first disobedience the foreseen Redemption comes into play. The more commonly accepted theology of the Incarnation can tend to suggest centuries of unsuccessful human progress in the learning of the Will of God, with a final and almost desperate Divine resort in remedy. The Incarnation of the Word is a deed of love and caring too perfect to be so misunderstood.

> 'The Incarnation of Christ was not foreseen as a contingent event, but was seen by God directly as an end from eternity. So Christ, in His human nature, since He is nearer to the end than other things, was predestined before them.' [9]

The Church permits the two ways of thought, without insisting upon one as against the other. She has always in mind the parable of the husbandmen and the Heir, attested by all three Synoptic Gospels in the same context. The context was actual and immediate. Our Lord was not here enunciating theology, but commenting upon current events to those who could not fail to see the force of His comment. The Son comes as the last and greatest of a line of representatives, through whom the Father is claiming a harvest overdue to His care and forethought. But He is not an afterthought. In all His servants He has been coming all the time, until they could do no more. The story is perfect in its place. It does not need to be regarded as defining the manner of the Incarnation. St. Thomas Aquinas writes :

> 'We say that the Son is sent by the Father into the world, because He proceeds from the Father, and is newly born visibly into the world, although He was there already: He was in the world, and the world was made by Him, and the world knew Him not.' [10]

The Divine Will that the sufficient love which binds the Blessed Trinity should overflow into the natural creation, carries as its consequence a Will to the perfection of His purpose. What fails of fulfilment in one setting will emerge in another. The Church makes this petition in the Versicle and Respond following the antiphon *Salve Regina*: 'Pray for us, O holy Mother of God, that we may be made worthy of the promises of Christ.' This is evidence of human longing to respond more truly to the Divine Will of her Son. The response must be seen in our own circumstances, and in our particular vocation. But behind such a limited view we know that the Beatitudes promised by the Word of God are the continual echo of a purpose and an intention which is the whole meaning of Creation. They define the goal to which a perfected humanity must be brought as a consequence of its perfection in His sight. The pure in heart are blessed because they are going to see God. That is the consequence of their purification, and therefore the purpose of God for all men. Would He desire to make beings in which He can never rejoice? 'The glory of God is a living man, and the life of man is the vision of God.' [11] So in the moment of the first assertion of pride—the first choice of the forbidden good— the foreseen Redemption has already begun. The cruel disobedience of earth strikes as a wound within the perfect obedience of heaven : there can be no other response from the Divine compassion but the placing of Love Himself in the lovelessness; the overwhelming of rebellion by the perfect obedience of the Son of God. If our sorry history can now look out upon its world and see indeed little beyond the vain assertion of human self-will—careless to the depth of ignorance of any realization of its doom—the eternal intention of Redeeming Love is still unvaried. Consequently we have a right and a duty to seek behind the declining years of our own twentieth century, and look back over the signs of its appearing. In so doing there is no attempt to escape from current realities. The nostalgia which adds to the world's backward look has no relation to the eternal *now* which is God's meaning for His chosen. Where we are able to find in history the marks of the emergence of the hidden life, it is not in order that we may hark back to the imitation of things that are past. To do so would be to miss the essential of any response that men have made to some existential moment that confronted them in their own lives and in their own setting. The setting cannot be restaged. We are not those people, and their place and manner of life are not our own. Yet apart from the discovery of successive moments of response, there is a common character which informs them all and enables their recognition. From the first rejection of the Divine intention until the Incarnate Word was conceived by the Holy Ghost in the womb of the Blessed Virgin Mary, the world had waited for an answer to the problem which human disobedience had posed. The true drama begins from the first obedience of Abram to the destiny shown to him. 'He went out not knowing whither he went' (Heb. 11 : 8). Out of each such obedience the foreseen Redemption is slowly prepared, and no surrounding disobedience can deflect the single intention of response. There can be 'no variableness, neither shadow of turning' (Jas. 1 : 17).

When, however, we read the history in the normal sequence of its unfolding, it is never easy to escape the illusion of spiritual evolution. The Fall, it will be argued, may have been a serious set-back, but every day and in every way we grow better and better. In each epoch of history men rise to a truer appreciation of the purpose of God and become more malleable to it. This is proved when at last the race can produce one who was called the Son of God. Such crude self-confidence may in fact be rare in modern days, but it is (or was) the temper of Liberal piety. Yet to say this is not to avoid it. We should not look back to irrecoverable past ages. We cannot in the modern world look forward with any facile optimism, as we watch the nemesis of human folly closing in upon us. But we can try to realize effectively the sole source of our being and doing. Man was created primarily, and now the process has reached to us. But Christian man is created anew in his Lord, 'for in him were all things created in the heaven and upon the earth, things visible and things invisible, whether thrones, or dominions, or principalities or powers—all things have been created through him and unto him : and he is before all things, and in him all things have their coinherence' (Col. 1 : 16–17). 'Beloved, now are we the sons of God' (1 John 3 : 2).

We have thought thus far of God's purpose in a perfected humanity. Since it is God's eternal purpose, ever-present in the Timeless Being, it is indefeasible. Mankind redeemed in Christ and sanctified in the Holy Spirit is still meant for transforming union with the Blessed Trinity. Even at this stage there must be in human history traces of the response which has made this transforming union a reality. Further, and more obvious, there are traces of a measure of union with God in souls who knew some measure of that supreme grace while they still lived on earth. Some of these the Church has named as saints. Their true number is known only to God.

As we consider these fellow-servants of ours, we give them honour and gratitude; we are moved to remember them in profound relationship; we invoke confidently their prayers and their aid. When we most know our own frailty in some particular, there will be one among them notably triumphant at that very point. When we are most conscious of our weakness in the massed pressure of the underworld, we rejoice in the numberless company of all saints, and in their midst find ourselves swept into the whole company of heaven. But these too are our fellow servants. Whatever we do in truest devotion, we do not adore (cf. Rev. 19 : 10).

Here the humanity of the Divine Word stands unique in all history. When the Godhead was veiled in flesh, the human mind and the human soul showed to men the unqualified perfection of Divine Being in terms of human conditions. The Incarnate Word is the beginning and the ending of all history. He is a peak towards which all before Him in Time ascends and strives. He is a watershed sending the living stream of an eternal well-spring back into all history before His coming, and forward into all history after His return in glory to the Father's side. The humanity of the Incarnate Word is here stressed. We are dealing with sublime truth, but that Word was made flesh, and entered a factual and historical sequence. And it is with that sequence that we deal, however it may be enflamed by the blaze of Eternity. There is a significant point to be observed in the Gospel of the Infancy. St. Matthew, with admirable purpose, begins the generation of Jesus Christ with an astonishing telescoping of history. He is presented as 'the Son of David, the son of Abraham' (Matt. 1 : 1). But then the Evangelist begins again more soberly from the said Abraham, and in fifteen verses climbs back through history to 'Joseph the husband of Mary, of whom was born Jesus' (Matt. 1 : 16). St. Luke, however, seems to have decided that the normal historical sequence is misleading for his purpose. He tells his primary reader that 'it seemed good to me also, having traced the course of all things accurately from the first, to write unto thee *in order,* most excellent Theophilus, that thou mightest know the certainty concerning the things wherein thou wast instructed' (Luke 1 : 3–4). St. Luke then proceeds to give a fresh genealogy in its spiritually logical order—the order which St. Matthew abandoned after one verse. St. Luke knows at any rate that the entropy of the time-scale in physics can be a misleading truth in the spiritual world. Whether as beginning (in the case of St. Luke) or as climax (in that of St. Matthew) we reach in the person of the mother of God the crucial moment of our study. Through her obedience all Redemption came into being. Such a potency of acceptance—such unwavering contemplation of the Divine demand upon her—can alone explain the proportion of the result. If it were possible to write adequately of the spiritual wonder of her life, the theme of this particular study would be unbalanced. But the statement of that theme must begin in the key of her obedience. Poetic licence often conceals inevitable truth. In this then she has been named by some writers, and hailed at times in the Church, as co-Redemptrix.

> 'Jewish thought was always directed towards the future. In the history of the past it sought an image of that which had not yet happened. Given a particular event, it would travel back over the stages that had prepared for it, traversing the chain of ages backwards. . . . But if this was the way of . . . the Israelite mystics, it was with all the more reason that of Mary also, for she was in possession of the definitive event. The whole Judaic time-scheme reached its climax in her; so did the time scheme of Abraham, the time scheme of Adam. . . . In her, the time before Christ arrived at its own source.'

As we have seen in the two gospel genealogies, the one processive, the other recessive, so

> 'one may think of Mary going backwards in the same way, passing beyond David, Messiah's royal ancestor, and so reaching Abraham, and beyond him Adam. . . . She ran through the whole chain of history in her mind; she saw its movement, all leading up to her own consent and the un-moved movement of the Divine thought, whereby God, having willed her to be the mother of Christ, conceived her as such and prepared her for this very end. She saw herself pre-existing in the eternal thought.' [12]

In this conviction the Church gives as her teaching-lesson in the Mass of the Nativity of the Blessed Virgin the passage from the Book of Proverbs :

> 'The Lord possessed me in the beginning of his way,
> Before his works of old.
> I was set up from everlasting, from the beginning.
> Or ever the earth was. . . .
>
> 'Before the hills was I brought forth :
> While as yet he had not made the earth, nor the fields,
> Nor the beginning of the dust of the world.
> When he established the heavens, I was there. . . .
>
> 'When he marked out the foundations of the earth :
> Then I was by him as a master-workman;
> And I was daily his delight,
> Playing always before him' (Prov. 8 : 22–30).

Living in this kaleidoscope of historical perspective, Mary knows the great event to which she is consenting, not only in its future con-sequences, but in its transforming effect on long past ages. The Church has honoured her in the beautiful hymn—*Ave Maris Stella:*

> 'Ave thou receivest,
> Gabriel's word believest,
> Change to peace and gladness
> Eva's name of sadness.'

Not yet does she know the full significance of her Magnificat, though in another sense she knows the whole in the first moment of accep-tance. In every way she is the great Reversal of human failure.

> 'Adam fell in Paradise, and with him all human nature. For he loved himself inordinately with a natural love, and therefore he turned himself away from God and in his pride despised God's commandment. And in his avarice he desired skill and wisdom, and in his gluttony he sought savour and delight, and through this he was stirred to lechery. But Mary was a living Paradise. She found again the grace that Adam lost, and much

27

more than he lost, for she is the mother of love. In charity she turned herself in her works towards God, and in humility she conceived Christ. and in mildness she offered him with all his sufferings to the Father. And she had no gluttonous savour of any consolation or of any of God's gifts. And all her life was led in purity. Whosoever follows her overcomes all that is contrary to virtue, and comes to that kingdom where she with her Son reigns eternally.' [13]

Without paradox we can speak of her as the source of a stream which reaches its destiny in herself. Before the Lord had entered the world in the human being He received from her, the new deed of Godhead had been wrought. That deed was to turn back the tide of sin; its scale outmeasured everything in human conceiving. But the very means must have appeared to be a violation of the life on which she had entered—of the normal hope and expectation of her betrothal and her coming marriage. On every level it would seem incomprehensible, and it is difficult for comment to overstate the issue.

'Never perhaps in heaven or earth had there been any moment like this. . . . This is the keystone of the arch in all the shifting architecture of time. This is the moment upon which all depends.' [14]

The quality of Mary's response to the Announcer is devoid of all self-awareness. It is an unconscious holocaust : nothing else would have seemed possible to her. The deed of God is not presented for argument, and yet no part of the Eternal purpose can ever have required so clearly the freedom of human consent. There is no compulsion, yet there is inevitability. 'Be it unto me according to thy word.' In that quality and manner of response there is shown to men their true relationship to the eternal purpose. The pulse of the hidden life is felt beyond mistaking, and wherever that pulse is felt the same vital stream is flowing. Whatever the actual times and conditions the question always comes from beyond Time. Everything depends on the recognition of its authentic note, and this recognition is often prepared by innumerable and insignificant details of the most ordinary living.

'Her answer to the angel when she said *"Fiat mihi secundum verbum tuum"* contained all the mystical theology of her ancestors, to whom everything was reduced, as it is now, to the purest and simplest submission to the will of God, under whatever form it presents itself.' [15]

The Annunciation affords the master-key to the contrast between the depth and quality of the demand, and the apparent simplicity and hiddenness of the response. Save in the secret dialogue of the Blessed Trinity, God can never speak to His equals. The very hosts of heaven are but things made as they face their Maker. And yet the Annunciation,

28

the birth at Bethlehem and the whole ensuing life seem to reverse the contrast. The very expression of Eternal Wisdom as it comes among men is not so much a condescension as a humble request. He speaks indeed to humble creation : but He speaks to His mother.

Such a response, even in this its most perfect form, implies preparation. The Annunciation is made to one that is highly favoured before our Lady has come into any public recognition as being what later generations have seen her to be in truth. God's choosing rests wholly in His own will, and it is not limited to notable souls. 'Not many wise after the flesh, and not many noble are called; but God chose the foolish things of the world that he might put to shame the things that are wise . . .' (1 Cor. 1 : 26f.). The calling of which St. Paul here writes is certainly the general calling of the Church, but it includes and is emphasized by those who are brought into this hidden life. Most notably has this been true of those who during the past century have received special graces through our Lady herself. It is to children in poverty, and with an unvarying demand for penitence, that she has spoken—not to mature saints in a blaze of glory.

No estimate of the significance of her response, however, can be valid if the response is thereby taken out of its historical setting. Our Lady is indeed highly favoured. Increasingly the Church knows the truth of her word, 'All generations shall call me blessed' (Luke 1 : 48). Yet there is the historical necessity that she grew up in a tangible tradition. The Church's realization of the unique condition of her birth emphasizes the certainty of God's choosing, but it does not make her an unreal or ghostly figure. Little is known in terms of normal history, but the Church has honoured St. Anne and St. Joachim, and in the light of our Lord's hidden childhood there is even more reason to acknowledge a normal if sheltered life in the childhood of His mother. Her immaculate conception, purifying her from the taint of original sin 'by the foreseen death of her Son,' helps to explain the beauty of her life : it does not diminish the humanity of that life. There are legends to be found, but they do not forward the purpose of this study, and are in fact best disregarded, lest they foster unreal imaginings in the life itself. If Jesus was subject to the proper disciplines of a devout Jewish home, it would be in her own home that Mary had learned what she was later to teach. Her parents, moreover, are not isolated in the Divine pattern. We know rather more from the gospel of St. Luke of a collateral line closely involved. Her kinswoman Elisabeth, the wife of a leading priest and herself a member of an Aaronite family, had reached an advanced age in childless marriage. The birth of John the Baptist inevitably suggests strong parallels with that of Isaac, but the story of the Visitation transcends any earlier historical links, or any degree of earthly relationship. Elisabeth and our Lady are bound in a common pattern for which the Annunciation provides fitting acknowledgment. The news is told to Elisabeth by her kinswoman's arrival, but the news is already known to her and confirmed by her welcome, and by the mysterious mutual greeting of the unborn children of Promise, themselves bound together in the heart of the mystery.

The circle of the miraculous is again enlarged by the Presentation of the infant Jesus in the Temple. Here we find Simeon and Anna, who are unknown, and unconnected with the past, and yet are drawn into the same pattern by the secret intelligence of the hidden life which they have shared for so long 'looking for the consolation of Israel' (Luke 2 : 25). Zacharias had been deprived of speech, not necessarily as a penalty for lack of faith, but rather as a measure of the significance of those things which he had so naturally doubted. Just so had Ezekiel been silenced—apparently for some long time—while he was still in the closest knowledge of God's purposes. The silence stresses the fact that the work is wholly God's work. Those who are fore-chosen for a part in it are not allowed any means of interference. To Mary's perfect faith and submission no such precaution was needed. 'Mary kept all these things, pondering them in her heart' (Luke 2 : 19). In their turn Simeon and Anna had been waiting, knowing the great purpose that was preparing, but knowing only that they must wait until it was realized and until their appointed part must be played. No interference was possible, but when the event matured they knew at once that they had seen the salvation of their God. Manson stresses the supernatural character of Simeon's assurance : he was seeing on earth what had at best been accepted in an eschatological future. The effect was precisely as he announced it :

(a) A light of revelation to the Gentiles (Isa. 42 : 6f.; 49 : 6; Matt. 28 : 19; Acts 1 : 8; Col. 1 : 27; Eph. 2 : 11–15).

(b) The glory of thy people Israel (Isa. 46 : 13).

But it is also the crisis for Israel through the denial of the glory. Many will fall who are on high : many will rise who are fallen. The child is the signal for controversy and abuse. 'Behold this child is set for the falling and rising up of many in Israel, and for a sign that shall be spoken against' (Luke 2 : 34). Anna's joy was no less, though her part was less conspicuous. She was but one among many 'that were looking for the redemption of Jerusalem' (Luke 2 : 38) and she could tell them of the evidence she had seen to confirm their long vigil.

The historical details of these two encounters have been studied many times, and those who need to learn more can find other and fuller treatments. Our present purpose can be served with but brief reference to the facts. The Gospel of Luke without comment or addition is sufficient to suggest a mode of human spiritual development which, in later Christian language, is clearly a contemplative spirituality. Its essential marks are already evident. The ordinary course of human life gives rise to situations in which unpredictable demands are made upon one and another. In the light of later understanding there is ample evidence to interpret the measure of inter-linking of persons in a common pattern whose delicacy they come to realize but slowly, as they find their own lives woven into it. The supreme and sufficient example is that which we have already seen in the pattern of our Lady's *Fiat*. However little may be known of the persons concerned, whether they be obscure or prominent in the eyes of the world, there is always evidence of an obedience and a submission, marked at every step by an increasing and an awed humility. No speculation upon the 'mysterious' or the so-called 'supernatural' is needed, for the deliberate quest of such elements would lead only into curiosity and a self-full pride. God lays His hands upon one and another, often as interpreters or messengers to others whose part is for the moment less clearly marked out. Among such chosen individuals there grows a wonder of certainty which makes outrageous statements appear natural and inevitable. A child astonishingly born to aged parents is named already, against the wishes of relatives and the tradition of their families. 'His name *is* John.' We may recall the ancient picture of the naming of the beasts in Genesis 2 : 19. The naming was not so much a proposal as a deed, and it arose from a perfect communion with God, and a perfect obedience. There is another wonder in a humble certainty of self-knowledge before God. 'All generations shall call me blessed. . . . He that is mighty hath magnified me, and holy is his name' (Luke 1 : 46–9). God is so near. There is a quiet and joyous interchange of praise between Him and the handmaid chosen to be His mother on earth. Degrees of perception will vary, but there is a common factor in them all which is to prove of immense importance in the creative future of the body of Christ. Already in this first generation—or rather in the circle of varying generations who were brought together in this supreme obedience —we find that the contrast is already prepared within a widening circumference. The common bond in what we have so far seen is undoubtedly the expectation of Messiah. Later on this element will recur frequently. But a critical analysis of Messianism at the time of the Christian era would yield so much of irrelevant material as to conceal the significance of the linking. Even so, Messianic expectation must never suggest—as it undoubtedly did in later Jewish history—an esoteric mysticism remote from contemporary life. The particular group at which we have looked were, after all, not 'disappointed in their

hope' (Ps. 119 : 116). Whatever was to be found, they at least had
found it. 'The rest may reason and welcome—'Tis we musicians know.'
The true mark of the hidden life is never mystical intensity, but a
quality of response to the present moment and to its demands upon
them. (It is here, as we shall see later, that the teaching of the Jesuit
de Caussade, and of the orthodox Jew Martin Buber, speak almost in
identical terms of a truth they share.) There are individuals to be
explained, and for each one there will have been larger numbers in
outer circles. Nathanael is singled out among the first disciples (John
1 : 43–51). Jesus has noticed him, sitting alone and waiting uncertainly
for an actual meeting. Jesus needs no introduction to His chosen. He
knew what was in men, and discerned in Nathanael a man of the
needed quality. Nicodemus was drawn in a similar if less decisive
way (John 3 : 1–10). Perhaps he had still too much to lose if he were
really to know the Spirit's heritage. At a later stage he offers a hesitating
plea for Jesus, but is overruled by the dogmatism of his fellow-
councillors (John 7 : 50). We hear no more until he appears with
Joseph of Arimathea to prepare the place of burial and the scene of
the Resurrection (John 19 : 39). It is more than the artistry of the
Fourth Evangelist which draws these three into the circle of those
chosen in spite of themselves. They find the pattern that awaits their
acceptance when their place is disclosed to them. But again they are not
isolated examples. The very prominence of Nicodemus and Joseph
suggests an environment, a circle of like-minded if even more hesitant
and wistful men, whose lives had been prepared for the task that
waited for them. There were others who had not to carry the burden
of public life or social position. One, however, had both these burdens
in a very different sense of the words. Mary of Magdala was evidently
known too well, even in the respectable house which she dared to
enter during Simon's dinner-party. But in the overturning of all her
life there was already a new life waiting for her, which she was able
to recognize, however far it seemed from the ways she must now leave
for ever. With her namesake who was His mother, she now stands for
the Church as the exemplar of the contemplative way.

All these were Jews—from the unknown and obscure to the leaders
of the Council. The claim which marked out the disciples of the man
Jesus as dangerous alike in the eyes of Church and State had answered
an awareness among many. If Anna were conspicuous in any way, it
would be for her great age and the astonishing persistence of her
devotion. There was purpose in it, and she would know and be known
by numbers who shared a similar purpose, and were likewise a familiar
element in the daily life of the Temple. But they do not appear as
sectaries. They are devout and recognized members of Jewish religious

life. They stand apart from any interest in a worldly or political
Messianism. They would be lost and bewildered if they could awaken
in present-day political Israel. They are not sectaries, and yet must
increasingly have felt themselves part of the tradition of the Remnant. The tide of Judaism had ebbed from them. The hope on which
they were nourished, which was never selfish or partisan, was a hope
that should have uplifted their people.

Yet the developments which now appear in modern Zion might
almost have begun in their time. The Messianism that should have been
the inspiring dream had become something to dread. In the prevailing
despair there was always the incipient popular movement. Often the
uprisings showed no stability, but sometimes there was more than an
echo of Maccabaean power. Each visionary who arose, each rebel who
incited Israel to take up arms, could count on a following who would
be ready to hail him as the long-awaited Messiah. It was the very
uncertainty and instability of such an atmosphere which continually
strengthened and seemed to justify the more conservative elements.
But it must be clearly understood that the conservative is safeguarding
a future—not merely preserving a past. He is so determined to hold
to the Messianic destiny of Judaism that he suspects, and almost seems
to condemn unheard, any suggestion that the hope has been fulfilled.
Any interpretation of the most distant past must point always to a future
—never to the age now in being. So it is that in our present decade
of the twentieth century, when the geographical setting of Old Testament Judaism is more than ever one of the immense potentials of
world affairs, one who is perhaps the greatest of modern Jewish spiritual
leaders finds himself at one not merely with the orthodox, but even with
the liberal and the irreligious. Dr. Martin Buber has said :

'He who acknowledges Jesus to be the Messiah already come cannot belong
to us : he who tries to weaken or divert our belief in a redemption still to
come, there is no agreement with him.'

This leap over nineteen centuries is not taken without relevance. We
shall realize later the close linking of Martin Buber's spiritual existentialism with the inner meaning of the hidden life that is here being
examined, and there is no desire to disparage the reality of the Jewish
contribution, nor to scorn its apparent present conclusions. The explanation for such a paradox of despair must be sought with a sympathy
and understanding which is intensely difficult to achieve against a non-
Jewish background. The effects of the psychology of rejection go very
deep, and we shall always have to remember them in judging any later
developments. For the moment there is more to be observed in the
actual setting of the first century.

C

The men and women who found their hopes so unaccountably fulfilled may already have become marked out among their contemporaries. With each phase in the slow disillusion the repeated rising and falling of hopes had intensified the emotional burden, and contrasts became more extreme. Those whose singleness of mind gave them little enthusiasm for the ebb and flow of popular thought were still carrying on a steady tradition of their own, which they had in turn received from their forebears. In the atmosphere of a worshipping life, which is always the hall-mark of the finest Judaism, it would be certain that special care was given to the training of children. In normal practice the individual Scribe, or a small group of Scribes in close co-operation, would be the leaders in a centre of personal education. Wherever some special religious genius was evident the particular *Beth-ha-Midrash* would become a centre of devotional life as well as a place of learning. The same practice of devoted study and corporate research clearly extended to the Temple, as we shall later note in more detail. The Temple would doubtless be a special objective for the countryman journeying to Jerusalem, if only as some devout parishioner in an English village would seize his chance of worshipping in Westminster Abbey. This temple privilege would be valued also by the teachers, and leading Scribes from outside the city might be welcomed in the Temple seminars. But the institution of the local teaching centre is the normal reality, and the devout families of Hasidic circles would be its true nucleus. We shall find this practice emerging at various points in the story, notably when we trace it in the totally different environment of Eastern Europe eighteen centuries later. Perhaps the best-known example is in the mystical centre at Safed in Northern Galilee, which followed the Spanish Exodus and is still a spiritual growing-point. In many such centres, some external crisis—as at the outset of the Maccabaean revolt, would draw the Hasidim into a vigorous or even violent defence of the law. When the immediate task is completed, however, the Hasidim fall back into the obscurity they desire, in which alone their true work can go forward. In any age the contemplative way demands hiddenness, and it is only drawn aside into the glare of publicity with regret and with some inevitable loss. Yet, as we have seen and shall see far more clearly, the impact of the present moment and the existential response to the direct encounter with the will of God, will always overrule him. The phases of return are not a relaxation of the principle of withdrawal. The *Starets* will attract large numbers for a time, either through his own perception of the need or even at the call of monastic obedience, as in the notable cases of St. Seraphim and the Blessed Silouan. The hiddenness of his inner life is unbroken.

As we seek to follow the traces of this response, the problem of historical sequence has to be faced if any normal logical thought is to be preserved. We have already touched briefly upon the question of continuity between Old and New Testaments. The type of exegesis implied in the general treatment of this book must be unacceptable except upon this clear Catholic tradition.

'The tradition that is properly Christian cannot rightly apprehend itself so long as its bonds with ancient Jewish tradition are ignored. . . . What has lived in the religious consciousness of the people of God before Christ as well as after Him, should be an authoritative source for Christians. . . . There is no reason to doubt the fact that the beneficiary and guardian of revelation, of the divine Word, is the people of God taken in its organic unity.'

Père Bouyer shows that the relevance of Jewish mysticism is a witness to this fact, and concludes :

'Who could deny this, who could doubt it when he has studied any of the documents of mediaeval Jewish mysticism, or modern studies by an Abelson, a Scholem, a Buber' [16] :

the present writer's debt to the Jewish writers named is obvious in the following chapters. Perhaps chiefly this debt is owing to the work of Dr. Buber, who is living the life here studied.

But the spiritual principle must not be felt to rely upon direct connections of date or of environment. We shall find notably, as the same response is found in Jewish history, that the logical reasons for the emergence of something that must be called Hasidism in medieval Germany, and far more widely in Poland and the Ukraine in the latter part of the eighteenth century, may defeat the historian, and yet be unmistakable to those who are of the contemplative way. That way is always the way of response and of obedience. There is an apparent suddenness, an unpredictable speed and variety of action, which can only be understood by those whose experience confirms it in their own lives. In consequence various isolated moments of historical time suddenly become luminous. These moments are later seen to be connected. It must be so, whether perceived or not, since the purpose of God is wholly and eternally present to His Mind, and actions and situations moved by His Holy Spirit can never in fact be spasmodic. This ruling principle is the primary reason for the necessary extension of this study into the Semitic field. In any Jewish spirituality it is clear that for every significant event—an event, that is, where meaning and interpretation transcend material and temporal fact, important and veridical though the outward event may be—the written historical record reflects

a far greater volume of personal knowledge widespread through un-
recorded speech and story. In the case of the *Torah* the term 'oral
tradition' is common and justified. In the case of many isolated responses
in the lives of individuals there may be no question of a formal tradition : yet the events marked out the individual concerned in such a way
as to cause continuing mention and remembrance. This fact emerges
at various periods of Old Testament history, but mainly through scattered individuals. Only later is it able to inspire groups and companies,
and then only through personal allegiance. These later growing-points
have briefly been noted in the methods of the local *Beth-ha-Midrash,*
in which the contemplative way would emerge among the continuing disciples of an organized school. We shall not lose sight of the
astonishing event for which we are waiting in the hidden life of the
chosen body—the human order in which, by the grace of union with
their Lord, the perfect life of the Incarnate Word is continued on earth
as it is in heaven.

For the present we may begin with the beginning of the Church—
with the call of Abram. Whatever be the light thrown by critical study
upon these early narratives, the emergence of the hidden life remains
obvious. We do not select signs of a fugitive sanctity in Abram, but
the marks of an attitude more abiding.

> 'Abraham is a man who has committed himself unconditionally into the
> hands of God; a man who does what God asks of him without hesitation,
> however paradoxical or self-contradictory it may seem, and who accepts
> God's promises, however mysterious and incredible they may appear. . . .
> Such an attitude presupposes that God has complete control of the world,
> and of the course of events in it: that He exercises this control in a
> manner which is purposeful : that human beings have a place in His
> designs, and that He communicates with them in ways which they can
> legitimately understand as commands and promises, and by which their
> hopes can be guided. This is the presupposition of Jewish and Christian
> thinking. . . . It is not a self-evident truth, nor a piece of knowledge
> gathered from experience, but a proposition made as the result of a basic
> acceptance.' [17]

'The Lord said unto Abram, get thee out of thy country and from thy
kindred, and from thy father's house, unto the land that I shall show
thee . . . and in thee shall all the families of the earth be blessed. So
Abram went as the Lord had spoken unto him . . .' (Gen. 12 : 1–4).
In the course of the journey it becomes impracticable for Abram and
his nephew Lot to continue their partnership. Abram sets aside seniority
in age and social rank, and is content to accept the use of apparently

inferior land. Lot, dwelling in the cities of the plain, found no gain from his bargain, but Abram restores the loss. They share in the symbolic meal presided over by Melchizedek, the priest of the most High God (Gen. 14 : 18f.). The priestly blessing is owned by the promise of a son, and a countless dynasty is founded in obedience (Gen. 15 : 5). The promise was marked by a strange quality (the term 'numinous' is not yet in currency) and Abram was cast into a deep sleep, and knew 'a horror of great darkness' (Gen. 15 : 12). In that single phrase from a primitive text there seems to lie a clue to the character of his experience. Rabbinic interpretation will find in the darkness reference to the tyranny of Ahasuerus, or to Alexander the Great who darkened the eyes of Israel with his decrees.[18] To the vocation of the single person such darkness is more immediate and more terrifying than remote history suggests. The authentic attitude of the soul to God may and will produce for the subject various well-recorded phenomena. But invariably they are but labels. The event is accidental—not to be valued in itself, and still less to be sought. Here the term 'darkness' suffices. With the later task of Moses there is the suggestion of an early perception of the Cloud of Unknowing. But whatever the phenomenon, it is more truly a signal for vigilant obedience. The place whereon we tread, the moment into which we are brought, is indeed holy ground.

The Covenant was clearly ratified and even detailed. It was not easy to accept, and the story of Ishmael is one of those waverings of faith too well known in such experience. Ishmael is not to suffer. Prosperity after his own manner will not be denied, but the promise is with Sara and Isaac. Its importance is marked by the contrasted doom upon Sodom, which Abram had renounced to his ambitious nephew. At once Abram is moved to intercession. The Judge of all the earth must not be gainsaid, but he pleads again and again that, for the sake of the least sign of obedience and faith, the doom may be averted (Gen. 18 : 22–33). The prayer seems unavailing : the conditions of promise could not be fulfilled. But the prayer had been made, and had shown the true contemplative relation to God.

In due time the fulfilment of God's own purpose is marked by the birth of Isaac 'at the set time of which God had spoken' (Gen. 21 : 2). But in the midst of Abraham's joy in the developing life of his son, the gift is made an occasion of testing. Under a terrible trial of faith the promise is reaffirmed 'because thou hast obeyed my voice' (Gen. 22 : 18). It is strange that so much disgust and criticism can be aroused by this account. To whatever extent Abraham's interpretation of the demand reflected the conception of his own times, this does not detract from the completeness of the oblation, nor from the faith with which

Abraham followed it to the utmost limits. 'Now I know that thou fearest God, seeing thou hast not withheld thy son, thine only son from me' (Gen. 22 : 12f.). St. Paul is content to base the main structure of his theology here : 'He that spared not his own Son, but delivered him up for us all, how shall he not with him freely give us all things' (Rom. 8 : 32). It is the obedience of faith—not the conformity to works of the Law—which alone can sustain the Church.

Next there is the quest of a suitable bride for the son of promise. Obedience still rules Abraham, and it is conveyed to the servant upon whom the mission is laid. The result is again of the same transparent quality. 'Blessed be God. . . . I had only to begin my journey for Jahveh to lead me . . .' (Gen. 24 : 27). The rich detail of the story only confirms its quality. We are already, despite all critical judgment on texts, in the familiar setting. The dazzling coincidences of the Visitation are foreseen in the whole of the events. This is what we shall learn to expect in the hidden life of the body. But we have still looked at more than a remote past, clouded in the mists of doubtful legend and conflicting tradition. Rather is it the timeless process in which the Body ever lives. 'Your father Abraham rejoiced to see my day, and he saw it and was glad' (John 8 : 56). In this saying our Lord gives all the authority we need for our telescoping of history. 'Before Abraham was, I am' (John 8 : 58). The Church which is His Body is the 'Church of Abraham and his seed. There never has been and never will be any other.' The continuing vocation is traced but fitfully, but the traces stand clear as they are found. The deception of Isaac and the supplanting of Esau do not commend themselves to our Western standards, nor appear the means of any true communion with God. But the vision at Bethel and the fresh dedication at Penuel before the reconciliation with Esau mark the true relationship, and 'redeemed me from all evil' (Gen. 48 : 16). At the end of his life the father of Israel can look back to trace the hand that has led him.

The same revelation of Being and of Relationship which we have seen as our starting point, sustains the mission of Moses. He stands at the outset on the holy ground, afraid to lift his eyes to what he might see. As with many among his successors he feels himself utterly unsuited (not merely unprepared) for his vocation. But the answering authority is imperious. I AM hath sent me unto you (Exod. 3 : 14). It is not the mouth or the thought of Moses which holds the coming revelation. 'Who hath made man's mouth; or who maketh the dumb or the deaf, or the seeing or the blind?' To this only the same answer is possible : 'Send by the hand of him whom thou wilt send' (Exod. 4 : 11–13). The well-known chapter in the *De Imitatione Christi* (III, 15 : 3) reflects and develops this supreme mode of the contemplative life. 'Let me ever do thy will and accord with it truly well. Let me be unable to will or not to will save as Thou willest or willest not.' (In modern literature the late Charles Williams rests his teaching upon the same spiritual perception of total submission to the will of God.) For Moses, the secret does not lie in the successive wonders of leadership or of miracles in Egypt, but in the constant understanding and dependence which is slowly built up. Moses neither desires, nor is he given, the posts of action. Amalek is to be withstood, but his task is on the summit of Horeb, where he carries the whole burden that makes action possible. He is held in the Cloud of Unknowing for forty days and nights, and returns, knowing what must be, and yet finding his task betrayed by those who should have learned its meaning. But the very betrayal concerns the work of God : it is not an occasion of protests, but of reparation. Forgive if thou canst, but if not join me also in the condemnation (Exod. 32 : 31f.). His time of departure is near, and like St. Paul he is ready to be offered (2 Tim. 4 : 6). He has been brought into the grace of the unitive knowledge, and God speaks to him face to face as a man speaks to his friend (Exod. 33 : 11). But for all such knowledge the assurance can come but slowly. The passing of the hidden glory spoke of mercy, long-suffering and forgiveness, but the covenant that is promised is terrible in its demands, and in its exclusive claim upon total allegiance.

'The historical importance of this text (Exod. 33 : 18–34 : 8) is immense. It has aroused numberless commentaries among the Fathers . . . (who) find it the key text for the whole Christian theology of mysticism. More generally, from Origen to the pseudo-Areopagite, including St. Gregory Nazianzen and St. Gregory of Nyssa, the entrance of Moses into the cloud appears to be the examplar of the whole mystical life. . . . For Jewish mysticism, this is the vision in the clear-obscure of the Shekinah : the highest communication to which the divine Presence offered to Israel can bring the man of God in the midst of the people of God.' [19]

The burden is laid swiftly upon a heathen soothsayer, who has watched the events from outside. But Balaam likewise finds that he cannot go beyond the word of the Lord, to do less or more (Num. 22 : 18). 'How shall I curse whom God hath not cursed; or how shall I defy whom the Lord hath not defied? From the top of the rocks I see him, and from the hills. Lo! it is a people that dwell alone' (Num. 23 : 8f.). The vision has not been wholly clear : it has been corrupted by divination and enchantments (Num. 24 : 1). But now his face is set towards the wilderness and his eyes are open (Num. 24 : 17). There is an unexpected gleam of a far distant vision—an anticipation of the Epiphany or of the Apocalypse. Our concern, however, is with the mode of seeing as well as with that which is seen. These aspects are of equal importance, since both alike are part of the wholeness of God. At first Balaam (from professional experience?) thinks that his own intention and his own will must prevail. He is used to being held in awe by a credulous audience. But then—'I have sinned, for I knew not that thou stoodest in the way against me. . . . Only the word that I shall speak unto thee shalt thou speak' (Num 22 : 34f).

So Moses must remind the people : there has been no such calling in the past. They may question through all earth and heaven, but to them alone is the immediacy of God's presence made known, and the meaning is as ever obedience (Deut. 4 : 32–40). At first the miracle may prevail in an unbalanced form : at first in all ages the contemplative may lose the proportion of things, and so mistake their meaning as to exalt the one to whom they are disclosed. But in all true perception the vision and the understanding are for His glory who is seen and known. 'Thou art a holy people unto the Lord thy God . . . the Lord did not set his love upon you nor choose you because ye were more in number than any people, for ye were the fewest of all; but because the Lord loved you hath he redeemed you out of the house of bondage' (Deut. 7 : 6–8). The condition of continuing is the same as that of beginning. The Exodus has been a testing and a humbling purgation that will guide them in the onset of pride in future prosperity. There will always be the parting of the ways—always the choice of a blessing or a curse (Deut. 11 : 26) and always the blessing will be found in the way of acceptance. 'Thou shalt rejoice in every good that the Lord hath given' (Deut. 26 : 11). The promise and the calling are presented in a detailed pattern of law, but when the subject has learned its true nature and purpose the deeper law is seen as a law of consequence. The world which God has made is proved only to work in the free will of conscious obedience. St. Paul will show later the contrast of law and grace, but he and all the faithful know the deeper law of consequence on which their obedience rests. 'The Lord shall give thee a trembling heart, and failing of the eyes and sorrow of mind : and thy life shall hang in doubt before thee, and thou shalt fear day and night, and shalt have none assurance of thy life : in the morning thou shalt say, Would God it were even! and at even thou shalt say, Would God it were morning!' (Deut. 28 : 65f.). This is the law of obedience and of acceptance, written not in ancient codes alone, but in the living heart of the contemplative in all ages. He looks upon the thing which is, and he sees in it the meaning of love, and is brought into the place of adoration. 'Ascribe ye greatness unto our God. He is the Rock, his work is perfect; for all his ways are judgement (Deut. 32 : 3f.) . . . The eternal God is thy refuge, and underneath are the everlasting arms' (Deut. 33 : 27).

As the preparing of the Redemption is thus working itself out, it is seen as uniquely personal. A people is called and chosen, and while its response is to the prophet's word and to the prophetic vision, obedience can be sustained. But soon the called and the chosen strive of their own will to become the choosing and the calling, and the hidden life is lost to them. The pattern begins to be reversed. Abraham, Jacob and Moses in turn have sustained their prophetic leadership at their own cost—by their own obedience to the hidden will. At every moment of that obedience the will became more truly established. The kingdom was coming, and the will was being done on earth even as in heaven. But now a change begins to appear. Another generation is arising which knows neither the Lord of Israel, nor the works which He has done (Judges 2 : 10). The ways of those among whom they live take possession of them increasingly. There are indeed moments when the earlier obedience is not wholly forgotten, but the demand of self-will has risen to a new climax. At the apparently crucial moment it is not Samuel whom the people have rejected. He is no longer allowed to resist their desires. He is to hear their voice in all that they say. The Lord Himself is bearing the pain of their rejection (1 Sam. 5 : 7).

It is already evident that we are not considering an established tradition, as in later centuries men speak complacently of 'Christian civilization.' We are dealing with moments of obedience in the midst of self-will—almost with moments of light in a prevailing darkness. We are far from the quality of Mary's response to the Announcer. Still less can we yet imagine the ultimate moment when the Light shone in the darkness with such invincible brilliance that the darkness could neither understand nor overwhelm what had happened to it (John 1 : 5). The Redemption is uniquely personal. There is never the established order which is entered from outside. In a true sense this is always so. In the fullness of time THE WORD will be made flesh—not the whole sweep of language. The Redeemer at our present stage is a holy people, and there is far to go before men allow themselves to dream of a universalism. When they do so dream, the awakening is often as from a nightmare. There is no vague, evolving process, but a pattern and a hierarchy.

But now factors are entering history which must be observed very carefully and with discrimination. They are factors which God will use in the triumph of His Will, but it is clear that they do not arise directly from the desire of that Will. They are used only by being remoulded and reshaped at unknown cost. The joyous acceptance of His Will changes to the assertion of self. We are returning to the mood which rejected Paradise. But the Divine purpose is established, and needs no discarding.

The vital change may in fact be nothing new, for it is only in man's perception that any change appears at all : yet now it seems that even God is obeying the present moment—that He has made Himself subject to His own law of consequence. We are being given a deeper glimpse of the true pattern of Redemption—the suffering of the Servant. There appears the thought of the Remnant—of the chosen within the chosen. They are themselves the Servants of the Will of God, and they are not allowed to escape from reality to serve some private preference. They are called to retain in being what would otherwise be lost, and suffering is inevitable in such a call. God is working more visibly in His own work. Abraham, Jacob, Joseph and Moses—to mention only the outstanding figures—have found themselves drawn into intercession for their people, and have begun to know its pain. They have stood in the gap between an inscrutable wisdom and the chaos of reckless folly. They have sought to turn back the tide of consequence, though from others and not from themselves. Later we see it truly called 'interposing for rebellious men' (Isa. 53 : 12—Moffatt). And now it is becoming clear that they were not resisting the Eternal Will in so acting. Rather were they co-operating with that will more completely than in any time of unclouded obedience. God Himself is seen to be bearing the pain of His own rejection. 'Ye have done it unto me.' In his first understanding man had to learn the reversal of the primal disobedience by the acceptance of all things at the hand of the Lord. Already we have looked into the future to see One who 'though he was a Son, yet learned obedience by all that he suffered' (Heb. 5 : 8). The rejection of His Love becomes the chosen pathway of His Love; and so it must be for all who are called into the same vocation. To anticipate what will constantly appear in this study, the contemplative way in Christian spiritual life is the way of reparation and intercession.

This principle gives a clue to the falling away of the chosen people. It is no longer merely disobedience and failure. These dominant facts are used to heighten the values of their reversal. A notable and early example is the tragic experience of Hosea. We are accustomed with good reason to believe that the Hebrew text is here so obscure that any translation of the words of his prophecy must be speculative. But for present purpose the course of the journey seems clear. Hosea is brought into a way of life—or finds himself in it—which becomes a vivid parable of the disobedience of the people. Perhaps the lesson is learned by some, but the destruction of the corporate life cannot be stayed. The prophet himself is brought into a strange obedience. His marriage and his family life become subjects of notoriety and shame (Hos. 1 : 2). He seems commanded to link himself with the evil and disordered cultus which is destroying Israel. He is to receive a son whose

very name recalls the struggle against the false worship (Hos. 1 : 3).
He is to receive a daughter uncompassionated—a son disowned (Hos.
1 : 6). The marriage takes its inevitable course, and Gomer returns to
the sinful life from which she had been rescued. But instead of enduring his loneliness, Hosea must once again bring her back as though
he were satisfying his own desire by paying the price of her shame
(Hos. 3 : 2). He cannot give her up, and he must still believe that the
scattering of Jezreel will be turned to a gathering together : that the
unloved and the disowned can again be owned and loved by right. The
people are blind in their deliberate sin, but Hosea speaks the voice
of the Lord to them even at this eleventh hour.

> 'I drew them with cords of a man, and with bands of love. . . . How shall
> I give thee up, Ephraim. How shall I let thee go, Israel? . . . Mine heart is
> turned within me. . . . I will not execute the fierceness of my anger:
> I will not return to destroy Ephraim, for I am God and not man—the
> Holy One in the midst of thee' (Hos. 11 : 4–9).

Dr. Pusey's commentary is instructive.

> 'Hosea, accustomed from childhood to obey God and every indication of
> the will of God, did at once what he was bidden—however repulsive to
> natural feeling—and became thereby the more an image of the obedience
> of Christ Jesus. . . . We must not imagine things to be unworthy of God
> because they do not commend themselves to us. God does not dispense
> with the moral law, because the moral law has its source in the mind of
> God Himself. To dispense with it would be to contradict Himself. But God,
> who is the absolute Lord of all things which He made, may at His
> sovereign will dispose of the lives or things which He created. . . . All the
> methods and parts of God's government are twined together, as so many
> twisted cords of love from Him, so ordered that they ought to draw man
> with all his heart to love Him again.' [20]

St. Augustine throws further light on what is admittedly a difficult
narrative :

> 'No man cometh unto me except the Father which sent me draw him. He
> did not say *lead* but *draw*. The violence is done to the heart, not to the
> body. Why then dost thou marvel? Believe, and thou comest: love, and
> thou art drawn. Do not suppose there is any rough or uneasy violence:
> it is gentle, it is sweet: it is the very sweetness that draweth thee . . . for
> unto Him who is everywhere we come by Love and not by travelling.' [21]

The form of the actual demand will often prove a stumbling-block
to those who are distracted by it. As always, it finds its true meaning
through a creative obedience to the present moment. There is no
intrinsic virtue in Hosea's continuance of a marriage doomed at the start
to failure. Likewise there is no intrinsic virtue in the sudden bereavement which falls upon Ezekiel.

'The word of the Lord came unto me saying: Son of Man, behold I take away from thee the desire of thine eyes with a stroke: yet neither shalt thou mourn nor weep, neither shall thy tears run down. Sigh, but not aloud: make no mourning for the dead. . . . So I spake to the people in the morning: and at even my wife died, and I did in the morning as I was commanded' (Ezek. 24: 15ff.).

The word of the Psalmist is a precise commentary and interpretation. 'Blessed is the man whose strength is in thee: in whose heart are thy ways : who, going through the vale of misery use it for a well, and the pools are filled with water' (Ps. 84: 5f.). The event might have its direct meaning for others when suffering came upon them. They were to lose the thing they loved—to be deprived of the temple and see it profaned. The pattern of their lives was to prove the very reverse of their hopes, their reasoning, and even of their will. But whether or no the lesson is in fact to be learned by others, for Ezekiel the hidden moment is recognized, and is accepted calmly and instantly. Such obedience is very often set in the context of suffering, but the two things must not be confused. In the experience of Hosea the entry into cruel suffering is the character of his obedience. With Ezekiel, as if in a more mature soul, the suffering is taken as incidental. But in both there is the note of what we may call exemplary intercession. This is perceived at once by Ezekiel's hearers. 'Wilt thou not tell us what these things are to us, that thou doest so?' God has already prepared the answer in advance. 'Say—I am your sign. Like as I have done so shall it be done unto them' (Ezek. 24: 19–21). There is no moral value in the presence or the absence of suffering as an intrinsic fact. To suppose otherwise would readily produce a morbidity and self-awareness. All the value lies in the quality of the response of the free will. It is, however, frequently proved that suffering is the context of the hidden life. It is never sought for its own sake, but may be expected without anxiety or surprise, since it often appears to assist or even to ensure the contemplative obedience.

The distinction here indicated becomes of greater importance when we turn to the Servant passages in deutero-Isaiah. Much discussion has ranged and still continues around the Servant Songs. Do they speak of the corporate destiny of Israel, or of a single victim-soul in contemporary history? The interpretation given by Philip to the prominent Ethiopian eunuch is naturally that on which the mind of the Church has fixed, if only because of the outstanding example of the miraculous encounter (Acts 8: 26–40). The man was familiar with the Scriptures. He would know the examples already given from Hosea and Ezekiel, who had conveyed their message through their personal sufferings. Here is a far more outstanding example. Is there some great event in

44

the present or the future, or does the prophet record far deeper experiences of his own time? The answer was precise. From the same text Philip could preach unto him Jesus, who for such a man is shown at once to be the expected Son of God. We are not concerned here with the important critical problems raised in the servant-songs. The individual vocation, for such as Hosea, Ezekiel or Daniel, can be understood by a devout reader, and can be faithfully fulfilled by those to whom it is given. The vocation of a suffering race is a far more difficult question. In our succeeding study it may well appear that the people of God's choice have either failed or have declined to understand what was asked of them in the prophetic message. We must not anticipate the discussion of what has been called by a Jewish writer the psychology of rejection. It is in any case true that the purity of obedience as it has so far been noted is not easily manifested in very varying examples. What we have already seen points to the fact that the hidden life finds its deepest roots in the response of obedience to a given moment, and that it is not long before that response takes on the character of suffering. The suffering shows itself, by the calling of God to an individual, in an exemplary intercession. There is a further quality in a purely vicarious character, which by the climax of the Servant Songs has become so evident that it can be seen as a very portrait of the Lord Messias when His mission becomes an accomplished fact. The problem of the one and the many finds its resolution in the practice of substituted love.[22]

Although the relevance of the Servant Songs to Christian Redemption may be doubted by some scholars, and of course notably by serious Jewish scholarship, it is held by others that there is no need to limit the question to those special passages. Père Sétillanges, O.P., puts this view very plainly. 'The whole of the history of the Cross and its consequences is written in the Hebrew Books.' In a full catena of passages he quotes : Gen. 49 : 10; Mic. 5 : 2; Isa. 7 : 14; 9 : 6; Mal. 3 : 1; Isa. 9 : 2; 35 : 5f.; 42 : 1–3; Zech. 9 : 9; Ps. 41 : 10; Zech. 11 : 12f.; Ps. 35 : 11f.; Isa. 50 : 6; Ps. 79 : 22; 22 : 8–19; Isa. 53 : 4f.; Ps. 16 : 10f.; 110 : 1; Isa. 53 : 12; 60 : 1–4; Dan. 7 : 13f. It is, of course, possible to question the relevance of some of these passages, but equally possible to enlarge such a catena greatly.[23]

The seeming asceticism of Ezekiel's example is not for its own sake. It is simply the setting of the task, in order that the Will of Jahveh may be exalted. As in a later age, 'He must increase and I must decrease' (John 3 : 30). The Servant is compelled to silence, and as a lamb before the shearers is dumb (Isa. 53 : 7). So is the Lord Messias, answering nothing to cruel accusation until an answer is compelled—not by His own judgment, but by obedience to the Father (John 19 : 9–11). We do not suppose that our Lord was deliberately echoing the Servant, or playing a part. The picture Isaiah draws is strangely convincing, and yet mankind waited for centuries before seeing the truth 'placarded before their eyes' on Calvary (Gal. 3 : 1). The purpose of God abides unchanged and undefeated, however desperate men's rejection may seem. The way of the Servant, with whomsoever history may identify him, is always that of atonement, of reparation, of substitution. 'Surely he hath borne our griefs, and carried our sorrows. He was wounded for our transgressions : he was bruised for our iniquities. The chastisement of our peace was upon him. . . . The Lord hath laid on him the iniquity of us all' (Isa. 53 : 4–6). In one sense we do not need to decide this particular identification. We do not say that no one could have imagined so accurate a portrait : it is however certain that the pattern made perfect in the Passion drama could not have been developed indefinitely. What God intended was in fact displayed by the Incarnate Lord. The servants of earlier ages had seen a great deal of the truth. Now it is embodied and fulfilled.

The earlier understandings meet face to face the revealed fact. The Servants of the Will of God follow their hidden life in the same but in far surer ways. The way of contemplation, of adoration, of oblation, of intercession and of reparation are aspects of one whole. All the way is marked by joy and by pain, and none can distinguish for long between the moments of the many-coloured pattern. By the faith of the Servants the world is sustained—is many times apparently saved from destruction—and is brought in the end to its unity in God.

> 'That which sin takes away from the world's worth, the Cross brings back, not in a fiction but actually and really, in the Servant perfect and individual, in the Servant Church imperfect and collective.' [24]

To that comment from a leading Protestant writer we must venture to add the words : 'The Church imperfect and yet obedient : the Church truly personal because truly corporate.' In a matter where so much seems to rest upon the solitary life, we must always assert the primacy of the Eucharistic Body in discerning the fullness of sacrifice. Later ages will yield many diverse examples of this one pattern. Whether there are only hints, or fully developed illustration, the principle will need little variation. The first beginnings are not to be discarded merely because a greater perfection of understanding is seen. God sees and judges all His servants in the wisdom and love which are Himself.

There is, however, one further example which appears far more exact and relevant in its detail. The account of the great intercession in Daniel 10 undoubtedly presents a more acute critical problem even than that of the Servant Songs, but the character of the demand and of the response, however rightly conceived, outweighs any detail.[25]

In a given time and place, dated with deliberate accuracy, 'a thing was revealed . . . and the thing was true' (Dan. 10 : 1) though its understanding might not immediately be realized. The call was of such demanding urgency that a fast of twenty-one days was needed to prepare the prophet for the opening of his task (Dan. 10 : 2). There was a chosen group of companions, but the actual impact of the vision fell upon Daniel alone. His companions saw nothing, but had every reason to fear. 'A great quaking fell upon them, so that they fled to hide themselves' (Dan. 10 : 7). All Daniel's strength seemed to leave him. There could be no brave resolution to give him an impression of self-reliance. His vigour of action was turned to corruption. But the sense of perception in hearing and sight were maintained, though he was prostrate on the ground and powerless to initiate any action. Suddenly there comes an imperative call to action. 'Unto thee am I now sent' (Dan. 10 : 11). He is made slowly to stand upright—to regain, that is, all the needed use of his natural powers, but no more. When God grants this kind of insight to a Daniel or a Paul, there is only one way of keeping them free from harm, or from any self-will. He makes them empty and impotent.

The messenger of God explains that from the beginning of the fast, from the first forming of intention in the dedicated will, Daniel's prayer had been heard (Dan. 10 : 12). Throughout the fast his messenger had been occupied in another phase of the battle : the archangel Michael himself had been with him also (Dan. 10 : 13). This is for Daniel's comfort, and for his proper humility. He had in no sense been forgotten, but he must not be surprised at his own impotence. The importance of what was at stake in the eternal warfare was again stressed, and Daniel returns to his silent intercession, prone again upon the ground by his own choice (Dan. 10 : 15). He is allowed to speak the thought which possesses him, but it is again only to confess his utter weakness and impotence, and his sense that one so weak is not fit for the intercourse commanded to him (Dan. 10 : 17). All this is well. There is a glory surrounding such insight into the eternal world which can harm the human heart. Only in his broken knowledge and in perfect humility of spirit can the servant be truly used. 'O man greatly beloved, fear not : peace be unto thee, be strong, yea be strong.' As with the young Isaiah— 'When he had spoken unto me I was strengthened, and said, Let my Lord speak, for thou hast strengthened me' (Dan. 10 : 19).

The answer brings little consolation to human weakness, but none is needed. The angel explains that he must return to his own part in the battle, leaving Daniel once more alone, with the prospect of a new attack to face (Dan. 10 : 20). The spiritual warfare of the Church takes place where a Daniel has been emptied of himself, where he has offered up prayers and supplications with strong crying and tears. But in this fact the battle is decided. The victory of the Cross of the Servant has been won. 'It is finished.' This is not a rumour that might prove mistaken. It is advance payment, with which the praying Church in this world perseveres for so long as God has ordained.

The unusual detail, and the obviously existential character of the whole story, makes it possible to pass from the historic past to the historic present without any straining of truth or false analogies. Yet in this remarkable instance the principle of the hidden life as we have already begun to see it stands out clearly. What is here disclosed will be echoed in the garden of Gethsemane : it is also the common knowledge of the Church in all ages, and the signal illustration of her hidden life. Here most notably can it be seen that the Lord Himself bears the pain of His rejection. If He will that the Church should bear His Cross, so let it be. If not, the chastisement of our peace is still upon Him.

A sequence of examples of the contemplative way at different stages of pre-Christian experience has shown an increasing element of reflection in all that is done. There is no need to accumulate many further instances. The problems to be faced appear to become more acute : the prospects of any fruitful issue seem more improbable. Obedience is sustained at greater cost, and the element of suffering becomes more and more inextricable from the whole pattern of the contemplative life. The experience of the martyrs is determined by the experience of the Cross, whether foreseen by prophetic insight or reflected in subsequent history.

The contemplative response, however, can be sustained only by a wholeness of conception which we have hardly begun to examine. In the light of developing Christian experience it is inevitable that the contemplative way is sustained and informed by contemplative prayer. It is not, however, necessary to leave the period of Old Testament spirituality to find the same truth, even if less clearly defined. One major section of Old Testament literature has yet to be brought into evidence. The book of Psalms is above all the bridge linking pre-Christian and post-Christian experience. It is the prayer book of the Jewish Church and the Christian Church alike. 'The voice of the Psalms is that of contemplation animating the great prayer of the Church.' It was noted in the introduction, and will be further developed later, that Jewish tradition and Jewish liturgiology have often been acutely suspicious of Jewish mysticism. No living element in that tradition, however, can ignore the principle of *Devekuth* 'which signifies "adhesion" or "being

joined" to God. This is regarded as the ultimate goal of religious perfection. *Devekuth* can be ecstasy, but its meaning is far more com-
prehensive. It is a perpetual Being-with-God, an intimate union and
conformity of the human and the divine will.' [26] If *Devekuth* is thus
the goal, *Kawwanah* is its essential means. Scholem defines this as
'mystical intention or concentration.' [27] A well-known Rabbinic counsel
reads : 'It matters not whether you do much or little, so long as your
heart is directed to heaven.' This term 'directed' speaks precisely of the
mystical intention. 'No prayer without *Kawwanah* is a prayer . . . if
a man's mind is disturbed he should first compose himself and then
pray.' [28] Centuries later the philosopher Maimonides will say 'A man
should clear out of his mind all thoughts of his own, and regard himself as standing before the Shekinah. He who prays must direct his mind
intently towards heaven.' [29] *Kawwanah* is further described as :

> 'mystical meditation on the words of prayer while they are being spoken
> . . . something to be realized in the act of prayer itself . . . the task of man
> is seen to consist in the direction of his whole inner purpose towards the
> restoration of the original harmony which was disturbed by the original
> defect. . . . The individual's prayers, as well as those of the community . . .
> are under certain conditions the vehicle of the soul's mystical ascent to God.
> . . . The process of restoring all things to their proper place demands not
> only an impulse from God, but also one from His creature, in its religious
> action.' [30]

The central place of the Psalter both in Jewish and Christian worship
requires a catholicity of understanding rather than a subjective selection
or preference. 'The Church loves the Psalms because in them she sings
of the experience of God, of her union with the Incarnate Lord, of her
contemplation of God in the mystery of Christ.' [31] There is reason for
this fact quite apart from the long tradition of worship in both
covenants. As the individual prays with the Church his personal
spiritual life is built up and made more effective.

> 'To the Psalmists God is, and ultimately no one else and nothing else
> need be reckoned with. God reigns, and everything else need be reckoned
> with only in reference to that supreme fact. God besets, in knowledge,
> righteousness and loving kindness : and every relationship of life merges
> itself in the primary relationship with Him. It was as they placed God there
> at the heart of all things, that they arrived at those central convictions
> concerning Him and themselves by means of which they have steadied
> and fortified the faith of saints throughout the generations, and will con-
> tinue to do so while time lasts.' [32]

The knowledge and its development are alike contemplative. This is
again affirmed by Mowinckel :

D

'In Israel silence and stillness (as contrasted with the noise of sinners and of the powers of chaos) become to some extent the typical religious attitude —a mark of piety and uprightness—the attitude which was characteristic of the ideal of humanity.' [33]

We are noting already two distinct aspects of the relation of the Psalter to the contemplative way. The Psalter is peculiarly the working text of the Church's worship—the basis of her liturgy—the material from which the *Opus Dei* is wrought. Consequently the use of the Psalms in the Church's liturgy, and especially in the Monastic Office, must be distinguished from their use as personal devotional material. This distinction does not establish opposition in any true sense, but the two uses have a different quality. The use of the Old Testament hitherto made, however, discloses one further difference. We have considered the Old Testament history to learn the spiritual temper informing certain specific actions. Such a man or such a group were confronted with an existential situation, and their response to it, when most effective, was a contemplative response. In the prophetic writings, teaching has arisen from specific events in the personal life of the prophet, or in the society which he served. The Psalms have a more generalized, more timeless approach. They are concerned more with reflection than with specific encounters. They continue to speak to conditions widely different from those in which they were called forth. The actual spiritual setting is more universally relevant. But the knowledge at its best is still contemplative in character. It is a calm reflection on facts, and goes through those facts to God. 'The waves of the sea are mighty and rage horribly : but yet the Lord who dwelleth on high in mightier' (Ps. 93 : 5). The knowledge is that of those who, as they pass through a parched desert 'use it for a well, and the pools are filled with water' (Ps. 84 : 6). This is a world of fact, and not a spiritual illusion which refuses to acknowledge contrary things. But it is also, and supremely, a world of ordered fact—the world of pattern and of supreme design. The contemplation, in E. I. Watkin's phrase, is a contemplation of form.

For this purpose the Psalter is not a code of reference. If scholars can agree upon a close dating for any Psalm or any group of Psalms, it may be easier for us to appreciate the spiritual setting which is reflected. But such dominant attitudes as praise and thanksgiving : adoration and trust : petition and penitence override questions of date and of historical setting. Nor need we be troubled with undue precision in separating the singular from the plural. The needs and instincts of the worshipping Church are those also of her members severally. If the liturgical meaning is obviously dominant, the soul alone with God need not refuse its lessons, nor reject its support in a personal life.

In such reflection upon the Psalms as a whole, it is natural to begin with the note of praise. So far is it dominant that the whole purpose of the Divine Office is an act of praise to God. Yet at once a principle of selection or even of preference appears to demand admission in the hidden life. 'The Lord is righteous in all his ways, and holy in all his works' (Ps. 145 : 17). For this or for that deed of mercy or deliverance —for this or for that benefit or reward He is to be praised. But it would be a mistaken mood which could work through such a catalogue of benefits, and conclude that at the moment there was nothing to merit our acknowledgment. Rather should we 'mean Himself and none of His goods.' [34] He is Himself, whether or no His action appears to relate to ourselves, to our circumstances, or even to the universe He has made (Pss. 115 : 3; 135 : 6). One of the great reflective Psalms of Praise builds up into an exultant catalogue of God's glories—the child's praise of all things bright and beautiful—and yet 'When thou hidest thy face, they are troubled' (Ps. 104 : 29). Selection must never imply either rejection or indifference. It is a perverted praise which cannot rejoice with the conies as they find refuge among the stony rocks, and cannot learn from these least their meed of praise and worship. All the little things with which the Creator blesses our littleness and our incomprehension—these must not be neglected or despised. But through them, and beyond them all, we give praise to the Lord because He is good, and because His mercy endureth for ever. St. Bernard says that to praise God thus is to live by the law of charity which is the law of His sons.

'There is a man who gives praise to the Lord because He is powerful; and there is a man who gives praise to Him because He is good to him; and again, there is a man who gives praise to Him because He is simply good. The first is a servant, and fears for himself: the second, a hireling, desires things for himself: the third, a son, gives honour to the Father. And so he who is afraid, and he who desires things for his own sake, both act for themselves. Only the charity that is found in a son seeketh not her own.' [35]

This is the only means of securing our love and our praise, lest it should ever be found that the place where our treasure was, in fact, hidden had been taken away, and that nothing was left to us—except, of course, God.

This point should be sufficiently familiar in Christian thought to need no further emphasis. To turn the thought into a basis of living is another matter, and is the essence of the contemplative task. To mean God and none of His goods is never to detach His blessings from Himself. The Psalms are often looking forward in a mood of praise for blessings which the individual who speaks the words may never see in this life. This is obvious in the Psalms of Messianic promise and of restoration. 'The Lord said unto my lord' (to the master I serve the

Lord's promise was given) 'Sit thou at my right hand until I make thine enemies thy footstool. . . . The Lord hath sworn and will not repent: Thou art a priest for ever after the order of Melchizedek. . . . The Lord doth build up Jerusalem; he gathereth together the outcasts of Israel' (Ps. 110 : 1–4). Though the Hebrew tenses may be questioned, they are indifferent for our purpose. The Psalmist here, and his fellow-worshippers everywhere, can understand that the past and future fade into the light of an eternal *now*. His outward circumstances may be scattered or captive; but his life and the life of his nation are gathered in one timeless moment in the stillness of the heavenly Jerusalem. We shall see shortly the fruit of those Psalms in later ages. The knowledge they disclose is hidden and secret, and yet it is a gospel to be proclaimed to all. For the Psalmist, the glorious future was so sure that it was already an accomplished fact. Just so for us, in the reversed pattern of the Revealer, 'in the world ye shall have tribulation, but be of good cheer: I have overcome the world' (John 16 : 33). 'As we read such a poem as Ps. 72, we know that the poets of Israel had reached their truest inspiration. Only one King is here, the King of the Beatitudes, and of the parables of the Divine Kingdom : the king of the Bethlehem idyll, and of the meek ride into Jerusalem : the king who gave Himself to the uttermost for His people, and who is gradually and surely subduing the nations to Himself through love.' [36] There is so much in this Psalm of concrete detail that it has been supposed to be an early adulation of some specific king—even of Solomon—in a kind of coronation ode. But the mood of the whole is clearly Messianic. The grounds of praise link its central section with the Servant Songs of Isaiah. The vision is one 'of the Golden age—not of the strong but of the weak made strong.'

In another closely related mood, the Psalmist reflects constantly upon the marks of God's glory in the actual crises of national history, or in personal trials. These aspects are for the contemplative inseparable. He is never tempted to say, 'This is for others, but I am given no part in it.' Still less, 'This is for me, but others are not worthy of it.' The personal and the corporate are at one, just because each aspect is the essential character of the other. Apart from the life of Israel, there is no hidden prayer. So the Psalmist can look out on history and see it through the eyes of God. 'If the Lord himself had not been on our side . . . the waters had overwhelmed us : the stream had gone over our soul' (Ps. 124 : 1–3). The stream may be the tidal wave in the Red Sea, from which his ancestors had escaped as a bird out of the snare of the fowler. The very memory of something so remotely personal to himself is a vivid strength in his present darkness. What has been, will be, for God is God. The symbolism of the Old and New

Covenants alike is truly archetypal, and was rightly so interpreted and developed by the early Fathers of the Church.

> 'God is, in their thinking, everlastingly going forth of Himself, giving of Himself. All things that are, are God creating, fashioning, relating. All things that happen are God guiding, providing, intervening for His good though often hidden purpose.' [37]

The value of such a spiritual application of past events is sure. It underlies the allegorical and symbolic interpretation of the Psalter, which was a main ground of scepticism during the liberal age, but which is being restored to its full and proper value by the recovery of a truly Biblical theology. The sermons of St. Augustine on the Psalms are perhaps the notable example, but only one example of the patristic habit. In his hands the words which were even fettered in the partial apprehension of the Jews are liberated into a creative meaning in the discipleship of Christ, who has broken the chains of sin and death, and has taken our humanity with His own into the heavenlies.

The result of any such reflection upon past history or contemporary experience should help the contemplative to establish a settled disposition of Trust. Whatever fluctuations of mood may continue in his human weakness, and through constant dwelling upon his failure and upon the penitence it evokes, he will constantly find himself falling not to disaster, but to an incomprehensible rest. This quality of trust can reach to deep levels. It may rest, as is natural, upon proved experience. The constant appeal 'For thy Name's sake' illustrates this aspect both personally and nationally. 'Our fathers hoped in thee: they trusted in thee and thou didst deliver them' (Ps. 22 : 4). Yet in this last very perfect example the historic memory can rise up as a challenge from the enemies of God. 'He trusted in God that he would deliver him: let him deliver him if he will have him' (Matt. 27 : 43). This challenge was actual enough on Calvary, and was accentuated by our Lord's own recollection of Psalm 22 as He returned from the three hours of darkness. There would appear to have been in His perfect trust the still deeper reality of that context. 'And thou continuest holy, O thou worship of Israel' (Ps. 22 : 3). Not for what God has done— not even for what He has proved Himself to be by His doing—but for what He is in His being. All hope may have seemed to fade. 'I cry in the day time and thou hearest not' (Ps. 22 : 2). Nevertheless God is, and what may happen to the Psalmist cannot affect the certainty of that perfect Being, to be known in the perfect relationship of His truth.

Dr. Oesterley has called attention to another depth of meaning in that trust—a trust not in past or present, but in an unknown future. Psalm 21 : 1–7 is 'an illustration of one of the finest elements in Israelite religion, namely a faith in the efficacy of prayer so deep and living that the certitude of prayer being answered is expressed by the affirmation that it is already answered.' [38]

The Messianic kingdom was apparently an idle dream in the circumstances of the writer : yet in the quality of his trust there was no past nor future—only the *now* in which the Lord reigned. To stress such a triumph of trust in time of adversity need in no way lessen the value of the same trust. 'Thou preparest a table before me in the presence of mine enemies' (Ps. 23 : 5). This trust is almost exultant. But in a later Psalm of somewhat similar mood the same trust is even demanded. The Divine power is seen in an aspect terrible to God's enemies. The scourge of war is ended by overwhelming victory, and because of such examples Israel is challenged to abandon not indeed its enmity, but the fear and anxiety which have led to nervous efforts in its own defence. 'Give in—admit that I am God' (Ps. 46 : 10—Moffatt). It is again the being of God, not His value or usefulness, which here compels trust. The contemplative may miss the familiar injunction to tranquillity in the phrase 'Be still,' but he gains a less obvious insight of the highest importance to his prayer. The trust more hardly won by experience proves very convincing. 'For this God is our God for ever and ever : he shall be our guide even unto death' (Ps. 48 : 13).

This same quality of trust is needed not only to bring men to prayer, but to sustain them in the stress of prayer. 'Take heed unto me and hear me; how I mourn in my prayer and am vexed. The enemy crieth so, and the ungodly cometh on so fast. . . . My heart is disquieted within me, and the fear of death is fallen upon me' (Ps. 55 : 2–4). He is tempted to wish for escape and rest, but that is not his true answer. 'As for me, I will call upon God, and the Lord shall save me. In the evening, and morning, and at noonday will I pray, and that instantly : and he shall hear my voice. It is he that hath delivered my soul in peace from the battle that was against me' (Ps. 55 : 17ff.). In much of the battle of prayer the positive consciousness of the task may sustain him against the knowledge of the danger in which he is placed. At other times, however, the sense of his utter weakness enters to compel a trust which is the only alternative to despair. The enemy seems to have triumphed with ease. 'These are the ungodly, these prosper in the world, and these have riches in possession : and I said, Then have I cleansed my heart in vain . . . all the day long have I been punished, and chastened every morning. . . . Then thought I to understand this : but it was too hard for me until I went into the sanctuary of God : then understood I the end of these things. . . . So foolish was I and ignorant : even as it were a beast before thee. Nevertheless I am alway by thee, for thou hast holden me by thy right hand. Thou shalt guide

me by thy counsel, and after that receive me with glory. Whom have I
in heaven but thee, and there is none upon earth that I desire in comparison of thee. My flesh and my heart faileth, but God is the strength
of my heart. . . . It is good for me to hold me fast by God, to put my
trust in the Lord God' (Ps. 73 *passim*).

The conclusion is the same, though the approach be less sure. He
finds ultimately in prayer the meaning of his desperate need. Beast or
no beast, foolish or not foolish, there is but one refuge for his wavering
will. This is a journey which very many souls must repeat again and
again, yet its ending is out of their power to evade. 'Hath God forgotten to be gracious, and will he shut up his loving kindness in
displeasure? And I said, it is my own infirmity, but I will remember
the years of the right hand of the most highest. . . . Thy way, O God,
is holy' (Ps. 77 : 9f.). The way indeed often seems to be lost, and yet
the Psalms give to the contemplative a reason for his trust in which
he can live in unending wonder—a trust that seems unclouded owing
to the brilliance of the Divine Light in which it is set. In two earlier
Psalms we could have noticed a forecast of this triumph of trust. 'In
the time of trouble he shall hide me in his tabernacle : yea, in the secret
place of his dwelling shall he hide me, and set me up upon a rock of
stone' (Ps. 27 : 5). 'O set me up upon the rock that is higher than I,
for thou hast been my hope and a strong tower for me against the
enemy. I will dwell in thy tabernacle for ever, and my trust shall be
under the covering of thy wings' (Ps. 61 : 3f.).

The image of the sheltering wings was in our Lord's own thought
from these same Psalms, and chiefly from Psalm 91, which above all
the Psalter is the charter of the contemplative. It is so intimate in its
understanding that it appears less as a reflection upon the surety of
God than as a dialogue between God and the soul. The poem, so
familiar in its daily liturgical use, must still be pondered closely in
order to realize the subtle changes of tense and subject. In two verses
alone out of sixteen does the writer admit his personal experience—
each time in the declaration 'Thou art my hope' (Ps. 91 : 2, 9). In nine of
the remaining fourteen verses the writer bases his assurance and his
exhortation upon his own knowledge. But in the climax of the poem
the Lord Himself appears with words of assurance confirming and
explaining the Psalmist's trust. 'Because he hath set his love upon me,
therefore will I deliver him; I will set him up because he hath known
my Name. He shall call upon me and I will hear him; yea, I am with
him in trouble; I will deliver him and bring him to honour. With long
life will I satisfy him, and show him my salvation' (Ps. 91 : 14–16). The
image of ascent, of a physical lifting out of the reach of danger, need
not be criticized. A modern age—even some of the medieval ascetics—

would warn us against so literal and limited a conception of the love and power of God. And alongside it is the exquisite figure of shadow and protection. 'He shall defend thee under his wings, and thou shalt be safe under his feathers.' In another aspect of the Psalm our Lord well remembered the Devil's distortion of its meaning as part of the temptation in the wilderness. So in this image of the sheltering wings Jesus wept over Jerusalem, when she had rejected too long the means of her redemption. 'How often would I have gathered thy children together as a hen gathereth her chickens under her wings, and ye would not' (Matt. 23 : 37).

The unique quality of this Psalm is known chiefly by the contemplative intercessor, and in the work of reparation. Much that we have already noted in the Psalter sustains a trust in God at times of special danger— a danger from which God will surely deliver, even though His chosen hour seem long delayed. But here is a situation of continuing peril, and there is no apparent expectation that things will change. The contemplative has been brought into the place of danger, in order that he may do the work laid upon him. He will have ever in mind the supreme surrender in which Jesus passed to Calvary for His own perfect work. Here the contemplative has not been suddenly assailed, nor does he expect to be released. He is simply held by God and nothing can be desired otherwise. This was the experience of the Lady Julian, to whom the Lord spoke : 'See, I am in all thing : see, I do all thing : see, I lift never my hands off my work, nor ever shall without end. How should anything be amiss?' [39]

As the argument of this book is developed, it should become even more clear that such experience is perfectly normal in the hidden life. It is not highly-coloured drama, but sober fact, that the work of God Himself in the spiritual warfare requires the calling of His intercessors into what would be unrelieved and deadly peril—were it not that He is God. The same certainty is made more general in Psalm 139. The writer is reflecting in a mood which seems full of doubt and of hesitation. It is, however, useless for him to attempt evasion. He has no hiding place from the searching of the Divine Presence. 'If I say, Peradventure the darkness shall cover me, then shall my night be turned to day. Yea, the darkness is no darkness with Thee, but the night is as clear as the day : the darkness and light to Thee are both alike.' A modern poet has written of the relentless pursuit of the Hound of Heaven. 'Naked I wait thy love's uplifted stroke—My harness piece by piece Thou hast hewn from me, And stricken me to my knee. I am defenceless utterly.'

It is often in the folly and the sin, not only in the obedience of men, that the adorable goodness of God is disclosed. 'He satisfieth the empty soul, and filleth the hungry soul with goodness. Such as sit in darkness and in the shadow of death : being fast bound in misery and iron, because they rebelled against the words of the Lord. . . . He brought down their heart through heaviness : they fell down and there was none to help them. So they cried unto the Lord in their trouble, and he delivered them out of their distress' (Ps. 107 : 9–13).

The same dominant quality of trust finds another and more personal support from the Psalms. The sense of the limitless Majesty of God can persist through the darkest hours of desolation. The human individual might seem wholly negligible—'a beast before thee.' 'I cry . . . and thou hearest not,' but 'Thou continuest holy.' Thus far we have seen already, but it is not the whole truth. The same sense of the majesty in itself is a sense of intimate nearness. 'The Lord is high above all nations, and his glory above the heavens. Who is like unto the Lord our God, that hath his dwelling so high, and yet humbleth himself to behold the things that are in heaven and earth. . . . Ye are the blessed of the Lord, who made heaven and earth' (Pss. 113 : 4f.; 115 : 15). But as the Church closes her liturgy for the day in the Office of Compline the point is stressed beyond doubt : 'The Lord that made heaven and earth give thee blessing out of Sion' (Ps. 134 : 4). The traverse of the experience is here complete. The incomprehensible glory seems to exist for this precise end : it is focused through all the darkness of earth to the single image of God in its littleness. This final assurance is very close to the teaching of our Lord. The Gospels for Passion Week show Him in a remote, apocalyptic mood. St. John's story might even repel us at times, as the Lord seems deliberately to set Himself beyond any hope of human understanding, and to sweep aside the Jewish leaders who were so soon to crucify their Redeemer. 'No man can come to me except it were given to him of my Father (John 6 : 65). . . . Ye are from beneath—I am from above' (John 8 : 23). In a liberal age this mood was discounted as belonging to a mythical figure called the Johannine Christ. But such critics would find it less easy to dismiss the record of St. Matthew. The Lord whom Matthew knew could be even more infinitely remote. 'All things have been delivered unto me of my Father, and no one knoweth the Son save the Father, neither doth any know the Father save the Son' (Matt. 11 : 27). What then can man do? The door to any spiritual longing seems fast barred. We can reach neither the Father nor the Beloved, and there can be no hope. Yet the Divine logic, reversing every conclusion of man's bravest despair, goes on : 'Come unto me, all ye that labour and are heavy laden, and I will give you rest' (Matt. 11 : 28). 'The Lord that made heaven and earth'—the Lord beyond all human conceiving in His self-sufficient Majesty—'give *thee* blessing out of Sion' (Ps. 134 : 4). And the blessing is given so as to reach especially the weary, the burdened and the hopeless—'Come unto me.' He is remotely far as we look at heaven from earth. He is infinitely and personally near as He looks at earth from heaven.

The Church has always found, and will never cease to find, the ground of her praise in the words of the Psalter. Yet the contemplative will always owe the deepest debt. His task is above all to look steadily and unfalteringly at the concrete facts before him. The sublimest vision of the saints will usually be set against the background of personal and national darkness. Always it is in the facts, and not in spite of the facts, that he must find his life. It is in the desert, rather than from the reservoir, that his thirst is most surely met.

'For as the heaven is high above the earth, so great is his mercy towards them that fear him. As far as the east is from the west, so far hath he removed our transgressions from us. Like as a father pitieth his children, so the Lord pitieth them that fear him. For he knoweth our frame—he remembereth that we are dust. . . . The mercy of the Lord is from everlasting to everlasting upon them that fear him' (Ps. 103 : 11–17). The ultimate rock of faith is the everlasting kindness.

CHAPTER THREE

THE MANY AND THE FEW

THE preparing of the Redemption has now been sketched in an attempt to indicate its hidden pattern; but we face the fact that the preparation was at best strangely incomplete in the mind of man. The stream of spiritual comprehension has been traced in its early beginnings, but has also been seen in flood-tide at the moment when, in the fullness of time, Israel should have received the promise for which she had waited so long. The strength of that flood-tide is a true valuation of the early beginnings. If we had not seen the perfection of Mary's response to the Annunciation, the beginnings might have been neglected as unimportant. We are still so unused to realizing the true continuity of our heritage. The perfect readiness for the coming of the Lord was the response of a spiritual *élite,* and yet the Coming was vouchsafed. We cannot pretend to have found in contemporary Judaism any general setting fit to display its perfection.

The Messianic hopes of the Old Covenant were fulfilled in truth, and beyond all expectation. But the tragedy of Israel which failed to change the rigidity of its mind and to enter into its unquestioned place, could not leave the course of history unchanged. The rejection of the Lord Messias was an act of frustration from which no people could lightly recover. As the story is seen to-day, the personal earthly expectation had become established. When the popular hope became ever harder to sustain, it was time to 'eschatologize' what could not be explained.

> 'The history of Israel is a tragic drama in which reality seems to gainsay faith—a constantly repeated disappointment. When faith rises up and over-comes the disappointment, the future hope and eschatology begin to be.' [40]

Let it be admitted that even in New Testament times, and still more in the theorizing of liberal theology, the Parousia can be similarly obscured. Men no longer expect keenly a renewal of Pentecost, save in erratic sects. This undoubted weakness in human perception throws into even stronger relief the small groups in Temple circles—'all them who looked for redemption in Jerusalem' (Luke 2 : 38). It was redemption that they sought—no temporary political alleviation.

59

This very fact in its extreme example demands an explanation which takes the whole of subsequent history out of the field of normal human analysis. The calling of God was rejected not only in repeated moral and ethical failures, but on an even deeper level. It is only in the present day, after nearly twenty centuries, that we have to face the terrible picture of a materialist and political Zionism—the apotheosis of the original rejection—and still realize at its heart a spiritual insight, and the continuance of the same authentic note of existential obedience demanded as a condition of the Abrahamic promise. Out of the heart of that movement, and in one of the darkest hours of the world, Dr. Martin Buber could write before entering his own exile :

'Already in the prophetic writings of the first Exile we find mysterious references to the succession of the Servants of God, who, arising in generation after generation, will carry and purify the defilement of the world, condemned and held in low esteem by their fellow-men. . . . Each of them was called; each of them denied his calling in some respect. . . . So God waits throughout the generations of men for the one in whom the absolutely necessary movement arising from the creative will was for him the decisive power. With the deepening of the exile of the world, which has occurred through the exile of Israel, the men who rise in each generation are no longer known to the world but live in seclusion : they do their work no longer in the light of accessible history, but in the darkness belonging to an inaccessible, personal work of suffering, of which no account . . . reaches the outside world. But the more the fate of the world becomes filled with suffering . . . the more do the lives of these men become filled with meaning and operative within themselves. They are no longer . . . foreshadowings of the Messianic form : rather in them is the Messiahship belonging to the end of time fulfilled by one of all time, poured out over the ages : without this the fallen world could not continue in existence. . . . The messianic *mysterium* stands or falls with its seclusion, not because it is kept secret, but because it is in itself a true actual seclusion which penetrates to the innermost existence. The men to whom it comes are those whom the nameless prophet spoke of in his own name, when he said that God had made him a polished shaft, and had then hidden him in His quiver (Is. 49 : 2). Their hiddenness belongs essentially to their work of suffering. Each of them can be the Promised One : none of them dare in their own self-consciousness be anything but a servant of God.' [41]

From the standpoint from which Dr. Buber speaks it might seem that we had taken his words out of his own context, and read into them not more than he intended, but (to a Jewish mind) far less. Yet the passage is saying precisely what we have tried to develop in the earlier chapters. The world's redemption is, for the Christian, accomplished once for all. None the less its fulfilment in the modern age, and perhaps in many ages yet to come, rests in the hidden life of contemplative obedience, and of the suffering intercession for which that life alone can find meaning.

It is precisely in this hidden company that we have already met at close quarters two members, who are presented to us in an immediate short range encounter with an infant child (p. 30f. *supra*). Both are at the end of their lives—kept alive only by their hidden intention and sheltered by their hidden task. Their lives were evidently not such as to offer excitement. There was no constant stimulus of events. Rather had they to suffer an environment of sullen resentment, of murmured criticism of their masters, and (in privileged circles) of continual scheming and intrigue. It was useless to hope for the defeat of Rome, but the skill of the official mind could use and manipulate the imperial power, and could maintain a state of political and civic strain which made the spiritual atmosphere of the Temple an uneasy one. The hidden life would be unquiet in such a setting unless it could manage to maintain an undistracted recollection. Men and affairs are of little concern to those who are simply looking at God. Their lives would be held in a silence which spoke to them constantly of the hidden glory of Israel— the holy Presence of a God unseen, but inescapable.

'What a Simeon or an Anna awaited, this consolation of Israel that made the hope of a whole life is shown . . . in such a book as 4th Esdras (A.V. 2nd Esdras).' [42]

The latter part of 4th Esdras 13 echoes the words of our Lord in Matt. 24 and parallels. 'And the time shall be when these things shall come to pass, and the signs shall happen which I told thee before, and then shall my Son be declared, whom thou sawest as a man ascending. . . . He shall stand upon the top of the Mount Sion, and Sion shall come and shall be showed to all men, being prepared and builded.'

For them there would be no strain in the vigil. The recollection in which their prayer was established was enough. There was therefore no reason why Simeon's hidden life should alter its course so long as life was granted to him—no reason save the fact that in the depth of his prayer he knew that God was keeping him for a single task. He had continued in Jerusalem waiting: one day he knew that the time of waiting had become a time of action. The time of waiting was suddenly alerted by the knowledge. Many can witness that even when the very theme and purpose of the action may be entirely obscure, a sense of the imminence of a Divine event keeps the soul poised for instant movement, though it may continue in its present task. The response of Samuel is a listening—not a hasty movement. In this case there would be no possibility of hesitation, nor does Simeon draw from the experience what men term a 'new lease of life.' There is nothing more to wait for. 'He blessed God and said, Lord, now lettest thou thy servant depart in peace according to thy word, for mine eyes have seen thy salvation, which thou hast prepared before the face of all people; a light to lighten the Gentiles and to be the glory of thy people Israel' (Luke 2 : 28–32). 'The glory of the Lord shall be revealed, and all flesh shall see it together' (Isa. 40 : 5). There is always a difference between idea and reality. Even to the mother of God there was a concreteness and actuality here which no angelic vision could have given. The Magnificat had been a song of utter joy, but here, so soon, is the promise of pain. 'A sword shall pierce through thine own soul' (Luke 2 : 35).

The brief sketch of Anna illuminates this note of expectation. The instant of joy and thanksgiving is part of a hidden life in which by law and custom use of time is closely defined, just in order to secure its true direction. No charge of formalism or externality need lie against the prayers of Temple and Synagogue. If there is, by modern standards, an excess of detail and provision, the same principle has informed the whole succession of liturgical worship through the ages. The natural distinction between corporate liturgical prayer and the private devotion of the solitary person need never establish a critical comparison between the relative values of the two practices. This false valuation was briefly noted in the introduction, and no excuse is needed for dealing with the personal devotion rather than with the more integrated and stylized liturgical pattern. It may, however, be useful to see further how the problem presented itself in the age we have reached. It naturally became more acute in the centuries when the focus of liturgical worship had been destroyed—still more when even the Synagogue was a target of persecution, and the family worship of the devout Jew could be sustained only under grave suspicion, so that at every side of the Jewish fortification there were inevitable points of potential weakness. For the Jew, as for the student of Judaism, there is the constant distinction between the *Mishnah Haggadah*—the exegesis of the preacher—and the *Mishnah Halakhah*—the regulated code of the Law. The act of distinction itself can produce merely subjective and unstable argument. The art of interpretation and commentary would seem far more significant than the regulations by which the art may be practised. In a cogent example, Père Bouyer points out that the Daniel figure of the Son of Man appears nowhere else in the Old Testament, and yet our Lord's use of that same term is clearly connected with Daniel's vision. It is impossible

'in the Old Covenant as in the New to separate the word fixed by writing under Divine inspiration from the word held living in the consciousness of the people of God. Without the tradition of the Book of Enoch or of 4th Esdras, Christ's own way of designating Himself and of explaining Himself to men would remain incomprehensible to us.' [43]

62

But the distinction, or rather the desire to distinguish, can itself become unprofitable casuistry. The same question can face the Christian in a more familiar field. Liturgical worship, whether in the *Opus Dei* or— for example—in the Propers of the Mass for a given feast, can be treated almost exclusively from a devotional standpoint. Yet it is wisely said that 'the discipline of ordered rite and obligation is needed to train the spiritual outlook and to save Prophecy from self-will and the empty fate of dreams.' [44] Reflecting upon such issues briefly, it is permissible and even important to consider the spiritual climate which sustained the fidelity of a Simeon. It is commonplace in Catholic theology to stress the place of Intention. In the discussion of rites and validity it has one meaning, and that a strictly limited one. But in the contemplative way its importance cannot be exaggerated. To say this is not to desire fervid enthusiasm. The divisive effects of any such mistakes have done infinite harm in rending the Body of Christ. The valuable *Rabbinic Anthology,* edited jointly from an Orthodox and a Liberal standpoint by Loewe and Montefiore, provides a source-book for such a study.

> 'How is a wayfarer to pray? He must not take the kingdom of heaven upon himself while he is walking, but he must pause and direct his heart to God with awe and fear, trembling and quaking at the proclamation of the Divine Unity as he utters the Shema, every single word with heartfelt sincerity (*Kawwanah*). And then he should recite the Doxology: 'Blessed be the name of his glorious kingdom for ever and ever' (R.A. 693). ('Taking upon himself the kingdom' means, of course, the actual recitation of the central prayer in which our Lord Himself acknowledged the life-giving injunction.)
> 'When God gave the law, no bird sang or flew, no ox bellowed, the angels did not fly, the Seraphim ceased from saying Holy, Holy, Holy: the sea was calm, no creature spoke, the world was silent and still, and the Divine Voice said 'I am the Lord thy God' (R.A.1).

(So in Christian devotion speaks the ancient hymn from the Eastern Liturgy of St. James : 'Let all mortal flesh keep silence.') A constant injunction in the same sense is given. 'It matters not whether you do much or little, so long as your heart is directed to heaven' (R.A. 690). The word speaks precisely of this pervading doctrine of *Kawwanah.* It seems to have become even more prominent in the period of major recovery after the great dispersion. The book of *Zohar,* which we shall consider in greater detail in due course, comments upon the cry from Psalm 130 : 1f. 'Out of the depths have I called unto thee, O Lord. . . . It is incumbent upon any man praying before the Holy King to pray from the depths of his soul, for then will his heart be entirely directed to God, and his mind entirely bent on his purpose.' [45] A further comment runs : 'No prayer without *Kawwanah* is a prayer. . . .

If a man's mind is disturbed he should first compose himself and then pray.' A prayer may be liturgically ordered and performed, but this is no excuse for formalism. 'Commandments demand intention' (R.A. 692a).

In the same sense another concept appears—that of prayer and worship for their own sake (*Lishmah*). 'He who busies himself with the Law for its own sake causes peace . . . he protects the whole world : he brings near the redemption' (R.A. 707). A somewhat later injunction, though marked with traces of the esoteric ideas which entered the purity of earlier teaching, comes from the philosopher Maimonides (Chapter of Bliss).

> 'He who prays should turn to God, standing upon his feet, feeling delight in his heart and expressing it with his lips, his hands outstretched, his organs of speech intent on utterance . . . concentrating and preparing himself, supplicating, bending the knee, prostrating himself, weeping because he is in the presence of the great and awful king. . . . The soul of the honourable man is humbled, and it freed him from the senses, so that he is as though withdrawn from them, and with his imaginative faculty he beholds and sees things in which there is no doubt. . . . He looks upon future events as though he were gazing at past events, and those things which he recounts are true.' [46]

We shall not assume that Simeon had time for such self-analysis, but the quotation is given to show the long continuity of this principle of *Kawwanah.*

> 'He who makes use of the crown of the Law is rooted out of the world. Do the words of the law for the doing's sake and speak of them for their own sake. Make them not a crown with which to exalt thyself . . .' (R.A. 707).

There is always a great emphasis upon restraint in the best period :

> 'He who recounts the praise of God more than is fitting will be torn away from the world.' The phrase in Ps. 65 : 1, 'Praise waiteth for thee, O God, in Sion,' is rendered, 'Praise is silent before thee, O God, in Sion. To thee silence is praise : silence is a medicine for everything' (R.A. 728).

'God wants the heart.' This reference to 1 Sam. 16 : 7 occurs very often. The dedicated intention gives meaning and value to all life, and especially to prayer. The Rabbinic mind is in full accord with the concept of the *Opus Dei* in Benedictine worship. The same note of solemnity is found in connection with the daily Benedictions (*Shemoneh Esreh*). 'One must not stand up to say the *Tefillah* except in a serious frame of mind. The hasidim of old used to wait an hour . . . in order to direct their hearts to the Father in Heaven' (R.A. 903).

The expectant prayer of Simeon and Anna is inseparable from the duties of the Temple (Luke 2 : 37). So it was in the company of the disciples, alike while they were waiting for their task in the Church, and after they had entered upon it. Peter and John went up to the Temple together at the hour of None (Acts 3 : 1). The first response to the teaching at Pentecost was the calling out in one day of a large company of the newly baptized, who 'continued steadfastly in the apostles' teaching and fellowship, in the breaking of bread and the prayers' (Acts 2 : 42). The common life and the hidden life must never be separated in our understanding. The Rabbinic use of Exod. 32 : 7 seems to forget the deeper note of verses 31ff. 'Get you down from your greatness : I gave you greatness only because of Israel : now that Israel has sinned, what art thou to me?' But R. Hillel—by tradition one of those who received the boy Jesus in the Temple (Luke 2 : 46ff.) is quoted in a more gentle tone in the same context : 'Israel will be redeemed only when it forms one single band : when all are united, they will receive the presence of the Shekinah. Therefore Hillel said : "Separate not thyself from the community" ' (R.A. 939).

The actual language of the Canonical Prayers is of course often very close to much that has come into Catholic use, but the brief liturgical notes often emphasize more clearly the spirit in which prayer is to be approached. 'Do thy will in heaven above : grant tranquillity of spirit to those who fear thee below, and do that which is good in thy sight. Blessed art thou, O Lord, who hearkenest to our prayer' (R.A. 961). The same note of acceptance (how far removed it is from resignation) is found in comment on Ps. 116 : 1f. 'I will call upon God in sorrow as in deliverance' (R.A. 1001). The full note of the contemplative, however, comes even more in the counsel : 'Let a man love God with a perfect love, whether it go well with him or ill' (R.A. 1010). And the searching prayer of the *De Imitatione Christi* (III, 15 : 3) is heard in the final note : 'Do His will as if it were thy will, that He may do thy will as if it were His will' (R.A. 1014).

As in contemporary Christianity, so in first century Rabbinism, the idea and practice of prayer can range from a total acceptance of the will of God—blindly and for His own adorable sake—to specific and urgent petition. The prayer-teaching of our Lord, exemplified for us in the prayer He commanded, is exceedingly brief. But the earliest days of the Church are already urging continuous, unceasing prayer (Acts 12 : 5; 1 Thess. 5 : 17). The motives of prayer may be precise, whether in the Temple Liturgies or in the Catholic Breviary, but simple, personal and almost formless prayer is equally recognized. If there are dangers, they can be traced to formalism, which in turn can breed an indifferent inconsistency of prayer and conduct. But form is not formal-

E

ism; it is the necessary framework of discipline—the scaffold within which a spiritual temple, fitly framed together, can be made into a habitation of God through the Spirit (Eph. 2 : 21f.). It is against the background of fact, and not of prejudiced selection, that we may try to understand the setting in which our Lord's earthly life grew from infancy to maturity.

CHAPTER FOUR

THE PATTERN OF THE DIVINE LIFE

THE continuing remnant has been seen to reach the climax of its patience and its hope in the song of Simeon. 'Mine eyes have seen thy salvation.' The vision of Isaiah—'All flesh shall see it together' (Isa. 40 : 5) is still for him a matter of proved faith, but even his eyes have seen the fact of which the faith is the fulfilment. Simeon and his associates have learned what we have seen. They have prayed as we have listened to their prayer. The fruit in their lives has been the poised devotion in which the coming of the Lord can be accepted in humility and in joy.

These are the teachings, also, and the prayers which the Divine Child would hear when He was first taken into the synagogue at Nazareth. Whatever the sources of certain knowledge that the faith of the Church is to discern, whatever the manner of that perfect communion with the Father which He chose or was allowed to know, the growing humanity is nurtured in this spiritual climate. It is only in apocryphal fantasy that men have been tempted to exalt His Divinity with tales of futile miracle : often they have only succeeded by such tales in lowering humanity to a mere weakness of character and instability of temperament. But it is just because the Catholic faith holds firmly to the revealed truth of His Person that there is no danger of our being scared by the ghosts of liberal humanism. In the life of a little town He is there as a boy among boys, and a man among men. As months passed into years, the people for whom He was an ordinary event, an accustomed part of their daily intercourse, a member of their religious fellowship, began to be puzzled (John 7 : 27). There was nothing to blame. His character seemed to them strangely enviable, since he would seem quite unaware of its obvious beauty and attractiveness. There would be some comment aroused from such exceptional gracefulness, but since it was precisely grace and not accomplishment, we need not think that the silence of the narrative conceals any envy or criticism. As to the formal training of the early years, virtually nothing is known by direct information, for there is no reason to assume any different pattern in the course of His education from that of any Galilean boy. The fact that in His case alone the perfection of human nature was joined inseparably with the fullness of Godhead, and that human time and human history have faded in the light of His Eternity, still leaves to us the duty of seeing the human facts objectively in the terms of our own age. From the miracle of His birth—a secret guarded inviolably by His mother, or by the very few to whom it needed to be known, we may assume a sense in them of what in our day might be called 'a unique vocation,' and that in His home, and in the planning and the care given to His upbringing He was a child uniquely dedicated to God. But the religious emphasis in that home would not stand out from the general environment of devout Jewish society. Nazareth as a human social community existed, and could be compared sociologically with its neighbourhood if such comparison were needed for our purpose. But whatever its quality, and whatever the reasons for the proverbial despite (John 1 : 46), it was still part of the wholeness of a Holy Land and of a chosen people. By comparison with our modern debased standards it was obsessed by God. 'The whole of religion was revealed—nothing was kept back in heaven—and the whole content of revelation was religion.' This fact is intensified by the prophetic warnings. The message of repentance laid upon John the Baptist, in his own 'unique vocation,' is not proclaimed to secular indifference or to godless vice, but to a people who have incredibly forgotten the only task which explains or justifies their existence. It is customary in the narrow field of English social history to remark that the early seventeenth century brought an atmosphere when religion was likewise an obsession in the popular mind. But the fundamental character of Judaism overrides all necessary criticism, and only explains all prophetic doom.

In that setting we may rightly imagine the training and education of the son of Mary. An overwhelming secret is hidden in her heart (Luke 2 : 19) but the local synagogue and its associated *Beth-ha-Midrash* would afford for her son a basis of education which would be fully congenial to her deepest desires for Him. What He is in the purpose of God may still be but partially comprehended. At the moment He is her son, her beloved, and nothing can be too good to give Him. There is specific material to guide our inferences, and it is certain that the mental and spiritual development which early became occasion for comment was nourished by a home environment perfectly suited to what lay ahead (Luke 2 : 40, 52). The elders of the congregation would not expect those qualities in the children under their care, and the scribe who presided at the *Beth-ha-Midrash* (let us say the headmaster of the local Church School) would know that here was an unusual pupil. The boy Jesus would become familiar with the Scriptures, and thus with canonical Hebrew, as well as the Aramaic vernacular. Without such knowledge He could not enter into any share in the synagogue worship.

68

At last He reached His religious 'majority' at the age of twelve. Liturgically He is no longer a child, but the youngest of adult men, and already charged with liturgical duties. (There must have been many Jewish homes in the European 1930s in which a child of twelve had to carry the leadership of the family worship and to bear the apprehension of the family life.) At last the annual passover pilgrimage finds Him in the temple at Jerusalem (Luke 2 : 41). He comes, as it were, from a village school to visit the university, attaches Himself to a seminar of far choicer quality, and finds Himself already at home. There he would hear nothing of the vernacular speech save among his family and friends from Nazareth. He must try to take his part in discussions and teaching in the sacred tongue. This was not to be expected even of an unusually mature child. It is a tribute to this one Child, but also to the teachers from whom He normally learned.

The synagogue and the school were departments of one unit. Just as the synagogue is the place of worship, in which education and study formed a natural concomitant, so the *Beth-ha-Midrash,* the school of language and of the sacred law, is also potentially the place of prayer, and what we would now call ascetic theology. It is essential to realize that the conservatism and the static forms of Jewish religious life, for which our modern concepts of religion and progress are to a large extent irrelevant—even a contradiction in terms—made it possible that the social and religious structure of first century life could be carried over into later years.[48] We need not anticipate the actual development that followed from the marked influence of later mystical thought, nor assume that all of the *Battim-ha-Midrash* of the first century would show the intensity of concentration on the spiritual life which we shall find at the famous centre at Safed in Galilee in the fourteenth century. But the Rabbinic teaching on prayer which we have briefly evidenced, is for the present sufficient to show that the teaching in the synagogue at Nazareth and in its own school would go far beyond the fundamental study of Torah, although that remained its true purpose. On every Sabbath Jesus would enter into the blessing of the Name of God, and would share the insight into the loving-kindness that had called them forth. The atmosphere of worship, of education, of devotion is as one : 'Thou continuest holy, O thou worship of Israel' (Ps. 22 : 3).

The background of this single-pointed education, and the pattern of obedience in his home, prepare the crisis of His Baptism (Luke 2 : 51f.). Already the Baptist is in revolt against the generation of vipers (Matt. 3 : 7) who are content to display the label of orthodoxy upon a life far from the reality it should denote. It is noteworthy that our Lord was later faced with the same symptom, and was able to bring a far more searching diagnosis (John 8 : 33–58). The children of

Abraham should do honour to their father. That should be obvious. But if they really valued their inheritance, as they protested, they would recognize Him whom God had sent. If they rest upon God, why is it so obvious that they do not know Him? But if it is upon Abraham after all, should they not join with Abraham in honouring one in whom Abraham had rejoiced? But now upon the banks of Jordan Jesus is content to place Himself with those for whom John's baptismal message of repentance is essential. The hesitation shown by John is clearly based upon a spiritual perception. Already, when still in His mother's womb, he had recognized the unborn Messiah. But the return from Egypt and the restoration of some political peace after the death of Herod, would have caused John to hear news of his kinsman in the normal course (Matt. 2: 13-23; 3: 14). Jesus is not a self-conscious example—still less a decoy to encourage a hesitant crowd. The Baptist's surprise is obvious in this. But it must be as He commands, for His own command springs from the deeper obedience. He cannot purge the religion of law until He has proved Himself subject to the law. This act of submission is part of the obedience He was learning in everything which happened to Him. It is the true son of Israel who can be truly Lord of the worlds. At once the truth of His command vindicates itself, and His penetration of spiritual necessity. The unknown is proclaimed from heaven as the well-beloved Son.

As He was in His home, so He is at once before men, a pattern of humility and obedience. He shows Himself to be upon the hidden way, and He will walk there to the end, whether in the demands of the crowd or in the solitude of the wilderness. The crisis of Baptism is past. He who needed no repentance has made His first self-offering in the sight of men. Even as the Lord Jehovah in ancient times had taken on Himself the wrath of the people against Samuel, so now the Lord Incarnate faces the sin of the world alone. The Baptism was truly part of His contemplative obedience, and yet He seems to have known His way through that crisis from the start. John was doubtful of its necessity, but was caught up within the power of such an obedience. In the Temptation we shall see something more prolonged, more personal to the soul. We see it again in more than one later crisis—as in the coming of the Greeks which showed Him that the real battle was joined. 'The hour is come that the Son of Man should be glorified' (John 12: 23). The glory is given to the Father, and in that act of oblation the immediate crisis has passed. We see it in Gethsemane throughout the Agony, and again in the oblation that brings His submission to the soldiers. There are moments in which the reality of the human spiritual warfare is made evident. They are not moments of 'doubt': that happens only to us. But they are moments of real choice, of real encounter, of real obedience. Disobedience is inconceivable, knowing what we know of Him. And yet in each encounter it must be possible. The choice is laid open, and the will is free until again in each moment it enslaves itself to the will of God. St. Augustine makes the distinction that is clear in his own mind. 'The first liberty of the will was to be able not to sin (*posse non peccare*): the last will be much greater—not to be able to sin (*non posse peccare*).' [49] In his great controversy he will not transfer to mortality and to time the first of the treasures of heaven. And yet He who was a Son—the heir of all the heavenly joy—learned obedience by everything that happened to Him (Heb. 5 : 8). The path of obedience must be real. Between any two points upon the road there is a distance to be covered, an energy to be expended, a growth to be realized. The single term that we must avoid in thinking of our Lord is perhaps that of 'progress.' The Jesus of liberal history is not found in the discipline of the Wilderness or in the Agony of the Garden. Heaven waits, and God is praying His way lest He should be less than Himself. In one verse of scripture (Matt. 4 : 2) six weeks of our time have passed, and we are shown nothing of their character. Yet such conflicts are of the essence of the contemplative way. If we are wisely silent for ourselves, the saints of the Church have sometimes been allowed to speak for our guidance. But such testimony must wait its due turn. One hesitation must be mentioned at the outset, lest at any time it should be obscured or forgotten.

As we have been considering the hidden life of the chosen body in the past, and shall shortly be tracing that same stream as it flows into the future, there must be a certain element of restraint at the point we have now reached. We spoke at the outset of the revelation of Being and of Relationship. That revelation was beyond our reach, and its unveiling was of necessity veiled, though we rightly longed to draw the veil aside. But now we approach the same Revelation in the person of the Incarnate Word Himself, and we cannot escape the sense of restraint. The Revelation is His Being. It is His perfect union with the Father. That which He tells of God, He shows of God. That which He speaks, He is. The word is God, dwelling among men in the precise terms used of the mysterious dwelling of the Shekinah. The prelude to the first epistle of John is emphatic here. 'That which was from the beginning . . . we have seen with our eyes, and touched with our hands, for the life made itself plain . . .' (1 John 1 : 1f.). There are many indications that our Lord responded to St. John's sensitive and loving understanding by letting him see what others could not understand. To call him 'the disciple whom Jesus loved' implies no favouritism. Where the response to His love is made more clearly upon the spiritual level of the gift, He is able to impart the gift more richly than to those who try in vain to understand. The heart of Jesus, a burning furnace of charity, is the centre of all things to His contemplatives. They know themselves ever far below the heights of the knowledge he imparts, but they alone perceive the manner of the giving. Yet we must beware lest, in trying to speak of His own hidden life, we presume to anything that He did not will to disclose to the Church. Himself we could not harm, but the secrets of the King must be guarded. And yet all may still be safe, since He would surely will that we keep our eyes fixed upon Himself [50] in the constant knowledge that He prayed for us the gift of the Holy Spirit to bring all things concerning Himself to our remembrance (John 16: 13f.). In union with that prayer, He will not permit that anything should be known against His will; whatever is the imagination of men, however sincere it be, will in its nature be less than the Truth which is Himself.

The long preparation is over. The days and nights of prayer, as so often in the future in His times of greatest activity, will have followed the course which was presented to the dedication of His will. It is a crucial point. The manner and character of His ministry is still not shown to men, and it is certain that His task would be laid out in the fullness of its possibilities before the Father. Yet from what His Church has learned, it is not well that such prayer should become an endless vacillation between external choices. The real clearness of action will not always arise from a fully conceived plan of action, though such a plan may be needed. Above all it requires a fully surrendered will to do or not to do, even as the Father wills. We have seen this precise direction of prayer, which would be very familiar to his mind.[51] The Church later learned the perfection of that Rabbinic counsel from Thomas à Kempis (*De Imitatione Christi,* III, 15 : 3).

> 'Let Thy will be mine, and let my will ever follow Thine, and accord with it truly well. Let me always will or not will even as Thou: let me not be able to will or not will save as Thou willest or willest not.'

It is small wonder that a task so stupendous, and so prepared, should produce in the Enemy of Truth a determination to confuse and to distract all that the Lord had resolved. He had been led to the wilderness so that the opportunity might be afforded. He had in fact been led into temptation. For our weakness He will later counsel a prayer that we may not be so led (Matt. 6: 13; Luke 11: 4).

The Temptation in the Wilderness (Matt. 4: 1–11; Mark 1: 12–13; Luke 4: 1–13)
The interpretation of the main lines of these accounts covers a wider

field than concerns us in this study. It is well, however, to realize that
no human witness could have been present, and that all knowledge of
the three points of crisis can come only from our Lord Himself. The
account raises many issues which we can leave aside. It is clear that the
impact of the Temptation upon our Lord's mind is closely affected by
the Messianic recognition at His Baptism. A similar recognition will be
seen also at the Transfiguration, but this first occasion is different. He
has come from the long discipline of the hidden years. His impact upon
His fellows in Nazareth may be inferred, but now He comes quietly,
unrecognized save by the Baptist. He has mingled with an eager crowd,
and has shared the purpose that brought them to the riverside; there is
no reason for Him to be noticed. It is not clear whether the heavenly
vision was seen by any one, though St. Luke's account is more objective,
and allows the possibility. But to our Lord, at least, the experience was
in total contrast to the anonymity of nearly thirty years. Whatever
measure of foreknowledge is assumed, the event must have been of
profound spiritual moment for Him. Even if it confirmed knowledge
long possessed, the confirmation itself is memorable. If, as seems more
probable, it was a wholly unforeseen but conclusive experience, it is
easier to understand the direct effect in the long ordeal of prayer and
fasting. Such a vocation demands a comparable vigil.

The actual points of impact which the tempter used are significant.
The clear analogies with the spiritual battle in our own time—the
claims of a purely materialistic estimate of life, the claims of pseudo-
spirituality and false mysticism, and the claims of the God-state—these
and similar readings of the Temptation only show how little the
spiritual warfare varies from age to age. The devil knows very few
themes, and is driven to infinite ingenuity in producing specious
variations upon them. The chosen variant is always precisely fitted to the
occasion. It is usually fitted also to the tempted soul. We may assume
that St. Matthew and St. Luke use a common source of recollection of
what our Lord had told the disciples on some occasion when He
wished them to know how temptation might assail them. His perfect
humility would not over-colour the character of the battle, and in this
case it is difficult to imagine severe allurement proving less attractive,
or being more easily repelled. The real battle must have been fought
out during the forty days, in reflection upon the whole future disclosed
at His Baptism. The devil is beaten before he shows himself.

The contemplative does not need to argue the merits of the case.
The fact of hunger and exhaustion are obvious, for the Incarnation of
the Son of God proclaims His humanity. It likewise assures that the
newly revealed Messianic destiny will be used for its proper ends alone,
and not for personal release. His trust is unmoved by any ordeal or

crisis. Through the now acknowledged Son, who is heir of all things, the very worlds were made (Heb. 1 : 2). He will know by right the ministry of angels, as is shown many times even in the brief Gospel narratives. He is also to refuse their ministry to rescue Him in the Garden. 'This is your hour and the power of darkness' (Luke 22 : 53). And yet a few moments ago He has known the consolation of the angel of the Agony. There are no apt formulas in the soul's relation with God. The single principle of trust covers all. 'Do or do not as thou willest' is the contemplative answer. He appears to be left alone, 'and yet I am not alone' (John 16 : 32). So now bodily hunger must wait upon the same unvarying trust. As with Elijah in his own wilderness and in fear of his life, the angels came to do what was their own appointment—to minister not only to the heir of all things, but also, as they do and ever will do, to those who are the heirs of His salvation —heirs of God and joint-heirs with Christ (Rom. 8 : 17).

The meaning of this trial for those brought into the hidden way needs no elaboration, for each is made to know it in his own life and after his own fashion. The sophistication of our modern world regards as fanciful, or as a theme for cultured literary pleasure, the faith of the negro slaves shown in one of their spiritual songs : 'He's got the whole world in His hands.' But this faith is unable to be sustained on an emotional level. It demands the constant discipline of the will-in-love, on which alone the prayer of the contemplative can be supported. When it is so founded, events or lack of events, action or passion leave the course of the life unchanged. There is no circumstance that reaches beyond the overshadowing meaning of Love. The Son of God cannot be deflected from His path by these small matters. But what of the great? To prove His power by means that would demand attention— to break through the natural order as a supreme demonstration of His faith in God. That, surely, would be permissible? To minds perverted by magic there would appear a sense in which the Truth itself might be made more true. The latent danger of a conscious mystical quest lies in the suggestion that the abnormal in religious experience has increased spiritual value—even increased moral value. Such notions, and their accompanying practices, are not well countered by supposing that they are fraudulent and delusory. They may be very much the reverse. Where there is unbalanced attention to the psychic element in human being, usually from a Manichaean notion that it works upon a higher plane, a distortion of the whole balance may result. Powers may be generated, and power may be encountered of a real and terrible kind. The self-induced mystical experience, built by human will from a purely natural foundation, can become an established indulgence even to the voiding of all natural power, and to an ultimate deprivation of being which does not stop with loss of sanity. Those who need to know more may consult Prof. Jacques Maritain's essay—'The natural mystical experience and the void.' In the process such things often attract great attention. The victim, and still more the literary exponent, of magical practices carries a terrible fascination for certain types of men and women, more honest but less intelligent than the evil they encounter.[52]

Only those who accept the psychic element in human nature as a mere matter of fact, just as they accept bodily capacities and use them in pursuit of a true goal, can be free from the dangers of such temptation. It bears many guises, but is a theme which might distract us from what we need to learn. The body and the human psyche alike find their completion and their safety in the love which is God—in the divine charity by which all true relationship and true being are satisfied. There is a love which is purely possessive, and another love which seeks its own enlargement and exaltation. Even in a sincere Christian intention 'the soul is too often loving itself and fulfilling itself in its desire for God.'[53] The psychic element in human nature often taints the Body of Christ with an element of excitement and mystery, but these desires can only distort the true relationships within the Body.

In considering the second temptation presented to our Lord, such things must seem alien to His pure being. They were, however, an active poison in the mediterranean world. In Judaism itself, as we shall later have reason to discuss, the growth of mystical religion arising in considerable part as a reaction from extreme legalism, but also arising within the later environments of the Dispersion, embraced elements of a dangerous Gnostic character, by which the character of Judaism itself became distorted. The time and place of our Lord's earthly ministry may have been more free, though recent documentary discoveries show some contemporary alien elements. In all His contacts there is the single emphasis on God alone, and the redirecting of newly released lives into the love of God alone. In anything that He did, and anything that the Church is called to do in His name, that is all-sufficient. His followers need no other powers, however real they be of their own dark kind, and however potent for their own perverted purposes. To seek such power is indeed to tempt the Lord our God—to play the part of the Devil. In the first temptation the lesson was one of unfailing trust. Nothing further needs to be learned for Him to overthrow the second temptation.

The final trial is yet to come. The Devil sometimes knows when he is beaten, though so often he appears to the Christian disciple to overplay his hand, and to become merely obvious. Here, in his master-struggle, everything is at stake. He will no longer cast doubt upon the

Messiahship. That vocation is accepted—even if in the irony of silence. But if the Messiah has really come to enter into His Kingdom, it seems needless that the Kingdom of Satan should oppose Him. Let Him therefore take what He will. Satan will withdraw from any claim upon the kingdoms of this world. He will, in fact, surrender and lay down his arms. There is only one minor condition. Let his authority be acknowledged before it is relinquished. 'All these things will I give thee, if thou wilt fall down and worship me.' It is a strange condition, perhaps relying for success upon its sheer impertinence. The suggestion is plain. 'You are the Christ of God. I admit it. As such, all things should come under your sway. But at the moment they still belong to me. Just acknowledge that one fact and then take what you will.' It is akin to the formal casting of incense before the image of the Roman Emperor —a trivial formality which cost the lives of many martyrs. The force of the temptation can be seen in a double aspect. It is in a strict sense political and secular, an assumption that the achievement of power was all that our Lord could wish. It was the attempted corruption of His mission. The term 'worship' has primarily the sense of homage— of the acknowledgment of authority. The things that are offered are not fictitious. On the tempter's own terms they could be granted.

But in a deeper sense the appeal to sheer ambition and domination is a truly religious temptation, and the homage desired as the price of ambition puts the soul in hell. History shows men to whom Satanism is a fatal infection. Even with such darkness as this our Lord's purity was assailed—in vain. He who knew no sin was indeed made to be sin—to have the mere possibility of such a fall placed before His mind. It is on this deeper level that the offer is instantly and finally rejected, by a stern challenge to the one being who for a like ambition has refused both homage and worship to His Creator. For our understanding also, this temptation is the climax. Our Lord had been assailed in body and in soul. Here the temptation is directed to the apex of the mind—to the intelligent will which is supremely the agent of our deepest prayer. A failure here is above all else defeat.

The Unfolding of Revelation

In the power of the Spirit privacy and preparation are now laid aside, and the public ministry has begun. But the hidden life remains with Him as His mystery, disclosed to those who are given to Him by the Father (Mark 4 : 11 and parallels). Much has been written of the visible from which we may learn. Our task is the tracing of the hidden life, and that will largely mean the teaching and practice of His prayer. From the outset it will have to be admitted that the external evidence is very slight, and in such a field imaginative speculation is misleading and unworthy. The stage of the contemplative quest is set for us by Mary Magdalene in the home at Bethany, and her silent adoring love is the good part which is not taken away.

In the traces of the hidden life which have been noted historically in the Old Testament, the element of faith was clearly marked. The writer to the Hebrews has, in fact, already done what we have tried to do for ourselves. The quality of obedience which showed itself in varied and often strange crises is summed up in a new obedience which is itself the completion, the final accomplishment of faith (Heb. 12 : 2). 'The uniqueness of Jesus, his distinction . . . from all who preceded him, including all the prophets of Israel, is that it depends not on faith but upon sight. No man hath seen God . . . no one hath ascended up into heaven, but the Son doeth what he seeth the Father doing : indeed there is no action of the Father which is hidden from the Son' [54] (John 1 : 18; 3 : 13; 5 : 19–20). The Fourth Gospel thus establishes a most important link. With men, obedience to the will of God is a means to contemplation. With our Lord, the contemplation in which His purity ever dwells is the secret of a perfect obedience—a union of the Will in Love. The unity of His Person, the mystery of the hypostatic union in the Divine Nature—does not render the obedience of His earthly life unreal or theoretical. The Fourth Gospel in particular stresses its centrality to the understanding of the Incarnate Word.[55] 'My meat is to do the will of him that sent me' (John 4 : 34). 'I can of myself do nothing; as I hear, so I judge, and my judgment is righteous because I seek not mine own will, but the will of Him that sent me' (John 5 : 30). It follows that will is the condition of knowledge for us, as even for Him (John 7 : 17). As He moves towards the Cross, love leads to obedience (John 14 : 31), while, on the other side of the veil, the chosen are assured that to obey is to be loved (John 15 : 10). Even in the Lord Himself 'the obedience is not automatic and passive, but a supreme ethical bending of the will to fulfil the commandment of God whatever the cost.' [56] This truth offers no false or presumptuous comparison. Rather does the perfect obedience put our imperfect striving into its true setting, showing the source and the spirit which must always characterize it, thus giving full justification to the principle of the hidden life as we have begun to see it. The special emphasis and understanding in St. John's gospel is sufficiently supported by the synoptic tradition. The acknowledgment of the Beloved Son at His baptism rests on the same conformity of will (Mark 1 : 11). If there be indeed more than we cannot yet understand, there is certainly not less than the goal of our own union. The same acknowledgment at the Transfiguration is a command to the Church's obedience (Mark 9 : 7). And if the clear vision of His coming Passion brings, as it will bring to

ST. AUGUSTINES COLLEGE LIBRARY, CANTERBURY

any true humanity, a sense of shrinking, the prayer for release is coupled closely with a full acceptance of the Father's will (Mark 14 : 35f.). The supreme authority of His Messianic claim rests upon the same unclouded vision and perfect union of will : similarly the moral authority that commands the world of evil rests upon the action of the Spirit of God with whom He is at one (Matt. 11 : 25–7). Most clearly of all, in that dramatic moment when the coming Passion seems to break suddenly upon His mind, 'the concrete obedience of the Son . . . marks the dethronement of the Devil from his tyranny over men.' [57]

The immediacy of union which so marked our Lord's life is not, however, the mature reflection of a later age. It was perceived and remarked by the disciples—not uniformly the most discerning of men at that time. Their request to learn the secret of His prayer will be considered later. He is unable to show them, at that time, all that they wish to know. But in direct connection with their destiny of union, he must state clearly the nature of the road by which His disciples can follow in His steps. The road to God is the knowledge of truth and the possession of life. Truth and life are no ideal abstractions. They are present concretely in the Incarnate Son of God who is both truth and life. He gives the Life which He is. He reveals the Truth which He is. Consequently He is the Way (John 11 : 25, 42f.; 14 : 6f.). Philip has seen beyond his power to understand. Moses and the prophets were allowed a vision of God (Exod. 24 : 9–11; 33 : 13–23; Isa. 6 : 1; 40 : 5). Can they not be favoured in the same way? Things would be much more simple. They would be content, and would not trouble Him again (John 14 : 8). But Philip has failed to realize that to live with Jesus is to see God. St. Paul's great assertion of the unitive state (Gal. 2 : 20) shows the completeness of the transformation worked in Him. 'He might see Jahveh in the veil of his glory, like Moses and Isaiah . . . but which of the Old Testament saints would have dared to say "I live, yet no longer I but Jahveh liveth in me"? The most intimate union of God with man could be achieved only after the Divine Nature itself had been united to a human nature in the Incarnation of the Second Person of the Trinity. The full mystical union presupposes the hypostatic union.' [58] The valuable point quoted here is not, of course, to be understood as though the mystical union which is the supreme gift of God presupposes the achievement or possession of the mystery that belongs to the Lord Messias alone. None the less, anything that men may be allowed to receive in heaven is made possible by the glory of the Son of God in His incarnate life among them.

The innate perfection of this union of the will-in-love is the secret of the prayer-life of Jesus. There is no speculative imagination in this judgment, nor any straining of scant material. The Christian knowledge of the contemplative way of life, and the prayer which is the energy of that life, proves itself constantly as that way becomes increasing unitive in its course. How far more certainly must the same truth appear in the life of our Lord. This view, however, leads us to face an important and difficult distinction. We are stating two apparently opposite truths : both are true, and the resolution is not in compromise or verbal adjustment. In His humanity the perfect form of our humanity is seen. Could this ever be said of a human being—one of ourselves, a sinner redeemed in Christ and living in Christ—we should unquestionably be able to trace a spiritual growth leading all the way into that perfection. Such a man would 'increase in wisdom and stature, and in favour with God and man' not merely in the manner for which all of us pray and strive, but in the manner disclosed in the humanity of Christ. He would be brought by the grace of God into the abiding life, bearing no fruit from His human stem but bearing much fruit of the true Vine (John 15 : 4–8). So would he become a true disciple, and a cause of glory to the Father. Now the writer to the Hebrews insists firmly on this element of spiritual growth also in our Lord Himself. He writes of an unfolding Humanity which 'though he were a Son, yet learned obedience by everything which happened to him.' This point is deliberately stressed and singled out by the unforgettable play in his words : *emathen aph hōn epathen tēn upakoēn* : which throws a spotlight upon the truth (Heb. 5 : 8). But it is not enough to record this splendour of the contemplative way for our example and encouragement. By such obedience the very Son became the cause of eternal salvation to all who likewise obey. This passage is central in the theme of our study. A listening obedience wrought in humility—a standing underneath the whirling events of life and listening to (nay, hearing) the voice of God speaking in each moment—is the perfect characteristic of the contemplative way in Christian spiritual life. It is the highroad of union and is therefore the purpose of our making. On that road the soul moves forward and upward, though in using such crude terms we are always warned by the author of the *Cloud of Unknowing* (Cap. 51)— 'Beware that thou conceive not bodily that which is said ghostly. . . . Heaven ghostly is as near down as up . . . the highest and nearest way thither is run by desires.' Yet we are permitted to pray for the grace of union, in the knowledge that nothing can be nearer to His Sacred Heart. And so we are entitled—nay, it is our bounden duty—to fix our eyes upon the Master of the life we seek to live, and to know that He has passed by the same road, and that in Him we see the fullness of the invisible God (Col. 1 : 13ff.).

But as we rest in that conclusion, and see it as an insistent goal, the words of St. Paul are inescapable. Both scripture and the tradition of the Church determine that goal for us. Both scripture and the tradition of the Church almost warn us away from daring to look up its meaning. This fullness of sanctifying grace, the fullness of our prayer and longing, is reached so perfectly by our Lord, and yet that is but part of what we must say of Him. In a sense it is not a partial truth, but the whole truth concerning His humanity, and thus the whole truth that can bear upon our spiritual discipline. Yet there is another truth to be known. While this perfection grows in Him by His contemplative obedience, His human nature was in its inmost being united with the Divine Word. The Incarnation was complete—'not by the conversion of the Godhead into flesh; but by the taking of the Manhood into God.' This well-known clause in the formula *Quicunque vult* is sometimes grossly misunderstood. Out of all deference to the context and to the historical setting it is thought to 'explain away' the truth of our Lord's Divine nature. Liberal theologians will conclude that He was 'after all' a man like ourselves, who by great virtue ascended to a moral status so lofty that His humanity merited divinity. The common formula of such thought is to call Him 'the moral equivalent of God.' It is further, and far more dangerously, concluded that such divinity is the natural and psychological right of all men, who can in their turn do likewise, even though it would be allowed that many miss their supposed potentiality! In the moment of the overshadowing of the mother of God by the Holy Spirit, the humanity thus conceived and still unborn was sealed into the Divine Nature who desired it for His dwelling place. The home was made ready, and was made inviolable. He speaks to us with a human voice and from a human being, and commands us to a unity of abiding in Himself. But Himself who so commands is for ever one with the Divine Word who speaks in Him and so speaks to us.

There are sure, if incomprehensible, formulas to guard this mystery, but for us it is important to be sure that we mean all He is meaning in terms of the task laid upon us. We acknowledge and affirm the full faith of Holy Church in these mysteries, confessing the true humanity of the Lord Christ and the hypostatic union with the Divine Word. In our own duty and for our own purpose, however, we speak plainly of the union in Himself to which He calls us, and may know in so speaking that we are called to tread a path known to Himself by the fullness of human knowledge, save only without a cloud of sin. We are called to set foot on His road, and in His company to learn obedience through all that happens to us, and in our measure we dare to obey Him. At the same time the humanity which is our only pattern was taken out of the very order of our being, since He was in His Being bound within the glory of the Blessed Trinity. We can only rest in the intention that in affirming one truth we in no way deny or neglect the other. Human language may struggle in the dilemma of that which is and also is not. Here we speak of Consummate Being—of Him who *is*.

The Prayer of Jesus

The union of which we have spoken is the secret of His prayer, but the record of that prayer in the Gospels must be studied carefully, and the information is always elusive. In the first instance we must distinguish between the recorded fact of His praying, and any direct teaching about prayer in itself. Save for isolated references, and the story of Gethsemane which is common to the Synoptic record, St. Mark gives us but little. St. Matthew groups his references rather mechanically, and places his conflation at a very early phase of the Ministry. His important section (Matt. 7 : 7–11) towards the end of his long account of the Sermon on the Mount seems to have been separated from Matt. 6 : 5–15 owing to the absence of the key-word 'proseuchē.' St. Luke, however, gives not only a fuller record, but notably gives a widely different context to the teaching.

This could, of course, be a matter for the details of critical and textual study, and as such would be beyond the direct purpose of this book. It will, however, be convenient to illustrate our comparison by the different treatments of the Lord's Prayer. St. Matthew brings our Lord straight from the Temptation into Capernaum : the first choice of disciples is made, and after a very short summary of a widespread ministry the detailed teaching begins with the Sermon on the Mount (Matt. 4 : 13, 18 25). Midway in this sermon an almost passing caution against insincerity and vain repetition in prayer leads him to record the Lord's Prayer in the full liturgical pattern since used in the worship of the Church (Matt. 6 : 9–13). (The doxology, though normally accepted in certain parts of liturgical practice, may certainly be ignored in the Gospel account, not from any disparagement but merely upon full textual authority.) The prayer itself is recorded almost gratuitously. There has been no direct request. There is no apparent reason for its appearance save as a liturgical comment upon teaching which precedes and follows in the course of the Sermon. As we have noted above a very important piece of teaching upon prayer (Matt. 7 : 7–11; Luke 11 : 9–13) has been separated in the first Gospel from the earlier section, though there is no apparent evidence of displacement in the manuscripts. The account in St. Matthew is almost casual and imperceptive, more particularly in its apparent assumption that our Lord's own conception and practice of prayer is fully expressed.

F

This comment may appear to ignore the mass of literature expounding the text of the Lord's prayer. No such disparagement is intended, nor in particular can we forget the use which St. Teresa makes of the prayer in the whole body of her ascetic teaching. This teaching will be considered later in due course (cf. chap. 11 *infra*). For the moment it is necessary to make the single point that the Synoptic record, without that of the Fourth Gospel, would give comparatively little basis for our understanding of the subject as we need to understand it.

In St. Luke's parallel account the situation is very different. The narrative moves far more deliberately, and with an obvious dramatic momentum which is compelling in its naturalness and in no way suggests literary artifice. According to St. Luke, the Temptation is followed by the opening of the ministry in Nazareth (Luke 4 : 16–21) where our Lord is well known, and by the formal submission of His vocation in His own place of worship. There is some confusion in the account, but the Nazareth encounter was evidently a critical challenge, as the whole record shows to have been clearly intended. By some it seems acceptable that 'this day this scripture is fulfilled.' The supposed slight to the importance of Nazareth (Luke 4 : 23) occurs more in what He adds voluntarily than in the central Messianic declaration. The anger which filled all those hearing these things in the synagogue (Luke 4 : 28) makes St. Luke's narrative at this point seem somewhat inconsequential, which is far from his careful and 'orderly' style (Luke 1 : 3). The first choice of disciples (Luke 5 : 1–11) is preceded by, and followed with, a series of important teaching miracles. A sense of burden is upon Him, and we find the first instance of many withdrawals into solitary prayer (Luke 5 : 16). Before long, with the sense of urgency still pressing on the Evangelist, the selection of the inner Apostolate is made (Luke 6 : 12–16) with a night of prayer and vigil to sustain it. The Sermon on the Mount is far more briefly recorded, and St. Luke's dominant motive in selection seems to be the growing tension of the drama. In the light of the account of the Baptism of Jesus, the messengers sent by John the Baptist have great importance (Luke 7 : 18–20). The Baptist's judgment is being confirmed; however significant his own mission, here is someone far beyond it (Luke 3 : 16). The first meeting with Mary of Magdala is heightened in St. Luke by a medical comment (Luke 8 : 2) which also found its way into the rejected ending of St. Mark's gospel (Mark 16 : 9). It seems reasonable to suppose that the spiritual crisis which accompanied her first meeting with Jesus (for the penitence is clearly shown at the outset) was for Mary a drastic reordering of her whole life. St. Luke's almost casual comment indicates that for him as evangelist this meeting is no special event in the growing tension. The miracles continue—some from the common tradition but all serving his own purpose.

The apostles are sent out, and return in the hope of some respite (Luke 9 : 1–6, 10). He takes them into a desert place, but it is hopeless to expect privacy. They must face the crowd, and the feeding of the five thousand is a memorable way of doing what He commands (Luke 9 : 10–16). Already (Luke 8 : 19–21) they have realized that His mission must separate Him from all His family ties, and in this demanding mission they are being caught up. And now the signs of coming crisis, becoming slowly more obvious to those whom He takes with Him into His hidden life, are pressing upon them. The marks are more familiar to us to-day. The hidden life is, in fact, lived in a continual expectancy. The calm recollection must remain undisturbed, for the contemplative cannot afford the distraction of excitement. But no great demand will ever be made without the clear warning-signal, silent and hidden though it rightly be.

In this case it is not the drama of the miracle which has laid hold upon Jesus. A matter of far greater moment is about to begin. He is praying alone, and the twelve are resting around Him (Luke 9 : 18). He comes from the silence of His vigil-prayer to turn their minds from their own mission to His. We are not yet in Caesarea Philippi, but the spiritual context of St. Luke's recording of the question has its own meaning (Luke 9 : 20). 'What are they saying about me?' St. Peter's answer is set in a simpler context than that of Matt. 16 and the immediate result of the answer in the other Synoptists is more commonly accepted. In all the accounts the narrative of the Transfiguration follows (Matt. 17 : 1–8; Mark 9 : 2–8; Luke 9 : 28–36). This was a spiritual event totally strange not only to the chosen three, but to all Christian experience. They were permitted to see, though hardly to understand, the reality of Him who had taken possession of their lives. The story of the Transfiguration is almost certainly the explanation of the setting in which St. Luke records the pattern prayer. The Messianic recognition at Caesarea Philippi is an accepted turning point in the Ministry. 'Before' and 'after' characterizes all exposition of Jesus' dealing with His disciples. But the single experience of the Transfiguration seems to account for St. Peter's confession. Many times Jesus had taken them apart when He needed solitude for prayer. This might appear but one more similar occasion. Often they may have watched His prayer with wonder, but now sleep overcomes them, as later in Gethsemane. He needs their consolation, but the flesh is weak. Suddenly they are awakened. It seems to be a dream, but all the disciples have seen the symbolic figures of the Law and the Prophet in intercourse with their Master. Three people do not dream the same dream together. So it must be real, although it makes Him more mysterious than ever. They have received 'a unique mystical experience,' and like all novices they seek to secure it as a possession. As their answer, the vision passes, and they are alone again with Him. But in this very natural fear they had learned an essential truth that could never have come in words. The reality of the hidden presence was made known to them. The Shekinah dwelling in the Holy Place accompanied their Master, and they had seen, because for His own sake they must know. Père Bouyer emphasizes the link between the Transfiguration, the Epiphany and the classical text in Exodus (33 : 18–34 : 8), and points out that Elijah, the third participant in the Transfiguration, was likewise tested on Horeb—the mountain of Theophanies.[59]

Almost at once the first apostolic journey is repeated on a far larger scale. The result gives to Jesus the true joy, not in the evidence of human mastery but in the knowledge of the joy of heaven. You are blind indeed, He reminds the chosen twelve : it is not the great and powerful who are shown the glory of God. Once again there is need for rest. As the burden increases upon Him, so is the refuge provided, and the home at Bethany is prepared to receive Him. The chosen few are beginning to understand. Here He finds the understanding to which even His perfect sufficiency can turn with relief. The restraint shown by St. Luke in his understanding of such elements in our Lord's life is of the greatest value. To any who are brought into the hidden life such consolation is given in one form or another. Both the use and the proper discipline of such spiritual friendships is a matter to be cherished and guarded. When, as can happen, they are valued for something less than the will of God, we can lose His meaning in grasping at the gift.

Thus far St. Luke's story goes. In its own right it is a remarkable narrative. It has been briefly resumed here because of what follows, and was meant by the evangelist to follow, in close and logical connection. The mission of Jesus and the preparation of the Church have steadily advanced. Events of marked spiritual significance have followed one upon another. Above all, the inner group have been allowed to enter into experiences which they may never fully understand but can never forget. However little they may realize it, they are entering a corporate spiritual understanding for which it seems that our Lord has been waiting. Consequently they are ready for further knowledge which, as we have suggested above, an earlier stage of experience would have been inadequate. St. Luke writes 'in order,' and he communicates in his writing an understanding that he has firmly reached.

Once again there is the setting of the familiar prayer (Luke 11 : 1). The disciples are growing accustomed to the idea that these periods of retreat are the times when the real work is done. The subsequent teaching, or miracle, or sharp encounter with hostile elements, can be handled lightly—almost gaily—when the groundwork of prayer has been so established. But what is this prayer, with none of the customary setting of familiar liturgy? He is alone in the darkness after weary days, and they know that even watching those days has left them too weary to stay awake. How often has He found it necessary to shed before God a load that is proving unbearable? These things had piled one upon another. It was all so far beyond them, and yet it was clearly necessary that they should understand. It seems likely that only the twelve were with Him, though this is not certain. Some one of them who had graduated from the school of John the Baptist would have mentioned the prayers that He had taught, and the memory gives a precedent for this request. 'We have been watching your prayer : we have never seen people pray like that. Can you teach us how to do it?'

The answer is immediate, and as the answer of a consummate teacher, who knows the innermost thought of his pupils, He begins just where they are. He cannot teach them His own prayer. They would not understand, and in any case the discipline of their spiritual life needs to be taken much further before they would rightly be ready for such a level of intercourse. So His answer is clear : 'When *you* pray—say . . . ' Nothing could be plainer—nothing less mistakable. They have heard Him warn men against the mistakes of the Pharisees, but the substance of this lesson is material which they would have heard constantly in the synagogue. He has warned them against repetitions of formulas, but the prayer He dictates is repeated to this day, and many times in every day. The elements of formality, or of direct requests which can arise too easily from their own will and their own choice, have largely obscured the way of prayer into which they will need to enter as they become more familiar with His Father in heaven. St. Luke's omissions from the full liturgical formula recorded by St. Matthew are interesting, and seem to be deliberate. The simplicity and brevity of what He chooses to record are scaled to the disciples' situation and to their need. As we have suggested, the prayer does not belong in the Matthaean setting. The limited development of the disciples' experience at that stage would hardly have produced the request to which our Lord makes instant response. The fact that He does not give the questioner the answer he may have sought, detracts in no way from the supreme importance of the pattern prayer. It gave an opportunity for teaching which was then needed. If the account is brief, it is surely because He wished to say no more.

There has been much discussion as to the connection between this prayer and the current Rabbinic teaching. The actual form in St. Luke must not be overlooked because it is seldom repeated.

'Father, may thy name be hallowed :

May thy kingdom come :

Give us day by day our bread for the morrow :

And forgive us our sins, for we ourselves forgive each one of
our debtors :

And bring us not into temptation' (Luke 11 : 2–4).

There follows immediately the vivid parable which teaches persistence
in prayer. Every one who asks, receives. He that seeks, finds. To him
that knocks the door is opened. You who are fathers give to your sons
what they ask—not what will harm them. And if you who are evil know
how to give good gifts to your children, much more will your Father
in heaven give the Holy Spirit to those that ask Him. The significant
points which St. Luke discards (as compared with St. Matthew) or
which are absent from his source, are these : 'Let thy will come to pass,
as in heaven, so also on earth' : and the concluding petition 'But rescue
us from evil.' The variation in the prayer for forgiveness has curiously
been held to take the prayer further from Rabbinic thought. This
suggestion would apply in a less degree also to the Matthaean version
'forgive us our debts in the measure that we forgive our debtors.' A
leading liberal Jewish scholar has said : 'In the Jewish liturgies a man
admits his sin and prays for pardon. He throws himself unreservedly
on the divine mercy and knows no limits to it. . . . Hence the Jew prays
for forgiveness *sans phrase.*' [60] The prayer for forgiveness (*Selihah*) in
the sixth clause of the Benedictions reads : 'Forgive us, O our Father,
for we have sinned : pardon us, O our King, for we have transgressed,
for thou dost pardon and forgive. Blessed art thou, O Lord, who art
gracious and dost abundantly forgive.' But there is no question that
our Lord would differ from this outlook. The lesson of the Prodigal
Son shows a contrition which hardly dares to expect forgiveness, but
seeks it from the only possible source. Yet He also makes clear, both
in the Matthaean version (Matt. 6 : 14f.) and in the parable of the
unforgiving servant (Matt. 18 : 32f.) that the Divine forgiveness, while
unmerited, places a moral obligation upon the one who is forgiven.
There is no possible suggestion of bargaining.

For the prayer itself there is no single and complete parallel. It is
original teaching, but teaching which draws upon the themes upon
which our Lord's own prayer-life was first built as He learned to
worship in Nazareth. It is not, however, merely a précis of old material.
There is far more than reminiscence. He is authenticating essential
points in a type of prayer with which they are familiar—possibly over-
familiar. Hostile Jewish critics will make two common assumptions.
One group will say that there is nothing original in the prayer : they
know and teach it all. Others, with a different hostility, will try to

present it as owing nothing to recognized Jewish sources. These judgments appear untrue. But at least they cannot both be true at the same time. They cancel each other, as did the later testimony against our Lord before the chief priests and the council (Mark 14 : 56–9). We do not diminish the Dominical power that lies in the prayer by examining in fact its undoubted filiations with the purest Jewish tradition :

FATHER

'Is not he thy Father which hath bought thee' (Deut. 32 : 6). 'Thou, O Lord, art our Father, our Redeemer' (Isa. 63 : 16). 'But now, O Lord, thou art our Father' (Isa. 64 : 8). In the Eighteen Benedictions Nos. 5 and 6 (*Return* and *Forgiveness*) invoke our Father. On the theme of cleansing and forgiveness R. Aqipa said : 'Happy are ye, Israel. Before whom do ye purify yourselves? Who purifies you? Your Father which is in Heaven' (Joma. 8 : 9). And again : On whom have we to lean? On our Father which is in Heaven (Solah 9 : 15). An even closer reference is in the well-known saying from Pirqe Aboth : 5 : 30 '. . . to do the will of thy Father which is in Heaven.' 'Hearken to thy Father who is in heaven. He deals with thee as with an only son if thou obeyest Him. . . When thou doest His will He is thy Father and thou art His son : but if not, against thy will and opposed to thy consent He is thine owner and thou art His slave' (Pesh. R. 132b). The words 'who is in heaven' have in them no suggestion of the remoteness of God : they remove ambiguity by distinguishing between God and an earthly father.

MAY THY NAME BE HALLOWED

The invocation of the name is frequent, if only because it reverences without actually pronouncing the sacred Tetragrammaton. In very many Old Testament references the Name is made holy. *Tractate Berakhoth 40b* notes that 'Any benediction which is without mention of *Ha-Shem* is no benediction at all. From the canon we may select almost at random : 'And ye shall not profane my Holy Name : but I will be hallowed among the children of Israel : I am the Lord who hallows you' (Lev. 22 : 32). 'Blessed be thy glorious Name which is exalted above all blessing and praise' (Neh. 9 : 5). 'Glory ye in his Holy Name' (Ps. 105 : 3). 'The Lord of hosts in his name, the Holy One' (Isa. 47 : 4). 'My Holy Name will I make known in the midst of my people Israel' (Ezek. 39 : 7).

MAY THY KINGDOM COME

The coming of the Kingdom appears in the Old Testament as linked with the sanctification of the Name. 'The Lord shall be King over the whole earth : in that day shall there be one Lord, and his Name is one' (Zech. 14 : 9). In this connection St. Matthew is fully Jewish in his preference for the term 'kingdom of Heaven' rather than 'kingdom of God.' Any benediction which is without *Malkuth* is no benediction at all (Ber. 40b). We have noted St. Luke's omission in this clause, but the correspondence between heaven and earth is a recognized Rabbinic use.

> 'There is an archetypal and celestial Adam analogous to the lower Adam, and made literally in the image of God. There is also a *familia* above corresponding to the human *familia* below, with respect to which it is said: 'He who occupies himself in Torah for its own sake (cf. R.A. 707, p. 64, *supra*) makes peace in the family above and in the family below. . . . It is as if he built a palace above and below (Ber. 16b–17a). . . . Moreover, he protects the whole world and brings redemption nigh.'

GIVE US DAY BY DAY OUR BREAD FOR THE MORROW

In this clause we have chosen, perhaps arbitrarily, one meaning of *epiousion* rather than another. It seems the more obvious sense. There is no conflict between the prayer and the dominical counsel in Matt. 6: 25. The disciples are not to get worried about their daily food, but are to realize that God who made them is aware of bodily needs. Anxious care is not the same thing as reasonable forethought. The adopted sense of *epiousion* in fact stresses the lesson of faith as against selfish hoarding.

The petition corresponds with the provision of manna in the wilderness (Exod. 16: 4, 16–18). The provision for the coming day alone is precise in that case, but the whole question arises elsewhere: 'Man did eat angels' food' (Ps. 78 : 24–6). 'He satisfied them with bread from heaven' (Ps. 105 : 40). 'Thou gavest them bread from heaven for their hunger, and broughtest forth water out of the Rock for their thirst' (Neh. 9: 15). St. John makes the point explicitly, though it is only part of a more significant purpose : 'Moses gave you not that bread from heaven : but my Father giveth you the true bread from heaven' (John 6: 32). The gift was also associated directly with prayer. 'For that which was not destroyed of the fire, being warmed by a little sunbeam, soon melted away (cf. Exod. 16: 21) that it might be known that we must prevent the sun to give thee thanks, and at the dayspring praise thee' (Wisd. of Sol. 16: 27–8).

FORGIVE US OUR SINS, FOR WE FORGIVE EACH ONE OF OUR DEBTORS

The principle of retribution of evil was common enough, and our Lord emphatically reversed it (Matt. 5 : 38ff.) and put in its place the retribution of charity. But in the Rabbinical use there was a definite approach to a better course. 'As thou hast done it shall be done unto thee' (Obad. 15). 'Forgive a wrong to thy neighbour, and then thy sins shall be forgiven as thou prayest' (Ecclus. 28 : 2). 'May it be thy will, O Lord my God . . . that I may not be harsh with my companions . . . that we may not make defiled the pure . . . that we may not bind the loosed or loose the bound, lest I should be shamed for this age and for the age to come' (T. J. Ber, IV, 2).

AND BRING US NOT INTO TEMPTATION

Examine me, O Lord, and prove me (Ps. 26 : 2). Prove me, O God, and know my heart : try me and know my thoughts, and see if there be any way of wickedness in me (Ps. 139 : 23f.).

A direct reference occurs in the prayer : 'And bring me not into the hands of sin, nor into the hands of iniquity, nor into the hands of temptation . . . and remove me from the evil man' (Aboth, II, 12–13). The variant in the Authorized Prayer Book may also be noted : 'Bring us not into the hands of sin nor into the hands of transgression and iniquity, nor into the hands of temptation nor into the hands of contempt. And let not the evil inclination (*Yeser*) have dominion over me, and remove me from the evil man.' A very moving comment is : 'Remove from me all that thou hatest, and bring me nigh unto all that thou lovest' (T. J. Ber, IV, 2). Whether the 'evil' against which we pray is conceived as neuter or masculine—as personal or impersonal —seems of less moment than the principle of prayer. James 1 : 13–14 is quite specific and inescapable.

It seems clear on this evidence that any instructed Jewish hearer would receive the prayer with a sense of familiarity in the material. Each clause would bring echoes of well-known words. By analogy a Christian to-day may for his own reasons prefer the Authorized Version of the English Bible, and yet feel at home under the guidance of any competent and responsible modern translation. But what of the prayer itself, and the teaching in which it stands? More particularly, how does it relate to the spiritual emphasis we are concerned to trace?

The prayer in St. Luke is, firstly, fitting scenery for the teaching in which it is given, while in the Matthaean setting it appears abrupt and almost irrelevant. This point is deliberately re-emphasized. It seems that a choice must be made between the two accounts in this respect, not so much on textual grounds, with which we are not primarily concerned, but on the ground of spiritual fitness. To English Christians the balance is in favour of St. Matthew merely through liturgical familiarity, but in either version the material has been shown to be both Jewish and Rabbinic. This fact surprises only those who imagine our Lord to have broken into this world as a being from another planet, and to be in revolt against the values of his new environment. Such men forget that he came not to destroy but to fulfil.

In default of any request for teaching, St. Matthew certainly stresses a hiddenness, or at least a reticence in prayer, as against ostentation or mechanical formulas. But the counsel 'enter into thy closet and . . . shut thy door' (Matt. 6 : 6) has a fuller meaning. It accords once again with the cardinal rabbinic principle of *Kawwanah*. It is the quiet freeing of the mind from distraction, and a quality of Recollection which the Christian ascetic theologian should not be surprised to find fully understood in Judaism. St. Matthew follows the prayer at once by underlining the clause concerning forgiveness, but in his somewhat mechanical treatment this point may be of less importance, for the prayer makes no further impact after two verses.

St. Luke's context, as we have seen, was that of an open request to Jesus. This is a case when one would say that he must be right. The point he singles out for reflective use—what St. Francis de Sales would call the 'bouquet' to be gathered from the meditation—is not in the prayer at all, but teaches in a vivid story the need for perseverance (Luke 11 : 5–13). He does not say, and surely would never say, that God answers prayer for the sake of being rid of importunate beggars. The teaching passes quickly to a related theme. The reason for persistence is the importance of the task. We must believe in the mercy of God, and know that His children never turn to Him in vain. Yet there is an important corollary. God will not give 'stones' or 'scorpions' because of His impatience with a demanding child. He knows far better than we know how to give *good* gifts. St. Luke's conception of the best possible gift is wholly original. To him, influenced presumably by some source unknown to St. Matthew, the best gift is the Holy Spirit. The Holy Spirit is first mentioned by St. John early in the 'Last Discourse' (John 14 : 16). We give this formal name to what is in fact an epitome of our Lord's spiritual teaching, of deeper value than the sermon which opened the ministry. Jesus is saving His opportunities—never wasting them by premature action. 'I have yet many things to say unto you, but ye cannot bear them now' (John 16 : 12)— even this is at a far later stage. The whole of the teaching belongs in its appropriate settings, and most chiefly the spiritual depths of that teaching which only St. John seems to have grasped. The spirit of truth is a gift which those separated from Him would never desire or understand—'whom the world cannot receive, for it seeth him not, neither knoweth him' (John 14 : 17). 'But ye know him, for he dwelleth with you, and shall be in you. . . . I will not leave you orphans, I will come to you' (John 14 : 17–26). Only the father or the mother can comfort a bereaved child, but who can replace them for an orphan? The phrase deeply underlines the dereliction that the disciples are approaching, though they know it not. It is a piercing identification of the Church with the hidden truth of the Blessed Trinity. I do not leave you: I come to you. When I leave you, you will know that I am in my Father and also in you. To the orphan the Father shall return. (This point is made even more vivid in Lutheran countries—the Danish word used for the English 'comfortless' is *'faderlöse'*). The Comforter, who is the Holy Ghost, whom the Father will send in My name—whom I will send from the Father—this is indeed the best gift, and He is Myself. When you have seen Me, you have seen the Father (John 14 : 9). We have had to use St. John's insight to explain that of St. Luke (Luke 11 : 13), but in fact the teaching given through St. Luke's gospel just before the Lord's Prayer (Luke 10: 21–4) is a partial explanation. The mercy of God gives this dazzling truth to His Church, and we rest calmly in the adoration of the three Persons in the one God. The hearers of the Sermon on the Mount may be judged unready for such heights, but this was the teaching given to them. A leading modern commentator on St. Luke dismisses it as 'Christian and secondary.' It may conceivably be one or the other. But it can hardly be both. St. Luke has been named the evangelist of the Holy Spirit, and why should we be surprised at this flash of pneumatic insight? St. Luke has given us the picture of the Hasidim who surrounded our Lord's birth, and the Holy Ghost is the theme of the whole Infancy narrative. He has given us Pentecost, and that Descent of the Dove which moved the history of Christendom rests on his words. He has given us the glory of the mother of God, and has given also Mary of Bethany, who chose the good part, for her choice was of Himself. She did not need to do things for Him. It was enough for her to be with Him and, in the majesty of His friendship, enough at times for Him to be with her. In that single cameo of her character (Luke 10: 38–42) she is marked as an exemplar of the contemplative way.

We may turn aside for a moment to notice another and an unexpected acknowledgment of this best of gifts. In Northern Bengal is a tribe of supposedly primitive, and certainly ancient origin, named the Baüls. Among them there is of course no writing, but a long oral tradition which certain Hindu scholars have recorded for its great spiritual value. Their traditions are in some ways similar to those we shall later study among the eighteenth century Hasidim in Eastern Europe; a modern Hindu scholar gave to the present writer this paraphrase of one of the prayers current in the tribe: 'If I ask him for a gift, he will give it to me, and then I shall have to go away. But I do not want to go away. Give me no gift : give me Yourself : I want to be with You, my Beloved.' Indeed the Father gives the Holy Spirit to those who ask Him, and He gives to the intention of the heart as well as to the correctness of the theological mind.

In passing to further evidence of our Lord's own prayer, as distinct from that to which His first disciples were first called, two passages may be noted from St. Luke. There is further reference to the persistence in prayer noted above. There is a judge, commonly described as 'unjust,' though St. Luke is more drastic in saying that he feared neither God nor man. He did not wish to be troubled by the plea of a widow, but finally gave her a verdict in order to be rid of her. Perhaps our Lord's primary motive is different from St. Luke's introductory comment. God will, they know, always uphold His chosen, though the ancient cry 'How long, O Lord' may still be heard. But here the persistence in prayer is clearly for a deeper purpose. Will they be faithful enough, and faithful beyond their fellows, in holding to their Messianic longing? What will the Son of Man find to greet Him at His advent? (Luke 18 : 1–8). Persistence is good, but its object must be truly directed and not stay fast in private needs. There follows immediately (Luke 18 : 9–15) the temple prayer of the Pharisee. 'I thank thee that I am not as the rest of men. . . . or even as this publican.' The publican is not condemned as irreligious, but is almost regarded as sub-human—something worse even than the unjust and the extortioner. All the presented facts may have been true of this Pharisee, and they appeared to him to be sufficient prayer. But the despised publican (whom St. Matthew's narrative might have been expected to include) could bring only a prayer of humility, on which one of the finest contemplative uses of the Church has been based from early days. The Invocation of the Holy Name, which has for centuries been a dominant devotion in the Eastern Church, appears to have begun among the Desert Fathers in a common form borrowed from this parable. 'Lord Jesus Christ, son of God, have mercy upon me a sinner.' But the general intercession, and the stress on personal penitence, were overshadowed in practice by the Holy Name itself. The murmured, or even unspoken silent breathing of the Holy Name of Jesus, and its quiet persistent repetition, disposes the soul to contemplation.[61] 'No man can say that Jesus is Lord but by the Holy Ghost' (1 Cor. 12 : 3). In such recollection we have, of course, left aside the form of the pattern prayer, but are close to its deepest spirit. The invocation of His Holy Name unites the soul with Him, and He is the only door through which to reach to union with God—the purpose and goal of all prayer.

At the outset of the Ministry we have seen that the disciples began by watching the Master's prayer before He could help them to understand; so now they are not ready to question or to learn by parables the burden that is laid upon Him. Very soon, however, they are again to watch and to wonder.

'They came to a place called Gethsemane' (Mark 14 : 32; Matt. 26 : 36; Luke 22 : 39)

The place is not yet that called Calvary, though soon it will be so. The drama of Calvary has begun, as it will continue and end, in the setting of prayer. We have seen the long preparation, arising from the mere incidence of the daily event, which led the disciples to the Mount of Transfiguration, and made them ready to learn some part of the lessons of prayer. Apart from an intensification of the teaching, outward events have moved swiftly. The entry into Jerusalem has given rise to strange disclosures of a future that puzzles them. It fills their minds with a sense of foreboding, in which there is still no fear. St. Luke is not content with the echoes of Daniel the prophet. 'The abomination of desolation' (Matt. 24 : 15) is not congenial to a scientific mind, and might convey only a sense of nightmare. 'Jerusalem compassed with armies' (Luke 21 : 20) is quite another matter. Armies mean swords, sharper than prophetic warnings, and swords mean fear. But for the disciples, 'when these things begin to come to pass, look up, and lift up your heads; because your redemption draweth nigh' (Luke 21 : 28). For all the evangelists the end appears very near, but the answer is prayer and watchfulness. Against this background the Passover is prepared. With this knowledge the fellowship is sealed with the new covenant, even while it is being purged of inner treachery. The adversary had left Jesus 'for a season,' but the respite has plainly passed. All are in danger, but most of all the one among them who is assured of his own strength. 'I have made intercession for thee, that thy faith fail not' (Luke 22 : 32).

They go out to a familiar place in a quiet garden, and the disciples take it for granted that He turns at once to prayer. For the first time, even more clearly than at the Transfiguration, the chosen three are given a share in the primary task (Mark 14 : 33). They may not have realized that it was also for the last time. A burden is laid upon Jesus which should not be borne alone. They are there to watch and guard Him. The prayer which follows is by now more familiar to the Church, and better understood, than it was by the disciples. The battle is won before it can begin—'Nevertheless not as I will but as thou wilt' (Mark 14 : 36). This governing intention sustains the whole prayer. It is not an afterthought, or a word of despairing resignation. But neither is it an isolated point in the prayer, after which the subject is closed. There is a human will—albeit a will so perfect as to be beyond our poor conceiving—a human will that prays. The issue is a crucial one. This is obvious to Him who prays, and there is no purpose in dissecting its various elements. (So much of our prayer in matters of urgency becomes an ineffective worrying on our knees.) All the time there is will not be too long; but the time that is allowed will be precisely sufficient. When the prayer has been finished He will find Himself completely prepared to meet the demanding moment. In consequence there is no element of doubt or of attempted escape from the issue. The prayer does not struggle on to a final point of surrender. It begins and ends in the same accomplishment. After about an hour He returns to His watching companions—for their sakes more than for His own, but not only for their sakes. They are asleep at their post. They are weary, and their own sense of what is at stake is too wavering for them to be sustained against the weakness of the flesh. He understands their real intention, but they have much to learn, and must be warned with an echo of the prayer He has already taught them (Mark 14: 38; cf. Matt. 6: 13). They are not so much in danger of being led (by whatever means) into temptation as of walking blindly into it. He returns to His prayer, and once again comes as if to see the result of His words; but by now the disciples are dazed and cannot even make excuse. Finally the prayer is completed, and there is no more need for their support. The situation is totally new. The interchange of life with the Father, however great the agony of the vigil, has established in His mind the whole course of His future action. In no sense has His prayer tried and failed, and accepted failure with good grace. The prayer is but the visible form of unbroken intercourse—as a small part of an iceberg standing above the sea is evidence of depths unseen below: the true meaning lies in those depths and not in the slowly melting surface. But we do well to note the signs, for prayer of this order is fraught with dangers for those who are not meant to bear it. What is disclosed in Scripture gives sufficient indication of the knowledge that is general. The verbal content of the prayer is presumably told to them by the Lord Himself, for even if overheard it would not then have been understood. But the saying of words is no more than an indication. If He spoke earlier of His lonely battle in the wilderness, we do not assume three separate moments of dialogue to be the whole material recalled from forty days. So here we are shown briefly what is happening, and no more. Those who are brought into the spiritual warfare can fill in the outline from their own knowledge. They do not need to guess at 'supplementary dialogue.' Nothing more needs to be said. The task is made known, and the soul shrinks from it for every reason save one. There is no desire to change, or to escape from, the Father's will. The searching test which purges any lingering taint in human motive; the test which guards against any movement of self-will away from (or even, strangely, towards) the task that has been shown; the test which makes sure that no lurking element of reliance on self is present to affect the clearness of understanding—

94

these and all other elements which appear conscious in the prayer com-
bine to form a single intention. For as long as may be needed, the
human will is held steady and unmoved alongside the will of the
Father. The result in action may be quite unknown at first, but it will
slowly become clear beyond the shadows of doubt. At that moment
of clearness, however, there is no hard decision to be put into effect with
all the strain and uncertainty of moral struggle. The prayer itself is
the supreme action. It must never be understood as the athlete's training
for a task yet to come. It is not so much preparation as accomplishment.
When the prayer is released, whether after endless hours or brief
moments of loving glances at the Father, the work is already done. In
Gethsemane our Lord does not strain every nerve, and key Himself to
face His arrest, as though the real struggle were still in the future.
The brevity of St. Luke's account of Gethsemane is quite as effective
as are the fuller details by St. Matthew and St. Mark.

The Fourth Gospel

The synoptic record relating to our theme has now been reviewed. But
the disciple whom Jesus loved has not yet spoken for himself, though
certain illustrative material has been borrowed. It has recently been
suggested in a book which we have rightly valued in quotation above,[55]
that the fourth evangelist paid less attention to the details of Jesus'
prayer, 'refusing to believe that Jesus needed special times of communion since . . . He lived in the atmosphere of communion and
prayer.' [62] This astonishing judgment must come from the somewhat
Protestant atmosphere of Dr. Davey's study : it could not conceivably
be the judgment of St. John. Any practical understanding of the hidden
life is sufficient to dispose of it. It is as though we should say that the
pervading spiritual atmosphere of a Charterhouse rendered any prayer
or meditation redundant.

It appears, rather, that the admitted difference of treatment in the
fourth Gospel reflects a deeper spiritual understanding. If we were at
all justified in suggesting that St. Matthew only recognized the centrality of prayer in his sources when he met the term *Proseuchē*, we
might conclude that St. John was so absorbed by it that he was really
writing of little else; apart from the doctrinal bed-rock which he was
charged to demonstrate. The few hours covered by the 'last discourse
and prayer' (John 13–17) were to him full of breathless wonder
to which his companions were less ready to respond. As with Mary at
Bethany, he had already chosen the good part. He realizes that Jesus
is bringing them to the Father by the means of their abiding in Himself. He is placing them under the sunlit shadow of the Comforter
who will be to them Himself—for ever. The brief unqualified instruc-

tions which the Synoptists have recorded can be better interpreted when they are recalled in this new relationship. 'Ask, and it shall be given you; seek, and ye shall find; knock, and it shall be opened unto you' (Luke 11 : 9–10) are the things which happen to those who are living in Him and are therefore speaking in His Name under the guidance of His Spirit. St. John gives the same teaching in his own epistles. 'These things have I written unto you, that ye may know that ye have eternal life, even unto you that believe on the name of the Son of God. And this is the boldness (*parrhēsia*) which we have toward him, that if we ask anything according to his will, he heareth us : and if we know that we have the petitions which we have asked of him' (1 John 5 : 13ff.).

We may agree with Dr. Davey at least in this, that such plain counsel differs in its character (never in its value for us) from St. John's reflections upon those hours of silence or on mysterious, allusive words in which he had learned the meaning of the Incarnate Word, and had known that he had walked with God. When we return to the narrative of the last events, the crisis appears to St. John to be longer drawn out : he had watched it coming while others were still carefree. He sees more clearly what is happening and what his Lord chooses to do. The treachery of Judas (John 13 : 2) is discerned by Jesus and himself alone. Instantly it is an occasion for the glory of God. There is neither place nor thought for worry and planning. All is well, and all will be accomplished. The same governing principle carries into our lives : it does not rest upon our Lord's foreknowledge, but upon the faith He forms in us. So, in the teaching which follows ,the assurance of accomplished victory which appears later in the Garden is already present and is made clear. The eleven seem almost dazed. They face something they can neither define nor understand. And so for their sakes at the outset the victory is announced (John 13 : 31). He is speaking of a spiritual task for which they are not ready. 'Whither I go, ye cannot follow me now' (John 13 : 36f.). (In St. Matthew's very detailed narrative (Matt. 24 : 9–12) the reason is made clear, but not clear enough for Peter's impulsive desires. It is a cruel but inevitable time for him to be convicted of his own coming failure.) But at once the scene is lightened. 'Let not your heart be troubled : ye believe in God : believe also in me' (John 14 : 1). He does not counsel that belief, as in the common imperative mood. He accepts it, and takes the faith of one and another according to their need, and founds it again upon Himself. There is every basis for the faith that He assumes in them. 'Whatsoever ye shall ask in my name, that will I do, that the Father may be glorified in the Son' (John 14 : 13). This is only possible through the accomplished interchange of will. All their relationship with the Father is to be as it has been with Himself. All their love for Himself calls forth an answering love from the Father (John 14 : 21). He has bound them to Himself with the bonds of a shared life. The coming separation does not restrict them nor cause bereavement. He releases them into greater freedom, and gives them the fruit of His accomplished victory. To them it will seem at first like parting and grief, but they will know a joy and a peace which is already His own, and has been won for their sakes. Whatever they find to bear in the future, the victory has been won. He has overcome the world. No comment could be adequate to cover these three chapters in which the hidden life is laid bare to those who can hardly grasp its meaning, but who yet will form the Body by whom that life will first be guarded. It is only in the light of these chapters that we can estimate the story of the synoptists in the same days. The synoptists have shown us what had happened. St. John demonstrates the fruit of victory. And so it is with the unique record of the High Priestly Prayer (John 17). It is all on the farther side of sorrow and pain. It comes out of a vast accomplishment—the over-coming of the world. Yet that overcoming has been wrought through-out His hidden life, and it shows *now* no trace of the cost. It is this fact, supported in every sentence of the seventeenth chapter, that makes us see how the prayer would come much more naturally as spoken from the Mount of Olives over against Bethany, from the scene of the triumph it reveals—the scene of victory and of the ascending glory. Such a change of setting has appealed to various writers, though it is here made under the compulsion of the theme of this study, and not as a critical problem. With the generally admitted elements of dis-arrangement in the text of the fourth gospel, it is conceivable that such a self-contained section of the manuscript could have been displaced. No editorial linking or cleverness is needed. John 18 : 1 reads perfectly in verbal and in dramatic sequence following upon 16 : 33. The spoken dialogue is, in fact, almost interrupted by the matchless monologue of the High Priestly Prayer. Nothing, moreover, in the seventeenth chapter conflicts in any way with the Ascension narrative, which is deliberately omitted under the editorial shadow of John 20 : 30f. Everything in the prayer is, in fact, more fitting when read after and not before the factual narrative of the Trial and Crucifixion. (Once again, the textual problem is no part of the present writer's purpose, nor within his competence to decide.)

In its present context the High Priest utters the Eucharistic Prayer following the oblation first made in the presence of the Church. The prayer bears no marks of a personal petition. From beginning to end it is uttered 'for their sakes' (John 17 : 19) with a note of compassion. But the solemnity—the majesty of its language—and the deliberately balanced liturgical form take it far beyond a demonstration of prayer in

97

G

the presence of those who must learn. It is an act of Creation. The words of the Word effect that which they declare, and by the spoken word He confirms and ratifies all that He has done with those entrusted to Him on earth (John 17 : 6). He brings into being the hidden life which the Church is to know in Him as it knows itself to be in truth His Body.

He has given to them the Holy Name (John 17 : 6) by showing forth its glory. He has entrusted to them the words given unto Him (John 17 : 8), the words which have not come from Himself but from the Father (John 12 : 49). There is a perfect interchange of gift and of possession (John 16 : 15), and in consequence of this fact the earthly unity is to partake of the heavenly (John 17 : 11, 21). He prays therefore 'that they may be one, even as we are one' (John 17 : 22). As He has communicated the gifts entrusted to Him, so will the Church communicate them to those who believe in Him. Nothing is contingent, nothing uncertain or speculative, in this prayer. Each clause is a declaration, and thereby the thing declared becomes existent reality. Thus will the unity between the Father and Himself be conveyed by the Church to those for whom it is meant, and they also will be one, not merely by adherence to an earthly unity, but in the Divine Order. 'What the Incarnate Son of God had once been to the Jews, the Church is now to the world—the incarnate charity and glory of God.' [63]

The range of this prayer seems boundless. Its power becomes more sure as it passes from petition to command. No longer is it the prayer of Gethsemane—'not my will but thine be done' (Luke 22 : 42). It is a creative fiat—'Father, I *will* . . .' (John 17 : 24). This contrast is the perfect archetype of the counsel we have already noted : 'Do His will as if it were thy will, that He may do thy will as if it were His will.' Only the contingent note 'as if' is now needless. The Rabbinic counsel knows the true way in which men may learn through willing obedience to remove the barrier between self-will and surrender. But now He prays from the knowledge of the Divine Union of which we have tried to speak. No achievement has climbed to these heights. It is a disclosure of what formerly had to be veiled (John 16 : 12). 'Not even now are ye able to bear it.' Yet now it must be spoken, and the prayer is the interchange of Truth with the Church. Before He returns to His glory, He rehearses with the Father the account of His Incarnate stewardship. But 'this have I done' has now passed into the fuller truth —'This I am.'

In the wholly new situation created for the disciples by the High Priestly Prayer we pass once again into the Garden. There is clearly no room for the narrative of the Agony. The majesty with which He meets His betrayer speaks for itself. To Judas there is no word. The farewell has already been spoken (John 13 : 27). For the other disciples there is a new note of concern, but the action of Simon destroys its meaning. The injury to Malchus passes unnoticed (contrast Luke 22 : 51). The rebuke to Peter is not for causing pain but for intervention in a predetermined course. The whole narrative is brief, written with a detachment that is almost distaste, as if for something out of place. It is therefore necessary to restore the balance by comparison with the synoptic accounts of the Garden. The brevity with which St. John writes is inevitable after his record of the prayer. The full Gethsemane narrative cannot follow such a scene, though we could not spare one word of it in its place. For St. John it has been overshadowed by a more complete event. The prayer is a final declaration 'out of this world'— as the popular phrase has it. Its bearing on the teaching of the Upper Room, and on the clearly convincing narratives of the Garden are admittedly far from proven, but the language of chapter 17 and its self-contained perfection are fitted to the final benediction (Luke 24 : 51) before He is received into heaven.

The Crucifixion of the King (Matt. 27 : 27–53; Mark 15 : 16–41; Luke 23 : 26–49; John 19 : 17–37)

The narrative of the Crucifixion cannot be separated into varying traditions. It is one whole. If for our purpose the central act of the darkness seems dominant, the story at its beginning shows a further fruit of the already completed victory. Even from the Cross our Lord commands the world He has conquered. He has been occupied with those appointed to execute the sentence. St. Luke tells us that Jesus kept on saying— 'Father forgive them' (Luke 23 : 34). He has received the prayer of the malefactor, who shall be remembered indeed, beyond all his hope or knowledge. 'To-day shalt thou be with me in Paradise' (Luke 23 : 39–43). These works of intercession must be done before the work of compassion (John 19 : 25–7) upon the solitary disciple and the Mother who waited at the Cross. They were, in one sense, least in need of compassion. They were to be bereft indeed, but they already possessed Him.

With those deeds of charity fulfilled, and the first three hours of His agony already passed, the contemplative act enters on its true course (Mark 15 : 25–33). For as long as need demanded, the sealing of the world's Redemption could wait with no sense of pressing haste. But now the time has come when He must give Himself to the work that He must do alone. That work is veiled in silence from the sixth hour to the ninth. Darkness has covered the whole land : the earth has been shaken and the temple rocked on its foundations, tearing apart the Veil which hid the innermost secret of Jewish faith and ritual—

the Ark of the Tabernacle in the Holy of Holies. There was nothing left to conceal, for the Living Reality of God was displayed, alike in the shattered temple and in the Crucified Messiah. And in this darkness three hours passed—silently for the watchers at the Cross—silent above all for Him with whom they watched. At length there came a great cry as the darkness lifted from the hill-side. 'My God, my God, why didst thou forsake me' (Matt. 27 : 46; Mark 15 : 34). The Revised marginal reading surely gives the true sense, and is in addition grammatically the more probable. The cry is addressed in the familiar words of a Psalm which almost reports what our Lord had suffered, just as the last of the Servant Songs was seen to do (Ps. 22 : 1). It is addressed to God, and He is, then as always, My God. It is the cry of a conscious mind with a memory of three hours of darkness from which He is now released. The words cannot be the lamentation of one who finds himself at that moment 'without hope and without God . . ' (Eph. 2 : 12). The dereliction has passed into memory. When all might have seemed empty and lost, 'Thou continuest Holy, O thou worship of Israel' (Ps. 22 : 3).

A consummate prayer of the will has been accomplished. Obedience to the Father's will has been the meaning of His life on earth (John 14 : 31; 15 : 10). In the full consciousness of the first three hours His compassion has enfolded those to whom He still ministered. But in this mysterious darkness we find Him bearing the burden of a reparation which He lays only upon His contemplative intercessors, and only as they are able to bear it for Him. There is a growing spiritual darkness, in which the mind has no longer power to act, nor the memory to sustain. All feeling is blotted out. But the will, long set by practised oblation until its disposition can no longer be deflected, prevails for a time in silent affirmation of the Being of God through the growing darkness, while it can still know its task. Finally, even the will, the ultimate citadel of the soul, seems to have been overwhelmed, leaving a void unutterable. Yet in the mercy of God the will so firmly rooted has in fact stood firm, even when it seemed to the intercessor to have been lost, so that nothing save negation could be found. Even for Him, for whom alone dereliction in fact was impossible—for Him who alone was very God, and could never be separated from His Being—the darkness had to be utterly overwhelming, so that He might know in His true humanity the worst that could ever happen to man, and in that knowledge might overcome the darkness.

With that victory of intercession, the task draws to its close. 'I have finished the work thou gavest me to do' (John 17 : 4). The final word from the Cross is *Infinitum est* (John 19 : 30). There is perfect consummation, and yet an infinite process of completion committed to the praying Church. He has done all. Through the hidden life of the Body, all is now being done. We shall never understand that hidden life save as we learn how time and space are gathered into the co-inherence which binds together all ages. The warfare of the Cross has ended in triumph in His own Person. The same warfare continues without end for the servants of His will on earth and in heaven. For them as for us it seems indeed without end. For us and for them it is in Him already completed.

But even the triumph of overcoming could not in itself account for the glory given to the Church. 'Father, into thy hands I commend my spirit: and having thus said, he gave up the ghost' (Luke 23 : 46). It was indeed an amazing death, but it was, none the less, death. The body was cherished, and all that could be done was done. The women followed and saw how His body was laid (Matt. 27 : 57–61; Mark 15 : 40–7; Luke 23 : 50–6; John 19 : 38–42). Through the Holy Sabbath they rested; the recollected adherence to God and to the commandment of God was their natural response, whatever had happened. In the early dawn (John 20 : 1) Mary Magdalene is alone at the sepulchre. The duty of love prepared for the Beloved could not be completed. The tomb is empty. Each one, and each of those to whom they brought the news, received it in his own way. There is conviction behind St. John's account—the only word from an eye-witness, since the Mark (Peter) narrative finds Peter very naturally far away. Mary Magdalene herself, and the beloved disciple, receive what is given to them, as is their way. The blindness of Mary's grief is pierced by the well-remembered tone of His voice as He speaks her name. The disciple, following in haste upon her news, is the first of those of whom His Master was to say 'Blessed are they that have not seen and yet have believed.' (One is tempted to recall, to an age that has forgotten him, the wistfulness of Renan's comment on John 20 : 16f. 'Pouvoir divin de l'amour: moments sacrés où la passion d'une hallucinée donne au monde un Dieu ressucité.') His word to Mary would have the same underlying force. He has not yet ascended, but the Ascension to the Father's glory, and the resumption of His own glory, have already begun in the Divine act that has raised His Body from the tomb. It is the same Body, for He speaks to them: the women fall at His feet in worship and long to embrace Him: He eats with them, in a private home in Emmaus and later in the Upper Room. Thomas is restored from doubt to faith by at least an invitation to touch His sacred wounds. Yet at the same time it is a different Body, of which we have no experience, and of which little if anything is known by Revelation. He comes as He will, unhindered by doors as by a strongly guarded wall of stone. There cannot be quite the same relations of intimacy if the abiding relation of union is to be developed. There follows, not so much in sequence as in consequence, the fulfilment of the promise of His priestly prayer (John 17 : 15). 'As thou didst send me into the world, even so send I them into the world, and for their sakes I sanctify myself.' The sanctification, the perfect foreseen oblation, has been made. The sending follows, and because they, like Himself, will not speak their own words or do their own wills (John 20 : 22) the Holy Ghost is given. The power and authority of the gift is complete in this divine, creative act. The public exercise of the gift is to await the time of His commanding. Without the knowledge of the gift, their preparation for the apostolic work would be but 'a pre-ordination retreat.' Now they are possessed of His Spirit, and await in obedience the order of release. The gift is secret. Nothing is declared. The release is public, and at last those who have waited long for the consolation of Israel know that their vigil has passed into the feast which it foreshadowed.

The interval is no strained or barren time—no waiting with un-fulfilled hopes. The forty days of our Lord's preparation have won for them a new strength. Obvious human weaknesses are made good, by the Master's restoration of the doubting disciple (John 20 : 26–9) and by the completion of the chosen twelve broken by the treachery of Judas (Acts 1 : 24–6). The series of 'appearances' suggested by St. Luke may well have seemed to the inner circle a continuing certainty, underlined or pictured at times by physical sight and awareness. Yet for them also there are moments when certainty cannot forget perplexity. At the lake-side the main body of the twelve return naturally to their familiar work. They had been called away from it—had left their nets and their boats—'We have forsaken all and followed thee' (Matt. 19 : 27). It is wholly understandable that they should not at first grasp the full force of what had happened. Clearly He was alive, with whom their lives had been bound inseparably, but equally clearly the old life is not to be taken up again on the old terms. Something must be done, and the work they well understand is a practical and sensible thing to do. One ventures to wonder if Hoskyns has overstepped the necessity of comment when he finds in it 'a sense of complete apostasy.' The story could bear such an interpretation, but does not seem to need it. He is, however, undoubtedly right in the character which he discerns in the lake-side meal. St. Luke's words 'being seen of them forty days, and speaking of the things concerning the Kingdom of God' (Acts 1 : 3) clearly implies repeated meetings, and there would have been common meals, if not quite of the former kind. The *Chaburah* had been restored, and its daily life must continue, unrecognizable only by reason of its depth and recollection. St. John recognizes in the lake-side meal the familiar benediction, and receives the prepared offering in loving memory, as His Lord had commanded. The matter of the sacrament at this Eucharist is not the fruit of their own labour. It has been given for their use by Himself, and is made to be Himself by His own hand (John 21 : 9–14). As at Emmaus, He is known in the breaking of bread. He knows that they know, and is content.

It seems strange that the final closing of the gap is left apparently uncompleted at what must be a crucial point in the Church's defence— the strategic spearhead of her attack. Our Lord reaches out at once to Peter for the return of 'the love wherewith thou hast loved me' (John 17 : 26). Whether from a continuing shock to Peter arising from his failure, from indifferent understanding, or from pure humility, all that is offered in response is a natural affection. At the final question the Lord Himself adopts this lower level of demand. 'The idea of the loftiest love is given up. It is as if the Lord would test the truth of the feeling which Jesus claimed.' [64] A question of ascetic understanding rather than merely textual scholarship seems to be involved. *Erōs* and *Philia* are two stages of human development, and whatever the necessity of each in its turn they are not the divine gift of *Agapē*. Hoskyns and Lagrange must not lightly be set aside when they discount the measure of difference in the two terms that St. John interchanges. The difference seems in the light of our theme to be significant and deliberate. If it is discounted, we have still to explain the result in Peter's attitude. The command 'Follow thou me' (John 21 : 19) produces a mood of undisguised jealousy. Peter is left with a word that re-echoes the Lord's reply to His Mother at the wedding feast (John 2 : 4) but here it is almost rebuke. It is well for Peter that 'I have made intercession for thee that thy faith fail not' (Luke 22 : 32) and in time he will remember the injunction that followed—'When once thou hast turned again, establish thy brethren.' The immediacy of the Divine purpose brooks no misunderstanding.

In the plain reading of a story which St. John records plainly and objectively, it is made clear that the perfect charity of the Son of God can and does know preferences. In the poverty of human love twisted motives may enter. His desire for us is that we love not only one another in His Church, but love also Himself with the divine *agapē* which is the climate of the contemplative union and abiding with the Father and the Son in the Holy Spirit.

CHAPTER FIVE

THE CHURCH ENTERS INTO HER HERITAGE

'AND now I come to thee.' It is impossible, as we have said, not to hear at the threshold of the Ascended Glory the words of the High-Priestly prayer. Every sentence takes on an added radiance in the light of that glory. He has manifested in recognizable bodily form His victory over death, and now God has highly exalted Him to the throne of the most high. He has resumed the glory which He had with the Father before the world was (John 17 : 5). For the first time there is a Human Being in heaven. In its only perfect exemplar, our humanity is already where His servants are meant to be, and are willed by Him to be. In the same sense, the all-loving humanity which now enters that glory must desire to bring with Him into the proper glory and at the appointed time the Mother from whom His human nature had been received. The Assumption of our Lady is not a fanciful doctrine imposed upon the faith : primarily it is a logical necessity of love. 'While on earth His presence was physical only, and therefore limited to the place of His visible sojourn. It could reach only those who could get physically near Him. . . . By the mystery of His Ascension . . . these limitations have been transcended. He is still physically present in one place only, and visible in the physical sense only to those who have gone where He is; but there is also a mystically extended presence of His Body in the whole Church, and a special sacramental presence of the Body and the Blood in the Eucharistic mystery.' [65]

To this larger Presence we have come—but not as the persons we once were. We of later ages have never seen Him nor touched Him. And yet the humanity we could not reach because of the walls of time, has in His Divine Person transcended those walls and every other separation. The humanity which is now ours belongs with Him in heaven. That which is so obviously bound in time and space is assured of its destiny in Eternity. But if for us it must be only destiny, only a hope guaranteed by the love of God to those who are content to remain in His Love (John 15 : 9–10), for His humanity it is accomplished fact. He has taken again His glory, but He does not rid Himself of the memory and the vehicle of His pain. Despite the judgment of the Church upon Manichaean delusions, we still so readily think of the material as inferior, as though the Lord had suffered a taint of Incarnation. We should not think in such a way of the condescension of the Word of God. Rather should we contemplate that glorious Humanity in all its strength and splendour, and dare to rejoice with Him that He has foreshadowed for us a 'conascension.' There is now a place in heaven for our bodies, when they have put on immortality and incorruption. 'I am my Beloved's and His desire is towards me' (Cant. 7 : 10). St. Bernard will allow us to use—and even to share—that word.

The Acts of the Apostles—the first volume, after the centuries of the prologue we have studied, in the history of the Church—begins triumphantly, without trace of anti-climax. 'A cloud received him out of their sight (Acts 1 : 9) . . . Then returned they to Jerusalem . . . a sabbath day's journey.' All the chosen are named one by one. The women who had sought to minister to His crucified body are there, and last of all the Blessed Mother is named (Acts 1 : 14). There is no record in Scripture of any meeting with her Son after His resurrection, and we cannot speculate upon the omission of so certain an event. (Luke 24 : 33 is too casual a reference to include such a reunion, though it can be read in conjunction with Acts 1 : 14.) As in many earlier instances, the reaction to their joy is an accentuating of simple duty. St. Luke at the end of his gospel, and again after the story of Pentecost, finds them daily and of one accord in the temple (Luke 24 : 53; Acts 2 : 46f.). The first converts, already tenfold of the number of the twelve (Acts 1 : 15) have become a formidable group of five thousand (Acts 4 : 4) before the first sign of interference by authority. Even then the action failed from sheer lack of evidence (Acts 4 : 21). The fact of pious Jews praising the God of their fathers can hardly be a crime. The fact of a notorious cripple now healed could not be gainsaid (Acts 3 : 1-9; 4 : 14). A miracle has been witnessed, but it was not their work. . . . It was done 'in the name of Jesus Christ of Nazareth whom ye crucified, whom God raised from the dead' (Acts 4 : 10). The priests could not deny it, but this kind of thing must not go on happening. 'They called them, and charged them not to speak at all, nor teach in the name of Jesus' (Acts 4 : 18). On their release, the work is resumed almost casually at the point where it had been interrupted. The curiosity of the world is only to be expected : it must not go beyond its own place. They return to their own company (Acts 4 : 23), whose attitude is naturally the same as their own. The new life is living in them all. The five thousand or so would be as diverse as their humanity makes them—as diverse one from another as Peter and John. But now they lifted up their voice to God with one accord. The prayer that Luke records (Acts 4 : 14-31) is the prayer of the Holy Spirit within them (Rom. 8 : 26f.). The Church does not yet understand the theology of intercession, but no one can escape the fact. They are wholly in God's hands. St. Peter has led up to this fact in his public words (Acts 2 : 23). The Church has no doubts in its private mind. What has been done 'against the Lord and against His anointed' is in accordance with 'whatsoever thy hand and thy counsel foreordained to come to pass' (Acts 4 : 26, 28). The prayer has begun in the mood of solemn invocation. It ends with an echo of the simplicity of the Annunciation. The signs and wonders have been done through the name of 'the holy child Jesus.' At the very outset of an unrehearsed challenge we are already in the mood of simple joy that will be seen much later among the Hasidim of Eastern Europe.

The dialogue of official protest and calm defiance goes on, showing in every episode the new world which the Holy Spirit had opened to men so lately scattered and afraid. A fresh arrest brings a new hint of the resurrection power (Acts 5 : 17–32). The gates are closed. The guards are on duty as before. But the prisoners are found to be missing. There has been no secret flight to safety, but the apostles are again in the full publicity of the temple, continuing their obedience where it had been interrupted. The same unanswerable word is spoken : 'We ought to obey God rather than men' (Acts 5 : 29). It is more than famliarity or boasting. 'We are witnesses and so is the Holy Ghost' (Acts 5 : 32), as though to say, 'We tell you, and God agrees with us.' But Gamaliel's cautious advice is followed, at least by the council. One of his younger pupils would appear to have followed his own judgment. This young man named Saul had natural sympathy with the Eastern synagogues, and the web of the divine pattern thus linked him with the deacon whom the Grecians had nominated (Acts 6 : 1–6). Stephen would appear to have taken his diaconate in wide terms, and the word of God increased (Acts 6 : 7). He is already speaking in the tones of Peter, but there is something else that Peter has yet to learn. The words of the accusation (Acts 6 : 11) were hard for the authorities to hear, but the crisis was not only in the words. Stephen had learned the truth of whom he spoke. The council of the Jews looked steadfastly upon him, and saw his face as it had been that of an angel (Acts 6 : 15). Stephen also looked steadfastly, but what *he* saw was the face of the Son of Man. The contemplative may not often be concerned with visions. If he should see, it is the Truth that is seen, and not the manner of the seeing, which God means him to know. For Stephen a long testimony leads only to martyrdom (Acts 7), but another is caught into the pattern of the hidden life—the young man named Saul, who had fully agreed with the action of his elders.

In telling the story long afterwards Paul declares that he had been born out of due time. The words reveal a deep humility. He is no more fit for the grace afforded to him than is an abortion fit to be ranked with a natural human birth, nor can expect to enter human life (Gal. 1: 13–17; 1 Cor. 15: 8). Everything that can rightly be brought in evidence against him only gives more glory to God, for such is his desire. It further serves to strengthen the contrast we have first noted. He has gained the confidence and respect of men far older than himself. He would have heard some of Peter's outspoken testimonies against the Jews, and perhaps have added to his Jewish fanaticism a scholar's disgust at the crudeness of these unlearned and ignorant Galileans. He had learned from Gamaliel, but apparently had failed to learn the lesson of his tolerance and patience.

The whole stage has ben set for an influential career, but the drama is rudely interrupted. The young man is blinded by a light from heaven (Acts 9: 3). All his plans have been made, yet he is caught up into a pattern totally different from that of his own devising. The single fact —the answer to his broken question—is enough for his trained mind, and more than enough for his stricken soul. Jesus is alive. He has risen from the dead, and that does not happen to a man. It is of interest to quote here the comment of Dr. Martin Buber on a very different story—the experience of Thomas in the Upper Room.

'He invokes the Risen One—My Lord and my God! Now the doubter believes, but he does not only believe that Jesus is risen: he believes also that He is his God. . . We can only realize anew that the resurrection of an individual person does not belong in the realm of ideas of the Jewish world. If an individual as individual has arisen, then here is a fact which finds no place in this circle of ideas. Thomas does not intend broadening this circle of ideas. . . . What he thinks in this moment is apparent: since no man can rise as an individual, then this is no man, but a god: and since He (Jesus) had been for him the man, his man, now He is his God. But with this the Jewish world of belief, which knows no god but God, suddenly collapses for the Thomas of the resurrection.' [66]

It may be that the Paul of the Damascus road had no time for such a logical deduction, but the result would not ultimately be different. A blind obedience leads through an unpredictable course to the beginning of a new life. Hardly is the fanatic baptized than he is given power to proclaim the message of the Son of God. The pace of events is breathless, and his three years' novitiate (Gal. 1: 18) was a crowded one. Yet in that time he seems to have come into the mature contemplative experience which he recalls to the Corinthians (2 Cor. 12: 1–10) fourteen years later. He does not boast of his visions. If he boasts at all it is of his sufferings for their sakes. Even these he only mentions in order to be more clearly understood. His hearers are used to boasting claims, and he has good reason in their eyes to speak their language. But the 'exceeding greatness of the revelations' is characteristically tempered by the stake driven into his flesh. It is a messenger of Satan (thus not ordinary illness but possibly some besetting moral burden explains the powerful metaphor). He has prayed to be rid of it, but the Lord has answered, 'It is enough for you to have my grace' (2 Cor. 12: 9). The whole manner of his approach shows a real and established humility. 'By the grace of God I am what I am,' and he does not need to pretend that the work of God is something of no importance. Again he writes (probably in a later letter) of the captives of God, led in triumph, and burned as incense in the pageant of Christ's victory (2 Cor. 2: 14–17). Nothing can be so foreign to the nature of Saul of Tarsus—nothing so eloquent of the grace of God in Paul of Damascus.

But we are faced not merely with conversion. The mind and character of Saul could have made a prominent Christian leader. The Abbè Frouard has said:

'The nature of the Scribe, although crushed, still survives under the action of the grace which has matured him: there is the same soul, the same fire in his words, the same spirit in his actions.'

We may, however prefer the comment of St. John Chrysostom: 'Cor Pauli cor Christi erat.' The quality and temper of mind which he now presents is not of his own invention. This is no actor assuming a new role, with the appropriate costume and make-up. This is transformation by the renewing of a mind (Rom. 12: 2). The meeting on the Damascus road leaves him powerless and blind. After a time he can realize in amazement that what he has known and has scorned among his earlier Jewish acquaintances has now happened to him. A modern poet has written of the early experience of the beloved disciple, and has expressed the same amazement there:

'. . . I only know
That as we followed Him that day He called us,
We were not walking on the earth at all.
It was another world
Where everything was new and strange and shining.
. . . .
I was not blind, and yet He gave me sight;
I was not deaf, and yet He gave me hearing,
Nor was I dead, yet me He raised to life.' [67]

It was in that sense that the eyes of Saul were opened (Acts 9: 18). It is truly part of his need that the violent self-sufficient leader becomes the man who is blind and has to be led by his own companions to the very men against whom he had come forth in hatred, and to be dependent on them for sight and healing. He awakes 'in another world.'

The awakening is the grace of Baptism. The agelong hope is now fulfilment, and his only reparation for the past can be to make men understand his Lord.

The task began very near home. The transformation was too complete to be believed by those who were ready for it. 'They were all
afraid of him and believed not that he was a disciple' (Acts 9 : 26).
Barnabas, the son of consolation, appears as a reconciler, but even so
for some long time the Jerusalem Church 'dissembled' under the slow
and unperceptive mind of Peter. It may have been with a sense of relief
that Paul was seconded to Tarsus, where the conservatives would feel
that he belonged. In the next phase of his ministry the same convictions remain clear to Paul. The separation from Barnabas closed a
valuable co-operation, but Paul sees his path too clearly. John Mark
was still subject to the Jerusalem taint, and Paul is never one to take
kindly to compromise. But the new journey (Acts 15 : 40 ff.) is not for
this reason an expression of self-will. We find a characteristic sensitivity. At two points the intended path is closed to them (Acts
16 : 6–7)—'The spirit of Jesus suffered them not.' The Church is
entering a new and wider phase. The conflict with the Jewish Christians is taking a secondary place, though Paul's own references make
one see how deeply it had impressed him. In every minor outpost of
Roman power Paul is confronting the Empire with the kingdom of
Christ. Yet he is ready to claim the protection of the Empire for its
citizens as their right (Acts 16 : 37; 22 : 25–8). This is not self-
protection : it is rather a true sense of timing, that will not provoke
a struggle prematurely. Later on he will ignore the prudent counsel of
Agabus (Acts 21 : 10–14). They are weeping, and breaking his heart.
He is already bound in the spirit, though not knowing what might lie
ahead. He is ready to be bound and to die at Jerusalem : this would
add no new fact. The same perception was shown to the Galatian
Church. 'From henceforth let no man trouble me, for I bear branded
in my body the marks of the Lord Jesus' (Gal. 6 : 17). Or to his
disciple Timothy, 'I am already being poured out as a libation, and
the time of my departure is come' (2 Tim. 4 : 6). Most notably he
sees the ministry of the Church and his own part pre-eminently, as a
triumphal procession in which the Victor-King displays the glory of
His conquest. The knowledge of Christ spreads through the world
as the savour of incense, but to make this possible the incense must
be burned out. Such sacrifice, the glory of this humiliation, is always
a cause of thanks to God, who triumphs in it even as the crucified
Lord made open show of the principalities and powers, triumphing over
them in the Cross (Col. 2 : 15). There is no false exaltation, nor any
blindness to the facts. When events seem to be stacked against him,

Paul remains quietly aware of the presence of the Lord. Whether this be through vision or through spiritual perception matters not, either to Paul or to us. It is the fact of the living Lord, the only fact in the new life of the servant. The humility of the man who knew himself unworthy to be called an apostle is never lost. There are so many who have 'been in Christ before me' (Rom. 16 : 7). But the humility does not and need not hinder the courage and almost the gaiety with which Paul continues the course marked out for him.

Luke the historian sketches the period of this long ministry, selecting for his purpose and not attempting a formal biography. For the hidden life of Paul we must read between the lines of his letters. As we have observed both in the sequence of Old Testament history, and also in the Psalter, our present purpose does not depend upon critical controversies as to sequence, dating and geography in these epistles. The man is of one piece. In all his early training he had set himself to destroy the heresy which had arisen to threaten the Messianic destiny of his people. Then he was confronted with the reality he had denied. There was no need for Paul to change his mind—to revise this or that aspect of a former standpoint. As he looks back upon the first experience its pur-pose has become more clear. 'For this cause have I appeared unto thee, to appoint thee a minister and a witness both of the things wherein thou hast seen me, and of the things wherein I will appear unto thee.' The essential fact is established, and the mind already dedicated to God continues, humbled by past faithlessness but the more determined in the course now seen (Acts 26 : 16ff.).

There is in consequence a mature grasp of the truth, which does not need experimental action or an evolving spiritual consciousness. The fruits of a contemplative awareness begin to be gathered before his old associates, or his new, have had time to realize that the tree is very different from what they had supposed. But these fruits are not 'visions' or 'mysticism,' any more than they are an ethical intensity. The fruits are those of a life of union with Christ in God, and a consequent quality of response to the present moment which we are learning to recognize in very diverse people. In their being and in their doing one thing only can make sense, a correspondence of wills in perfect obedience.

It is necessary to understand that the obedience and its counterpart in humility are solid facts—not merely ideals. We do not seek in Paul his old self-assurance and competence, yet no disciple was ever more sure of his course of action, or less uncertain in carrying it out. The very energy in which he faced the delaying conservatism of the Jerusalem Church makes it necessary for him to disclaim any copy-right for his Gospel. 'Neither did I receive it from men nor was I taught it' (Gal. 1 : 12). His moral castigation at Corinth is not given to ensnare them, or to get them under his personal influence, but 'that ye may attend upon the Lord without distraction' (1 Cor. 7 : 32). The counsel is admittedly very exacting, but 'I think that I also have the spirit of God' (1 Cor. 7 : 40). On occasion he can speak even more forcibly, when his sole personal judgment is not in question : 'We have the mind of Christ' (1 Cor. 2 : 16). Such certainty is not confined to dealing with opposition. It is clearly marked in the heritage that he shares with his friends. 'Of him are ye in Christ Jesus, who was made unto us wisdom from God. . . . We speak wisdom among the perfect . . . not in words which man's wisdom teacheth, but which the Spirit teacheth' (1 Cor. 1 : 30; 2 : 5f., 12f.). This hidden wisdom is remote from the *gnosis* that has deceived men, and the certainty of conviction rests in the knowledge of Christ, the power of God and the wisdom of God (1 God 1 : 22–4). He interprets spiritual things to those capable of receiving them (1 Cor. 2 : 13). Babes they may seem to be, in their sectarian rivalries which miss so sadly the coinherence of Christ (1 Cor. 3 : 1ff.) and yet, by no merit or claim of their own, 'all things are yours, and ye are Christ's and Christ is God's' (1 Cor. 3 : 23).

But there is something deeper than personal modesty. Any glory given to them is something which he might long to share. The Apostles are on exhibition for the derision of the world (1 Cor. 4 : 9). But if this were not so—if the apostolic ministry were signally exalted by its prophetic gifts and knowledge, all would still be useless. All such gifts are but partial. The full-grown live only in the love which is God (1 Cor. 13 *passim*) and in which alone they find each other. In Him all things have their coinherence (Col. 1 : 17). Within it, 'we are your glorying even as ye also are ours' (2 Cor. 1 : 14). Sufferings and consolations alike are of God, and are for His purposes in the Church. If the suffering appears more obvious, it only makes God's glory more sure. We are 'bearing about in our body the crucifixion of Jesus' (2 Cor. 4 : 10). The Lord had prayed directly for this very gift for us. 'I will that where I am they also may be with me . . .' (John 17 : 24). If it is happening already, let thanksgiving abound to the glory of God. That is what the coinherence is for, and for this reason he is able to write freely to them, and to commit himself to their understanding, though he seems to speak as a fool (2 Cor. 5 : 12–13). The life into which he calls them is not what men would choose. To the world it seems dishonour, shame, obscurity, chastening, sorrow, poverty (2 Cor. 6 : 8–10, 16). But they are called to stand clear of the world's judgments. 'We are a temple of the living God, even as God said, I will dwell in them and walk in them.' 'I say it not to condemn you. Ye are in our hearts to die together and to live together' (2 Cor. 7 : 3). The

THE HIDDEN LIFE OF THE BODY OF CHRIST

picture of the new life into which he has come still astonishes even Paul himself. As he brings his own record as evidence, it stands in stark contrast to what he has now become. All that his old companions have done against him—all the perils which have best the vocation laid upon him—these things would formerly have produced indignation and arrogance. Now they are the life he expects, and a life in which he cannot but glory, even though it brings weakness, persecution and want (2 Cor. 12 : 10). And so he crowns his argument with the statement of a man who is speaking plain truth. As the symptoms of nervous hallucination the account is meaningless. As a factual disclosure it is unequalled. In all the later records of the hidden life, where so much has been written, few passages can carry such conviction. St. Teresa of Avila and the Dialogue of St. Catherine of Siena afford our best commentaries. But Paul had no Fourth Gospel, no apocalypse, no library of Christian mystical writings on which to form the chosen mould of his faith. The living Christ had laid hold upon him. There was a total reversal of the past. The actual course of the hasty confessional preaching, and of the prolonged spiritual retreat in Arabia cannot alter the facts. From the threatening and slaughter to the unspeakable words in the third heaven may require a time-interval of two or three years; but no one can say that the time was adequate to explain the result. From the vision of the Risen Lord to the revelation in Paradise is but one moment in the hidden purpose of God (2 Cor. 12 : 1–4).

The transformation of the dedicated self-will of the fanatic into the humble obedience and the tranquil possession of the Lord Christ is the cause and explanation of the doctrinal experience recorded in the central section of Romans (5 : 8). Writing to the Church he has never seen—to persons he has never met face to face—the closely knit argument lays open to them the man they have not yet known. Paul does not have to consider the impression that he will make. He is already bound with them, the beloved of God (Rom. 1 : 7) and he thinks of them as bringing an added strength to his own faith, as he to theirs. They with him have been brought into the same pattern of obedience. They are sharing with him the reversal of that self-will which had caused the slavery from which they have been delivered. But it is not a reversal which he or they could have achieved for themselves. The life of Christ, the life of Christ in them, brings to them a sharing in all that happened. St. Paul has entered into the meaning of the hidden life which Jesus had laid open to His chosen, but which the Church has not yet made known. He has already known his full share of the darkness (Rom. 8 : 17) but its counterpart is the light. 'Where I am, there shall also my servant be' (John 12 : 26). The Spirit of Him that raised

Jesus from the dead dwells in them (Rom. 8 : 11) and as a result they are brought into the Divine Sonship. Such is the love of the Father that the children who had no conceivable claim to this sonship are brought into its truth, alike in suffering and in glory.[68] They are brought, likewise, into the intimacy of the famly. They may know the elements of the language that is spoken, but they do not yet know those subtleties of intercourse that are exchanged in the family circle. It is the same divine and life-giving spirit which enters into their weakness, not only with understanding and pity, but from a Divine necessity. The children are in the Father's house : they are not relegated to a nursery where their childish games will not disturb their elders. The hidden life is lived with Christ in God, and each one of its members has his share of the weight laid upon that redeeming intercession (Col. 3 : 3). In this life the eternal Divine purpose works itself out without change. As in the supreme moment of human response to that purpose—the obedience which turned back the tide of disobedience—so continually the created order waits in pain and travail until now (Rom. 8 : 22). The 'now' is the moment of God's fulfilment, never of human climbing and achievement. Consequently those who are brought into the hidden life find in it that single quality which has appeared throughout this study. 'All things work together for good . . . to those that are called according to his purpose' (Rom. 8 : 28). 'The activity of the Spirit on our behalf points to the ultimate security in God of those whom He has chosen.' [69] The chosen must accept a mystery they cannot understand. The foreknowledge of God can be met only by that acceptance. They are brought into the image of His Son—which is also the image of Himself with which all creation is summed up (Gen. 1 : 27; Eph. 1 : 10).

As the majesty of this structure grows, it is necessary again to recall that St. Paul is writing to people he has never seen. In his dealings with Corinth there are the reflections of detailed personal knowledge, of exhortation or rebuke in specific matters. But in the main body of the letter to the Romans he is claiming the coinherence of the Christian family, and is taking for granted their share in the life into which he has been reborn. But he is still aware of those whose fellowship he lost when he was 'arrested by Christ' (Phil. 3 : 12). The contemplative is marked as the intercessor. 'I could wish that I myself were anathema from Christ for my brethren's sake . . . whose is the adoption and the glory' (Rom. 9 : 3ff.). He marks the tragedy in the way he now must. Of these his brethren according to the flesh springs even the incarnate Messiah—God blessed for ever. God did not cast them off—Paul himself is the proof of that. There is, in fact, a strange compensation. 'By their fall salvation is come to the Gentiles. . . . If their

H

fall is thus the riches of the world, how much greater would their fulfilling be?' (Rom. 11 : 11f.). He need not be afraid to glorify his new vocation. Some at least may be saved by realizing what they have lost. Yet the new heirs to the promise must bear the weight of this intercessory pattern. Nothing must be taken for granted. The grace vouchsafed to them must call forth a holocaust of sacrifice [70] (Rom. 12 : 1–2). This is more than reasonable, the sacrifice is measured to the grace, at least in their desire. It is in their being that the new life rests, not in conventional guise. It is in their being that the new life is proved, until they are perfected into one body (John 17 : 23).

Nowhere else is St. Paul's mission so elaborately stated, and yet, in the closely reasoned argument, he is saying but one thing and praying one thing. The prayer of Jesus likewise centred on a single desire—'that they may be perfected into one, I in them and thou in me, that the world may know that thou didst send me' (John 17 : 23). There is a life to be lived, and the one life flows from one living centre. It flows in them and in the Church which is His Body, and brings them alike into the suffering and the glory which belong to that Body. At one time they are reminded (Phil. 2 : 8) that this life is found in the form of a Servant, in obedience to the Cross. This humble obedience, and the pain that accompanies it, is a grace bestowed upon them for the sake of Christ (Phil. 1 : 29). Again he would have them understand (Col. 1 : 15ff.) that He who lives in them is the image of the invisible God, the meaning and source of all that is, and the living fullness of heaven and earth, who is none the less being fulfilled in that Body of which they are part (Eph. 1 : 23). But this incomprehensible glory is nothing that must inflate them with an empty wisdom. Whatever they were, or for that matter whatever he himself had been, is of no significance. 'You died' (Col. 3 : 3). They possessed their life no longer, if indeed they had ever possessed it. It is out of their reach and out of their sight, lest they should gaze on it with admiration. The new life is a hidden life—hidden with Christ in God. But wherever his counsel reaches that point, the fact of the hidden life demands that they be 'unblameable in holiness,' for that is the fruit of the given charity (1 Thess. 3 : 12f.; 4 : 3). Their sanctification is the will of God, for they are living in critical days, and the mystery of lawlessness that is growing up against them is real and present (Eph. 6 : 10–18). Yet their wrestling is not against flesh and blood. The enemy is not so simple, nor his power so obvious. When the whole armour of God is taken, it will in the end be found to have its use in the work of prayer—the prayer of the coinherence for which the Spirit Himself longs. St. Paul's words are written from within the hidden life. Practical news of him will help to inform their prayer, but the task belongs alike to first century Asia and twentieth century Europe. In all such life the spiritual warfare will be evident. For St. Paul, through years of imprisonment and insecurity, there was every chance to learn and to master the secret of holy indifference which it demands. There are glimpses of personal crisis, which surprise us by their variety as well as by their vehemence. One (or perhaps more than one) Alexander was an occasion of stern rebuke and stern action (1 Tim. 1 : 20; 4 : 14). When he recalls an occasion of 'delivering to Satan' one who has made shipwreck of the faith (1 Tim. 2 : 2) even the tireless Paul can ask the Church to pray for tranquillity and a quiet life. Yet in fact hardship and endurance are always his lot (2 Tim. 2 : 10). The very vigour of his struggle is itself an intercession. 'All who would live godly in Christ Jesus shall suffer persecution' (2 Tim. 3 : 12). There is acute perception of grievous times to come. For himself his own part seems to be ending (2 Tim. 3 : 1; 4 : 3, 6). His life is even now being poured out as a libation, and the time is short. His course is really finished, and he looks with joy, not to personal reward but to the benediction of those who with him have looked for their Lord in love. We recall Simeon and Anna in the temple. The hidden life is imperishable, and very precious. It joins together those who waited for His appearing, those who knew it in the days of His flesh, and all those whose life is now bound in Him. For them all it brings a common task and imposes a common character. For them He is unchangeable : He abides for ever the same (Heb. 7 : 24f.). From the character of His oblation they are to learn their own, and in Him they share the life of intercession that belongs to His Body for all time. 'To you it hath been granted . . . to suffer in his behalf, having the same conflict that ye saw in me. . . . You endured a great conflict of sufferings . . . and now ye have need of patience that, having done the work of God, ye may receive the promise' (Heb. 10 : 32). The epistle to the Hebrews is faithful to Jewish tradition

'when it presents all the wandering of the people across the desert as a quest for the lost paradise, or better for the heavenly city in which man will dwell with God for ever: while this Epistle also sees the completion of Christ's work as being His ascension as our Precursor into the sanctuary of heaven. . . . The Incarnation, understood according to Scripture, far from establishing God upon earth, only causes Him to come down in order that He may bring us up after Him, seeing Him from behind, like Moses, in an ascension in which . . . "He who truly rises up must always continue to rise: to him who runs towards the Lord a vast distance will never be lacking. Thus he who ascends never ceases, going from beginning to beginning by beginnings that have no end." St. Gregory of Nyssa' (Migne: P.G. Vol. 44, 876c).[71]

While they are still waiting, they have entered into the long succession of the hidden life which we have tried to study, finding only one substance in it all (Heb. 11 *passim*). Can they not rejoice and wonder to think of all that prepared their own inheritance? This is indeed the coinherence—the foretaste of the communion of saints. And as always it demands the same task—the sanctification without which no man shall see the Lord (Heb. 12 : 14). This is not only for ourselves and for our own destiny. Our faith and our love are needed by those who have gone before, and have waited for our perfecting. In the intercession which is the life-task of the hidden body, we at any moment enter only upon our own part. The prayer which is demanded from us by the Spirit is given simply to God, for whom all the times of all His children are but one moment. He will use that prayer as He wills, and where He wills. In so living, 'the God of peace who brought again from the dead the great shepherd of the sheep . . . even our Lord Jesus, will make us perfect in every good thing to do his will, working in us that which is well pleasing in his sight' (Heb. 13 : 20–1). The contemplative intercessor must not choose his battle-ground. He goes straight to God, and then the work is accomplished.

The Epistles of St. John

And now, in the historical growth of the Church's visible life, we return to the personal teaching of the beloved disciple. He lived with the incarnate Lord long years ago. He was present, and listened as if alone to the unfolding of the inner meaning of those years when he had shared his Friend with a group who understood so rarely and so little what it was all about. In the freshness of his mature faith he now writes against the background of that revelation. He speaks of 'things which we have heard, which we have seen with our eyes, which we have gazed upon and our hands have handled' (1 John 1 : 1–4). He is talking of the living God, and doing it so that we may know ourselves within the coinherence of the Church.

At once we find the same inexorable command which we have heard also from St. Paul. If we talk of fellowship with the unshadowed light while all the time we live in the darkness, the truth is not in us (1 John 1 : 6). But, on that inexorable condition, we are of the Body of Christ, and St. John will let us listen to what he has heard, and look at what he has seen. One does not have to judge evidence of this quality. It is inconceivable unless it is utterly true. It does not matter, says St. Paul, what I say, for I am speaking truth, but I forebear lest any man should realize how unworthy I am (2 Cor. 12 : 6). St. John does not even need to stress such safeguards, for in every line of his record they speak for themselves. Failure in charity destroys the fellowship. Weakness or confusion in the faith leaves it unprepared for the final issue—for the last hour. Yet he writes with confidence within the family life. He writes in order that they may not sin, and yet because he knows that their sins are forgiven for the Holy Name of Jesus. The hidden life is no self-righteous exclusiveness. It is the life of those who are forgiven, and who live in the power of the True God— having been led by the Holy Spirit into an abiding possession of the Son and of the Father (1 John 4 : 13–15).

The inseparable sequence of Divine Revelation appears more clearly, perhaps, in the Fourth Gospel than anywhere else. The writer is always in the presence of *pleroma*—of fullness. His mind can never forget, as the Prologue shows, the great sweep of human experience. 'What we have seen with our eyes and our hands have handled' is the Word made flesh—the Word which was in the beginning with God—the Word which *was* God. It is suggestive to allow that Prologue to remind us that the intimate dwelling of the Word with us (*eskēnosen*) is not only the translation of the brooding Shekinah of the ancient people, but is even a transliteration bridging a great gulf of language. The Shekinah (*Shakhan*) pitched its tent among men as the Holy Presence descended in the shining cloud upon the Ark of the Covenant.[72]

St. John speaks in full confidence, on the authority of the Truth made known by Jesus through the Father (John 15 : 15). The family was established so that it might draw its life from the Father in His Name : and now the same assurance stands. Whatever they ask, they receive, because they are living in His love. But there is even more. In the burning flame of charity which is the heart of all things to the contemplative family, they sustain one another (1 John 5 : 16). In answer to their prayer God will give them life for another's need. 'The normal action of intercessory prayer is within the responsive Body.' [73]

In the closing words of this first epistle, St. John recalls what is the closest binding link of all. He will never forget the great declaration of faith which is made in the High-Priestly Prayer. 'O righteous father, the world knew thee not, but I knew thee' (John 7 : 25) (*egō de se egnōn*). And now he affirms its human counterpart. 'We know that we are of God, and the whole world lieth in the evil one. And we know that the Son of God is come, and has given us perception whereby we know him that is true, and we are in him that is true. . . . This is the true God. This is life eternal' (1 John 5 : 19–20) .

As we now pass once again to the Jewish scene, it is well to recall Dr. Martin Buber's penetrating comment on this passage :

'The definite article before "true God" has obviously to express the fact that here no new image of God is set up; but the old, until now partly hidden one, has been revealed in its completeness : until now, that is, eternal life has been "with the Father," but now it has appeared unto us (1 John 1 : 1) yet not as something added to the true God, but as He Himself.' [74]

PART II

CHAPTER SIX

THE PARTING OF THE WAYS

THE Church has completed her Canon of Scripture, and goes forward to live the life expressed in it. But she goes forward in a weakened and divided state, wherever the fault may lie. The crucial revelation was worked out by St. Paul, though the Gospels later show it to have been first the mind of Messias. Our purpose does not lie 'in attempts to make a picture out of the dissected puzzle of prophecy, nor in the eschatological nightmare of the apocalypse.' [75] But whatever the balance of Jewish Messianic hope in various ages, we are faced by the great and tragic fact that the vineyard was prepared for the chosen body of Christ, and at the moment of its due acceptance was scorned by those for whom in all history it had been made ready. The rest of us went forward alone. The incalculable weakening of the Church by this parting of the ways is only less than the loss suffered by Israel.

'The kingdom of God shall be taken away from you, and shall be given to a nation bringing forth the fruits thereof. And he that falleth on this stone shall be broken to pieces, but on whomsoever it shall fall it shall scatter him as dust. And the chief priests and the Pharisees . . . perceived that he spake of them' (Matt. 21 : 43ff.). 'They that were ready went in with him to the marriage feast, *and the doors were shut*. Afterward came also the other virgins saying, 'Lord, Lord, open to us! But he answered and said. . . *I know you not*' (Matt. 25 : 10ff.). Two phrases of monosyllables, but surely the most terrible expression of the Truth of God that we have yet heard.

The failure, the blindness, as in all the revelation of the Word made flesh, is shown as due to moral failure, to ethical irresponsibility, to sin. But there is no moment in which we who walk with Him still can rest in the thought that *we* are pure, *we* are faithful. Even if this were true, our only thought as we consider these events would be that we are infinitely weakened. We may at this moment learn from a prayer attributed to Dr. Martin Buber shortly before his exile from Germany : 'O God, how can I come to thee without these others?'

The false choice was brought to the point of action by Judas in the upper room. 'He went out straightway; and it was night' (John 13 : 30). This was not the first moment when 'many of his disciples went back and walked no more with him' (John 6: 66). But here is planned action—not misconceived impulse. Judas understood well enough. He received the sop from his Master's hand. How often does it seem that the body and the blood, or that which they mean to men's understanding, offered as the pledge of unity, are still the mark of division—the neglected signpost at the parting of human ways. It is from the same Eucharistic act, and the teaching that is loaded upon it, that the defection in St. John's account takes place. 'It was not Moses that gave you the bread out of heaven, but my Father. . . . For the bread of God is that which cometh down out of heaven and giveth life to the world' (John 6: 32f.). The listening Jews here make the first false step. 'Is not this Jesus, the son of Joseph, whose father and mother we know? How doth he now say 'I am come down out of heaven'? 'How can this man give us his flesh to eat?' Jesus will not let them take refuge in vague notions, as in later years men 'spiritualize' the realities of the Eucharist. The simple verb *phagēte* of verse 53 becomes the harsh *trōgōn* in the following sentence. The evangelist, with all his evident Hebraism, could not have dared to invent such a change as a literary device. The Jews have questioned the eating of His flesh: now they know. It is a deliberate stone of stumbling, and has its predicted result. No one but Jesus could use the stark literalness of these words.

The sons of Zebedee were also confronted with the same dividing cup (Matt. 20: 20–8), though their fellows (including Judas himself) appear to have been shocked at such blindness of understanding (Matt. 20: 24; cf. Mark 10: 41). There is more than coincidence here. There is a clear index to truth. In each example the gravamen of the Lord's word and action lies in His destiny of suffering. From the passing of another crisis of decision 'He began to show to his disciples how that he must go to Jerusalem and suffer many things . . . and be killed. . . . And Peter . . . began to rebuke him saying, Be it far from thee, Lord. This shall never be unto thee. But he turned and said to Peter, Get thee behind me, Satan . . . thou mindest not the things of God but the things of men' (Matt. 16: 21–3). What Peter can say from loyalty, from eager emotion, or even from fear of coming terror, the serious thought of Judaism has already built up and documented:

'In the rabbinical apocalyptic literature the conception of an earthly Messiah is the prevailing one, and from the end of the first century of the Common Era it is the one officially accepted by Judaism. . . His mission is, in all essential aspects, the same as in the Apocalypses of the older period: he is to free Israel from the power of the heathen world, kill its ruler and destroy its hosts, and set up his own kingdom of peace.'[76]

Writing for a later and more philosophical age Maimonides likewise rejects the idea of suffering from Messianic thought.

'R. Akiba was among the great sagfes of the Mishnah, yet he was the armour-bearer of Ben Kozeba (*sc.* Bar Cochba) and acknowledged him as King-Messiah. Both he, and all the other sages, thought him to be the King-Messiah until he was slain for his sins. When he fell in battle it was known that he was not the Messiah.' [77]

Yet this normal and expected comment is modified, if not reversed, in another work :

'Knowledge will increase, as it is said: "For the earth shall be full of the knowledge of the Lord" (Isa. 11 : 9). Discords and wars will cease, as it is said, "Nation shall not lift up sword against nation" (Micah 4 : 3). Great perfection will appertain to him that lives in those days, and he shall be elevated through it to "the life of the world to come." But the Messiah will die, and His son and His son's son will reign in His stead. God has clearly declared His death in the words: "He shall not fail nor be crushed till he have set the right in the earth." ' [78]

But to this Rabbinic conception our Lord has already added the deeper one of the Son of Man.

'There is something higher than a merely national leader. . . . Manhood is not limited to the Jews : the Son of Man will judge all nations. The Son of David is the Jewish Messiah : the Son of Man belongs to the whole world. A merely national Messiah is inadequate. Jesus the true Messiah is Man and for men. And therefore will He suffer and therefore will He triumph and therefore will He judge.' [79]

Whether we think of His destiny as known before His time, or whether we are content to see it growing in His mind from Scripture or from current experience, our Lord's humanity is the perfect exemplar of the hidden life of the Body of Christ. He does not seek the bitter cup, nor does He pray that He may escape it. Yet He would rather be in the suffering and the agony than out of the Father's will. In that same resolve He continues to the ultimate oblation of the Cross. His face is set steadfastly toward Jerusalem. He does not look at fear or apprehension : he is looking into the will of the Father. But it is this Messiah who is scorned by Roman and by Jew alike. Pilate has caused the accusation (*aitia*) to be nailed to the tree of the Cross. THIS IS JESUS THE KING OF THE JEWS (Matt. 27 : 37). The same King, the Davidic Messiah, is clothed in a scarlet robe; no sign of majesty this, but a mark of shame (Apoc. 17 : 4; 18 : 12), and He is beaten with a reed that mocked His royal sceptre (Matt. 27 : 28–31). It is this Messiah who was announced to the wondering Joseph before his marriage to Mary (Matt. 1 : 20). 'Thou shalt call his name Jesus, for he shall save his people from their sins.' Yet when, as we shall consider later, the Hasidim of Eastern Europe were in danger from a false presentation of the Messianic character, the leading historian of Jewish mysticism can comment : 'It is one thing to allot a niche to the idea of Redemption, and quite another to have placed this concept in the centre of religious life and thought.' [80] Finally, it is this Messiah who meets His disciples in His risen majesty, and speaks to them out of the remembered suffering and out of the conquered death : 'All authority hath been given unto me in heaven and on earth. Go ye, therefore, and make disciples of all nations, baptizing them in the name of the Father and of the Son and of the Holy Ghost, teaching them to observe all things whatsoever I commanded you; and Lo, I am with you alway, even into the end of the age' (Matt. 28 : 18–20). This task was laid unmistakably and concretely upon men of Israel by the Messiah of Israel. It is small wonder that many who still were hoping and praying for Messianic fulfilment should turn away in disappointment (Luke 24 : 21) from one who was by every sign too great to match their narrow desires. And yet a people which has suffered so long and so cruelly in every age of history since that time, and in every country of Europe and the Near East—how can they fail to recognize such a Victim as their own pattern?

The answer to that crucial question cannot come from Christian minds, still less from converted Jews, if it is to be truly objective. The national isolation of orthodox Judaism is such that the best Christian analysis must verge on intrusion, and thus entirely defeat our own purpose. The question is central in fulfilling that purpose, since the answer cannot be a bland comment upon history. Those who cannot forgive their Messiah for suffering, reject themselves as His suffering servants, and thus refuse to share in His intercessory life for which alone the Body is continued upon earth, until He shall at last see of the travail of His soul. For this reason the Christian Church must turn in full charity for her answer to the best of Jewish Orthodoxy, by which term we emphatically do not mean a liberal modernism. An obvious difficulty is that much of the relevant Jewish writing is not designed for this purpose. It is not primarily apologetic, and is often defensive. In consequence there is no need for translation, and it remains in Hebrew. There are, however, two books at least, from our own time. Both come out of the Hebrew University at Jerusalem, and both have been translated by able Christian Hebraists. The first of these is Dr. Klausner's *Jesus of Nazareth* written between 1907 and 1922. The second, after the MS. had been destroyed during riots in 1929, was rewritten by the author from 1934 to 1939. Its title *From Jesus to Paul* naturally betrays its character, for many scholars seem to follow the chimæra of a Christianity torn from its roots and replanted by the malign influence of the apostle of the Gentiles. The book seeks to answer our primary question, 'How was Christianity separated from Judaism?'

From the former study one summary comment may suffice :

'To the Jewish nation He (*sc.* Jesus) can be neither God nor the Son of God, in the sense envisaged by belief in the Trinity. Either conception is to the Jew not only impious and blasphemous, but incomprehensible. Neither can He, to the Jewish nation, be the Messiah: the kingdom of heaven (the Day of the Messiah) is not yet come.' [81]

In the later study we find, of course, a much fuller expansion of this brief statement. St. Paul is the villain of the piece.

'There is nothing in the teaching of Paul . . . that did not come to him from authentic Judaism.' [82] Yet 'it is not to be supposed that Judaism could accept the teaching of Paul, with its phantasms and its mysteries, with its asceticism and abandonment of life, the results of its loathing of the flesh and its deep pessimism.' [83]

Such generalized contradictions, however, need not concern us, for Dr. Klausner's argument deserves far more attention.

'It soon became apparent that the Jews in general, for all their sects, would not believe . . . in a crucified Messiah. . . . The Jewish Messiah had to be both a warrior, and a man filled with the spirit of wisdom and understanding; he must redeem his people from poltiical servitude and bring about justice and goodness in a liberated land. Only then shall "all nations flow unto it" and only then shall he redeem, by his wisdom and by the spirit of God which is in him, the whole world from evil and sin . . . and shall bring it about that "nation shall not lift up sword against nation, neither shall they learn war any more." All this is very far from what Jesus actually did, so how could an ordinary Jew believe that one "hanged" had risen from the dead and would appear "at the right hand of power" and only then would bring about the kingdom of heaven upon earth? . . .

'In the last analysis any Messiah is King-Messiah: that is to say, He is to free the people from subjection to foreign powers, being therefore also a son of David, from the liberated and liberating royal house of Israel. . . . But in the last analysis, Jesus died an unnatural death, and in His last moments cried out "My God, my God, why hast thou forsaken me?" God did not answer this prayer, nor deliver His Messiah from going down to the grave after such an unnatural and shameful death: so how could faith in a Messiah like this be perpetuated? To the rescue of the disciples from such disillusionment came the belief in the resurrection of the dead. The first disciples came from the Pharisees . . . moreover they were from those circles from which came the authors of the Jewish apocalypses—books . . . filled . . . with all sorts of mystical beliefs in a Messiah whose actual person preceded the creation of the world, and in a Messiah who will stand at the right hand of God and judge peoples in the day of judgment. . . . Thus it was not difficult for them to believe the story of Mary Magdalene that Jesus the Messiah had risen from the dead. . . . Thus the primitive community was saved from disillusionment, and Jesus as Messiah was saved from oblivion.' [84]

Dr. Klausner is evidently and naturally disturbed by the supposed conflict between Jewish monotheism and the Christian revelation of the Unity in Trinity. He finds in this latter doctrine, and in the characteristic Pauline stress upon the life *en Christō*, something impossible of acceptance. We have quoted above from one of his colleagues at the Hebrew University a strong hesitation over any stress on the concept of Redemption (p. 124). Dr. Klausner further writes :

> 'The Jewish Messiah is above all a redeemer of His nation from subservience to foreign rulers. Sin shall cease in the days of the Messiah among the Jews first, and afterwards among the Gentiles also, when they have acknowledged the one God, the God of Israel, and His Torah. . . . The Jewish Messiah redeems not by His blood but by the spirit of God, the spirit of righteousness that is in Him.
>
> 'Judaism could not accept . . . this view (*sc.* Christian Messianism) with its hard and factual conclusions which fetter the spirit and still the joy in living and the potential energies of man aspiring to greatness and performing miracles in our time. . . .' [85]

It is hard to escape the conclusion that we are here listening to the materialist energies that have absorbed modern Zionism, and not to a Jewish prophet. Dr. Klausner writes again of

> 'the stubborn opposition of orthodox Christianity to the revival of Israel in its own land : for the realization of Zionism, strengthening Jewry as a nation possessing its own cultural-religious life, serves to frustrate the faith in the Parousia. . . . But the people Israel is an eternal people, an everlasting people which can neither die nor be transformed. Therefore it refused to modify or change the politico-spiritual, national-universal, earthly-heavenly Jewish Messianic idea which Paul . . . attempted to take over by introducing into it elements foreign to Judaism, and close in spirit to the pagan peoples of his time.'

Yet the same writer was just now asserting that 'there is nothing in the teaching of Paul that did not come to him from authentic Judaism. Finally :

> 'Judaism will never become reconciled with Christianity . . . nor will it become assimilated by Christianity : for Judaism and Christianity are not only two different religions, but they are also two different world-views.' [86]

Alongside these drastic judgments from Klausner, we may wish to turn to yet another of his academic colleagues. Dr. Martin Buber writes, discussing the meaning of Judaism in dialogue with a Christian :

> 'Your expectation refers to a second coming, ours to a coming which has not been forestalled. . . . Until the Messiah comes, our destinies divide us. Until then the Jew is to the Christian the incomprehensibly obdurate man, who will not see what has happened : and the Christian is to the Jew the reckless man, who in an unredeemed world affirms that its redemption

is accomplished. This is a gulf which no human power can bridge. But it does not prevent the common watch for a unity coming from God to us, which, soaring above all your comprehension and all our comprehension, affirms and denies, denies and affirms, what you hold and what we hold, and which substitutes for the credal truths of earth the ontological truth of heaven—which is one.' [87]

It is not possible to brush aside the judgments quoted unless we can find some more penetrating answers to our primary question. It is not for a Christian to discuss whether they are worthy of the people of God, since we are convinced from the meaning of our own faith and the life of our own Church that there is, despite all contrary evidence, an indefeasible continuity between Judaism and Christianity. The charity displayed in all Dr. Buber's writing may give us some encouragement, and still interpret to our minds a truly orthodox Jewish faith. We can for the moment only remember that such judgments as those of Klausner are the fruit of a tragic national history in which Christians must carry a large share of blame, not only in a supposed hostility to modern dreams, but more deeply in the persecutions of the past. It may be that through a reorientation of the Zionist movement a way might open for recognition of spiritual forces that have become obscured. 'For lo, days are coming, saith the Lord, when I will turn the captivity of my people Israel . . . and I will return to them the land which I gave to their fathers, and they shall possess it' (Jer. 30 : 3).

The Exodus itself is to be transcended : 'The days are coming, saith the Lord, when they shall no more say, "As the Lord liveth who led up the children of Israel out of the land of Egypt" but "As the Lord liveth who led up and brought the posterity of the children of Israel from the northern land, and from all the lands whither I drive them away, and they shall dwell upon their own soil" ' (Jer. 23 : 7f.). The apparent echoes of these words of prophecy have already sounded, but it is hard to recognize the shape of the imagined fulfilment. The exile from which the people were to return has been prolonged by centuries of chaotic Dispersions. Not even could an uprooted community form a settled life and accept its new environment. Some wholly external political factor, such as the expulsion from Spain of the Sefardic Jews in 1492, could intervene to destroy any social and religious structure which had been established. Apart from the history which the present generation can study, there are also two world wars, resulting in a major reversal of the pattern of Europe, against which the Jewish wandering took its main shape. An external return to 'the land which I gave to their forefathers' may even seem, in the event, to have proved void of its intended form in the purpose of God. What has come back resembles a political hysteria rather than 'the zeal of thy house.' The nation has brought with it, and discovered all around it, the infection of the contemporary world, and only those who are without this taint could dare to judge.

We have traced briefly through the Old Covenant and the New the marks of what must still truly be called the hidden life of the Body of Christ, though the race to whom the life was first committed find such a name unwelcome. In this sense our quest has reached the parting of the ways. A journey begun in common must apparently be continued in loneliness and separation. One of these now divided ways could be followed out with sureness and confidence. The record of Christian contemplative spirituality is clear, and fully documented. There is a life of union with God in Christ whose expression varied only with the outward circumstances and the individual vocations of those whom God had brought into it. It might even be thought that this record needs no detailed examination through its history, since the canon of the New Testament was completed : the continuing Body could be left to go forward with its present life and calling, lest there should be danger of a self-conscious *mimesis*. On the other hand, since any age is very close to its own learning of the will of God, there may be advantage in linking the present to the earlier stages. If, however, we have this Christian record clearly in mind, and remember that it is continuing in a living body from day to day, we may with advantage start with the harder task, and trace first any continuity that may be found with the contemplative experience of post-Christian Judaism.

CHAPTER SEVEN

THE EARLY PHASE OF JEWISH
SPIRITUALITY

WE will begin, therefore, from the historical point already reached. A continuing body of Christ, still in large part closely linked with its Jewish forebears, finds itself separated from its first roots. But the growth begun in the call of Abraham still goes on, and it is that growth that must first be studied. Messiah was rejected by those who were His own, and who received Him not (John 1 : 11). By the turn of the first century two generations had grown up in separation and enmity. Is there still a hidden life for the once chosen body that can be traced even to the present day?

The course that has hitherto been followed has been delimited by dealing, in the main, not with movements, but with persons in actual situations. It will become increasingly difficult for a non-Jewish judgment to be accurate, but this underlying principle should stand.

'In the religious life of Judaism primary importance is not given to dogma, but to the remembrance and expectation of a concrete situation—the meeting of God with man. . . . Israel's experience of the *you* in the direct relationship, a pure singular experience, is so overwhelmingly strong that any notion of a plurality of principles simply cannot arise within it. . . . A man is a heathen to the extent that he does not recognize God in His manifestations. "Turning" is not a return to an earlier, sinless state : on the contrary it is a turning of the whole individual—the individual being carried on to the way of God in turning round. . . . The man who turns finds himself standing in the furrows which the living God has made on His way through the world.' [88]

Despite the strong sense of sharp division between the two ways that has already been noted, we are here still in the spiritual temper which has determined all the past story. Yet it is well to be warned that 'the religious life means concreteness itself—the whole concreteness of life without reduction. The history of the world is a real dialogue between God and His creature. . . . In this conversation God speaks to man with the life that He gives him . . . again and again.' By accepting this clear existential pattern we may safely test any evidence, knowing that we are not trespassing idly upon holy ground, and therefore need not cause our brother to stumble. The comment must,

I

however, serve as a guide rather than as a rigid test. In a period where the history is so confused, where continuity is always difficult to establish, and documents are so elusive, it may seem impossible to focus clearly upon 'this man in this situation.' We may have to look rather at a general spiritual environment. We have seen that, as between Judaism and Christianity, at least in the early periods, a charge is laid of neglecting the ceremonial of the law and substituting a general ethic. This, at least, is Klausner's indictment of St. Paul. But within Judaism itself, and increasingly during the period from A.D. 500 to 1500, there was evident a different, if a related, problem. We have already noted briefly the supposed tension between a liturgical and a spiritual life. The contrast is not confined to Judaism, but appears throughout Church history. But it is, for present purposes, the key to any evaluation of the hidden life in medieval Judaism, so far as we have hitherto observed its character. This contrast is described as a 'tension,' since the strain occurs between the two extremes of a single structure, rather than as a choice between two rival and separated systems. To the Jew it is a commonplace, to the Christian a fact less obvious, that the whole religious and social system rests upon the corpus of Rabbinical literature. When we face the invasion of mysticism in the later Kabbalah, there is still a claim to continuity with the original Talmudic period, and its own documents (notably of course the *Zohar* itself) are held to be simply an extension of *Midrash*. To look for traces of the hidden life by ignoring, in any part of the period, elements which are cardinal to Judaism, would be to admit the failure of the inquiry—to ask that Judaism should be false to itself.

> 'The Rabbinic Jew who lived the life advocated by the Torah felt that that life and no other satisfied the deepest quests of his soul. The Torah enacted certain ordinances, and made their obedience obligatory to him. The Jew correspondingly felt that his only means for bringing God near to him, and for realizing this nearness to God, was this obedience. It was only as a son of Torah that communion with God was possible to him.' [89]

The Christian must conclude that in the purpose of God the fullness of time had not been delayed: the faithful adherence to the life of Torah had depended on a progressive and finally culminating revelation: the indefinite futurity was beyond human enduring. The demand for release from the stern weight of the remoteness of God was emerging, as was surely inevitable in the deprivation of the visible focus of Jewish life and worship. 'A Jewish mysticism exists: there is in Israel a desire for God, for His immediate presence, for a presence the sight of which will be salvation for His people, because it will give back the original resemblance of man to God.' [90]

Such demands, however, could be met, and for a long if interrupted period they were met from the accepted tradition of the Torah, and from the Rabbinical literature which expounded it. There is a weight of Rabbinic evidence for an understanding of the immanence of God. But it was not understood as opposed to the Divine Transcendence. The scriptural and Rabbinical teaching regarding the Shekinah speaks in terms which become personal, though never departing from the basic conviction of the Divine Unity. The Rabbinical writers were not philosophers, and cannot be made to think in the mood of the later speculative periods. They speak in religious terms. 'The Tabernacle in the Holy of Holies was filled with the light of God and with His Glory.' The Hasidim were so intent upon the Glory of God (*Kawod*) that they did not need to trouble themselves with any problems of relationship. As for Moses, the glory was itself Revelation. 'Shew me thy glory' is the aim and the reward of Hasidic asceticism, and they had no need to discriminate more clearly between 'emanation' and 'revelation.' The Holy Presence is not bound : He is present with the individual as with the nation : He is present in the Holy Land and also in the Dispersion which has scattered them. This is stated plainly, and is taken even further, in Ps. 139. 'Whither shall I go from thy Spirit, or whither shall I flee from thy Presence? if I ascend up into heaven thou art there : if I make my bed in Sheol, behold thou art there. . . . If I say, surely the darkness shall cover me, and the light about me shall be night, even the darkness hideth not from thee, and the night is as clear as the day : the darkness and the light are both alike to thee' (Ps. 139 : 7–12). Even those who would seek to evade the presence of the Transcendent God find it impossible to do so. The presence is inescapable. Though we are far (at least in the Rabbinic period) from any false notion of pantheism, the Shekinah dwells with Israel even though they be impure. This point is made in its extreme form in the experience of Hosea. 'When Israel was a child, then I loved him : I taught Ephraim to go; I drew them with cords of a man and with bands of love. . . . How shall I give thee up, Ephraim; How shall I let thee go, O Israel? I will not execute the fierceness of mine anger, for I am God and not Man' (Hos. 11 : 1–9).

'The Old Testament taught preponderatingly the truth of the Divine Transcendence. But the individual and national experience brought him (the Rabbinic Jew) round to the truth of the Divine Immanence. Instead of the monarch wrapped in impenetrable isolation, God became the Shekinah. No longer the great unapproachable, the great unknowable. He became the Father, with a father's love for his children. And his worship sprang, not from a feeling of external obligation, but from the impulse of the Holy Spirit. . . . It is only through experiencing the fact of God's immanence that we gain the assurance of his transcendence.' [91]

The point is made clearly in one of the Hasidic tales, and in a Midrash from which the legend doubtless arose. 'They asked Rabbi Pinhas: "Why is God called '*makom*,' that is, place? He certainly is the place of the world, but then He ought to be called that, and not just 'place.' " He replied: "Man should go into God, so that God may surround him, and become his place." ' [92] The same question is raised in reference to Ps. 90: 1. 'Why is God called a dwelling place? Because He is the dwelling place of the world, but the world is not His dwelling place.' [93] The wider question is illuminated by Père Bouyer.

'The Ark is sacred because it is the place of the Presence of Yahweh. But it is upon its cover, upon the preparatory, that the Presence is situated: . . . The best way of understanding the symbolism of the Ark . . . is . . . that the people of Israel were ruled by an invisible presence. . . . The only possible epiphany of the Shekinah who rules over Israel is the luminous cloud. But, in it, the ruling Presence veils itself as much as it gives itself. The *Deus revelatus* . . . only reveals himself as being the *Deus absconditus*. . . . This presence is a grace, an unheard of condescension of the Divine *hesed*, lowering itself to man so far as to come and dwell with him.' [94]

While, however, it is true that for some centuries it was possible for the mystical emphasis to continue within an accepted framework, the development of symbolic interpretation of the Torah, however it may take externally the required form of *Midrash,* leaves a very wide and uncontrolled field of development.

'The exodus from Egypt, the fundamental event of our history, cannot according to the mystic have come to pass once only and in one place: it must correspond to an event which takes place in ourselves, an exodus from an inner Egypt in which we are all slaves. Only thus conceived does the Exodus cease to be an object of learning, and acquire the dignity of immediate religious experience.' [95]

It is thus easily understood how a silent revolution became possible as the Rabbinic teaching began to develop in Dispersion. At every stage towards the full emergence of Kabbalistic mysticism it could appear (or be made to appear) that the traditional origins justified, or even demanded, the growth.

'It would be too much to say that the Kabbalists leave the meaning of the *Haggadah* intact. What makes them differ from the philosophers is that for them the *Haggadah* is not a dead letter. They live in a world historically continuous with it, and they are able therefore to enhance it, though in the spirit of mysticism.' [96]

Problems which figure largely in Christian Church history—the emergence of the independent sects, with claims to essential doctrines out of relation to the Church's creeds: the vital claim to the private interpretation of Holy Scripture: liturgical freedom in the ordering of ministry and of sacramental life—the whole range of issues which have broken the unity of Christendom: these problems appear to have emerged in Judaism in a far less disruptive way.

The history of this period represents something more than an immanentist or a liberal trend in Judaism. It would be a mistake for the Christian student to assume the research of liberal Jewish theologians such as Abelson and Montefiore as being an assimilation towards Christian Trinitarian theology. Here, as we have so often had to take note, the firm orthodoxy of Dr. Martin Buber maintains for us, owing to his great charity, a more balanced estimate of what we may in fact read into Medieval Judaism. At its best the immanentist trend served to save Judaism from a period of intellectual aridity or even of rationalism, under the influence of philosophical speculation. Even with the large element of Gnostic influence, the stress was still religious rather than merely speculative. This is perhaps notably the case in the devotional world. The theology and practice of prayer may prove of significant importance in tracing the hidden life through a very complex period. There is a large volume of material seemingly remote from the classical forms of liturgical and corporate prayer, and it is for this devotional element that the period must be remembered, far beyond some of its admitted extravagances.

Long before any impact of alien ideas had begun to affect the Dispersion, there are colonies or settlements widespread in Europe seeking not only to secure some mode of existence in adverse conditions, but also to conserve as far as possible the realities of their traditional Judaism. Even in the Holy Land itself Roman domination had not destroyed all these hopes, but already the first stirrings of speculation were to be felt. It is said of R. Akiba-ben-Joseph, to whom we have already referred briefly as the leading Rabbinic figure under Hadrian, that 'he left the paradise of mystical speculation safe and sane as he had entered it.' [97] The religious destiny of Israel as a people for union with God was the central theme of his teaching. The well-known stanza from the Canticles—'My beloved is mine and I am his' (2 : 16) occurs often. But, as we have seen, he met Simon Kozeba, and before long this 'Son of the Star' was proclaimed as Messiah, and Palestine flamed into revolt. For a moment Jerusalem was regained, and hopes rose to apocalyptic heights, only to fall in three years of bitter warfare with the final desecration of the Holy Site under the pagan name of *Aelia Capitolina*. Despite the situation in the essential colony of Palestine, Rome had known an established and self-supporting Jewish settlement from about the same period. The strange religion was winning more than wistful support, despite phases of imperial hostility. The

Roman exiles held their ground, and many synagogues had been established with their own normal administration. Morality was rooted in a
pure worship, and the whole Jewish outlook spoke of a quality beyond
pagan reach. Many were drawn to varying degrees of commitment, and
the proselytes of righteousness included leading courtiers. It has been
perhaps justly said that the vanquished imposed their laws upon the
victors. For the dark story of Christian persecution and massacre had
not yet begun. The official policy in pagan Rome was a reserved tolera-
tion and, more and more, Judaism began to express its own spirit,
receiving stimulus both in scholarship and in personal migration from
Palestine and Babylon. From this unlikely centre great spiritual
developments reached out; both in France and more notably in the
Rhineland, principally owing to the influence of a single leading
family.

> 'A consensus of traditions handed down by the disciples of Jehudah the
> Hasid determine the new mysticism as the final link in a chain which reaches
> back through the Kalonymides to Italy.' [98]

The younger generation of this family were early marked out as
Hasidim. They taught and practised the vigorous and practical piety
which came to mark the Ashkenazim as distinct from the perhaps more
brilliant and intellectual growth in Spain among the Sefardim.
Geography affects national temperament similarly even to-day. Their
mystical outlook, and the element of the new learning, did not at this
stage isolate them.

> 'The Hasidim were intimately connected with the whole of Jewish life, and
> with the religious interests of the common folk. They were recognized as
> representatives of an ideally Jewish way of life even where their principles
> were never completely translated into practice. Side by side with the great
> documents of the *Halakhah* . . . the classical literature of Hasidism attained
> a truly canonical prestige—not indeed among the representatives of Talmudic
> learning, but with the average Jewish householder.' [99]

There is a collection of Hasidic legend from this period translated by
Moses Gaster in 1934, entitled the *Ma'aseh Book*. The main collection
remains in Hebrew—the *Sefer Hasidim,* which though seemingly disjointed and legendary in style became one of the major forces in
Ashkenazi Judaism. 'No other work of the period provides us with so
deep an insight into the real life of a Jewish Community in all its
aspects. . . . The book records in plain words the actual conflicting
motives which determined the religious life of a Jew in medieval
Germany.' [100] Comparisons have been suggested with the Franciscan
movement, but there may be no need to speak of derivations : similar
causes produce similar effects. Mysticism was in the air, and its seeds

fell on fertile soil both among Jews and Christians. The true piety of the Hasidim, as seen in its mature developments, lies precisely in their detachment, their complete serenity, and a consistent altruism and practical charity. They were not principally marked for learning—rather for an idealism which transcended it—and the foundation of their life rests on prayer. However faithfully the corporate liturgical prayer may be sustained, as was the unquestioned aim of those who refused to surrender their religious life despite all persecution, the personal life of the individual Hasid needed a total setting of prayer. The practice of *Kawwanah* is commanded as the necessary setting for any true prayer, but for the Hasid it is more. He is living in the midst of the battle, and it speaks to him of the intention of the heart, the precision of the mystic will by which the prayer is moved. The modern term 'Recollection' in ascetic theology largely covers the meaning. But where *Kawwanah* is an all-important means, the goal is God Himself. The Hasid is making a complete oblation. His prayer is no longer encumbered by detailed petition. He stands before God alone, with empty hands save for the fullness of his desire. But he is clear in his unspoken aim—that he may be held close to God in a true union of moral will. The concept of *Devekuth* is his goal. As we have seen, ecstasy is a mere accident in such a prayer-life. *Devekuth* is a perpetual being with God, an intimate union and conformity of the human and the divine will. In later periods, under the malign pressure of Gnosticism, *Devekuth* could become debased into a self-willed intention by various practices of magic to merge the soul with God. Such false mysticism holds the fatal error of being careless of the essential humility and creatureliness of all our prayer. Such error can only takes us away from the hidden life. From the same family of the Kalonymides, R. Eleazar of Worms is noted in an ancient *Mishnah* of the Hasidim :

> 'The soul is full of love for God, and bound with ropes of love in joy and lightness of heart. He is not like one who serves his master unwillingly. . . . For when the soul thinks deeply about the fear of God, then the flame of heartfelt love bursts in it, and the exaltation of innermost joy fills the heart. . . . The lover thinks not of his advantage in the world; he does not care about the pleasures of his wife or of his sons and daughters : all this is as nothing to him, everything except that he may do the will of his Creator, do good to others, and keep sanctified the Name of God. . . . And all the contemplation of his thoughts burns in the fire of love for Him.' [101]

We shall find that, in the beginnings of Polish Hasidism in the eighteenth century, this same analogy is used by the founder Baal-Shem-Tobh, as witnessed by Saadia. 'If the force of sensual love is so great, how great must be the passion with which man loves God.'

When such convictions appear, the power of the hidden life is surely evident.

'All that is necessary is to have a soul united within itself, and indivisibly directed to its divine goal. The world in which you live, just as it is and not otherwise, affords you that association with God that will redeem you, and whatever aspect of the world you have been entrusted with. . . . All the contradictions with which the world distresses you are only that you may discover their intrinsic significance. . . . All innate sorrow wants only to flow into the fervour of your joy. But this joy must not be the goal towards which you strive. It will be vouchsafed to you as you strive to give joy to God. Your personal joy will rise up when you want nothing but the joy of God—nothing but joy in itself.' [102]

The extract quoted from R. Eleazar might seem congenial to later ages of a purely Christian mysticism, save that the Christian stress, in the Spanish mystics, regards love in its most exalted terms as an act of the will, far more than mere desire and longing. But the thought is still more truly representative than either Messianic speculation or social philosophy. It is, of course, expressed in a common-sense and practical mood. It is, in its measure, a contemplative act. The material standards of the world are set aside in no false Manichaean sense, but in a spirit of holy indifference. The attitude of serenity, which has been supposed to show Stoic influence, would for the Hasidim appear in the light of a truer faith than anything known to philosophy. The affairs of daily life are controlled not by self-advancement but by a real altruism—the essence of community. The concept of meekness under suffering, which so deeply colours the thought of the Old Testament prophets, is prominent here. The Hasid was always conscious of the role of the Suffering Servant. He was a dedicated man—a religious in the world. With no desire for a false Pharisaism, he was in fact living beyond the claims of the *Halakhah* upon him. The *Mishnah* of the Hasidim is no pious theory: it bears the very character of *Hasiduth*. An early Spanish extract (*c.* 1300) could belong equally to Meister Eckhardt.

'He who is vouchsafed the entry into *Devekuth* attains to the mystery of equanimity, and he who possesses equanimity attains to loneliness, and from there he comes to the Holy Spirit and to prophecy. . . . If you can still feel the sting of insult you have not attained to the state when you can connect your thoughts with God.' [103]

There are clearly major aspects of Judaism for which the normal canons of the Rabbinic life—the clear framework of the *Halakhah*—would appear to be ignored by these Hasidic emphases. The principles of *Hasiduth* do, in fact, go far beyond the strict demands of Torah. The position is similar to that of much piety in Christian sects, which may in fact co-exist with ignorance of creed and neglect of liturgical tradition. The Hasid was less concerned, however, to protest against the preferences of others than to pursue the course that he knew to be binding on himself. The simplicity of this character of devotion further preserved the Hasid from falling into certain dangers which can beset the contemplative life. He is not trapped by the fascination of magic which weakened others. 'The magician prides himself on his control of the elements : the humble Hasid craves no form of power.' [104] The early practice of prayer itself became confused by aberrations of numerical and literal calculation (Gematria): but if we cannot find widespread in German Hasidim the prayer-life that might be hoped from it, at least some of its leaders were prepared to withstand firmly the worst fantasies of the Merkabah. Whether or no there was any taint from non-Jewish sources in their Christian environment, there were many better aspects. The true ethical note in Hasidim that has been noted was marked by an emphasis on penitence to a degree and in a manner which is certainly new. This was a safeguard against the 'heavenly journey of the self-absorbed ecstatic' which in any religious system is a horrid portent. Scholem may rightly find 'after effects of Christian influence,' for it may well be that much in the early penitential discipline of Christianity needed drastic reform, and in consequence brought such influence to bear.

We must not, however, seek to imagine this western Hasidism as remaining untouched by any theosophical trend. Even from Saadia himself it could enter. There are, moreover, emphases which we might be glad to receive as evidence of the continuity of the hidden life, but which the modern Jewish scholar might rather assign to heretics and sectarians. The relaxation which we have noted above does, however, receive a more orthodox support in the Hasidic *Song of Unity* :

'Everything is in Thee and Thou art in everything: Thou fillest everything and dost encompass it. When everything was created, Thou wast in everything: before anything was created Thou wast everything.' [105]

The very words almost echo Duns Scotus Erigena in *De Divisione Naturae* (P.L. 122 : 876). But if we cannot retain the simple ethical quality already noted in German Hasidism, it is useless to expect precise philosophic thought. Elements interlock and contradict one another, and this fact must be accepted. There may, for example, be presented to Hasidism various manifestations of God which are supposed to exist and to give precision to their prayer. But, on the same authority of R. Eleazar, while the Hasid may indeed call to God as King, his true intention is to contemplate the hidden holiness of God —His infinite and formless glory. 'The finite word of man is aimed at the infinite word of God. By the same token, however, the Shekinah —itself a created light—is the true aim of prayer.' [106]

Scholem's summary judgment upon this question of continuity is of great importance :

'There is little to connect these old Hasidim of the thirteenth century with the Hasidic movement which developed in Poland and in the Ukraine during the eighteenth century. . . . The identity of name is no proof of real continuity. After all, the two are separated by two or three great epochs in the development of Kabbalistic thought. The later Hasidism was the inheritor of a rich tradition from which its followers could draw new inspiration, new modes of thought and new modes of expression. And yet it cannot be denied that a certain similarity between the two movements exists. In both cases the problem was that of the education of large Jewish groups in a spirit of mystical moralism. The true Hasid and the Zaddik of later Hasidism are related figures . . . prototypes of a mystical way of life which tends towards social activity even where its representatives are conceived as guardians of all the mysteries of divinity.' [107]

He is prepared to modify this judgment in an earlier chapter:

'There is little resemblance between the earliest mystical texts in our possession, dating from Talmudic and post-Talmudic days; the writings of the ancient Spanish Kabbalists; those of the school which later flourished in Safed, the holy city of Kabbalism in the sixteenth century; and finally the Hasidic literature of the modern age. Yet the question must be asked whether there is not something more than a purely historical connection uniting these *disjecta membra.*' [108]

As we pass from this early period and meet in its more mature expression the invasion of mysticism, these judgments of the leading Jewish scholars in this field must have full weight. It is obviously true that the situation facing the Polish and Ukrainian dispersion, which created the latest and greatest Hasidic development, was in no way a conscious historical revival. Such documents as did exist would represent a largely different social and economic environment. There was only the common factor of suffering. The later Hasidim would not be likely to have known the records of their Ashkenazi forebears, but the suffering which beset their common life led them to turn to the same God in the same way. The continuity is not one of written records nor of intellectual achievement. We must wait for the re-emergence of the original motives—where men and society are again living in God and are seeking humbly a way of life pleasing to His will and purpose. These things are real, and they are as ever in His hands.

Meanwhile a different development has had time and space to become established. For centuries past, Spain and Northern Africa has been the home of the Sefardic Jews. In the vision of Obadiah it was promised that 'the captivity of Jerusalem, which is in Sepharad, shall possess the cities of the South' (Obad. 20). The actual origin of the settlement is a matter of legend, but a community was certainly established early in the fourth century, when the Council of Elvira made regulations to limit established practices of peaceful contact between peasant groups, and even intermarriage between Christian and Jew. The later third Council of Toledo, having renounced the Arian heresy, strengthened Christian resistance, and was the cause of many coerced baptisms. But by the early eighth century the whole country fell to Islam, and for the Jews there was now respite enough to allow considerable growth of scholarship and the consolidation of the Scriptures. It is necessary, however painful in the light of present-day understanding, to realize that almost any culture gave to the Jews a greater security than they could hope to find under Christian rule. This is most notable in the common declaration of the Divine Unity between Jew and Moslem. The facts of physical violence and of intolerance do not cancel the unChristlikeness of Christendom.

As Moslem control weakened, Talmudic research and the circulation of manuscripts increased, especially in Granada and Saragossa. The poet-philosopher Solomon-ibn-Gabriol left his mark upon the Sefardic liturgy, and sang of the longing of Israel for redemption—the longing of the soul for union with God. Neo-platonism began to enter the pure stream of Jewish piety, but we may find in R. Bahye-ben-Joseph a closer connection with our own study. He held public rank as a judge in the Rabbinic court, but served his people chiefly as a spiritual man, showing great humility and charity. He was himself a contemplative and a solitary by *attrait,* but in writing his *Guide to the duties of the heart* he showed himself strictly orthodox. There are links with the Sufi mystic Al-Ghazali, and to some extent with Maimonides.

The worship of God, for Bahye, in its strictest prescribed form, is of value in giving a practical *via media* between the ordinary standards of the common man and the extremes of world-renouncing asceticism. Yet without true *Devekuth* the worship and observances are but dead forms. Men seek power, whether openly, or by the forbidden and secret ways of alchemy and magic. But true power comes from trust in God.

> 'He alone who confides in God is independent, and satisfied with what he has, and enjoys rest and peace without envying any one. . . . All that the world offers will disappoint in the end, and for this reason the saints and the prophets of old often fled their family circles and comfortable homes to lead a life of seclusion devoted to God only.' [109]

Humility and true repentance both arise from a true conception of God. The Hasidim are the true penitents. The same note of penitence that had sounded for the Ashkenazim, and had been stressed also in their German Christian contemporaries, appears here not from any tradition, but by the inner nature of Hasidism in any period.

'R. Bunam was asked: "We confess our sins so many times on the Day of Atonement. Why do we not receive a message of forgiveness? Now David had hardly finished saying: I have sinned, when he was told: The Lord has put away thy sin." He replied: "What David said was, 'I have sinned against the Lord' and what he meant was, 'Do with me according to your will and I shall accept it with love, for you, O Lord, are just.' " ' 110

Bahye himself comments even more directly. 'Were you altogether free from sin I should be afraid of what is far greater than sin, that is, of pride and hypocrisy.' He exhorts to self-examination in order to a state of purity, a state reached only by the Hasidim, the chosen ones of God. Yet he turns to the prescribed forms of the Law in prayer and worship, as the sure means of elevating the soul to those heights of contemplation of the Divine which are accessible only to the pure in heart. His book ends with a meditation on the Love of God—the longing of the soul for the fountain of its life, in which alone it finds joy and peace, even though the greatest pain and suffering be inflicted on it.

Bahye's *Guide* was translated into Hebrew, and was widely used among the Spanish dispersion as a Treasury of Devotion. Successive Muslim pressure had led, however, to a great weakening of Spanish Jewry. The most famous of the exiles—R. Maimun (Moses Maimonides) —fled to Morocco, and finally reached Palestine. It is perhaps understandable from his writings that he found no stability there, and soon joined the large Jewish settlement in Cairo. His main work was in the nature of an *Eirenicon,* written in Arabic as *A Guide to the perplexed.* These 'perplexed' may well be thought to have been partly his own restless desires. A number of his successors clearly did not wish to be disturbed by the impact of neoplatonism and its kindred sciences upon the Jewish faith. The teaching as a whole appears reasonable and sober and, if it opened a door to greater extremes of Kabbalism, it does not in itself greatly offend. It brought, in fact, a certain spiritual purity to contemporary Jewish mysticism. It has very little bearing upon the hidden life of the Hasidim, since it is concerned so far less with practical adoration in daily life, and so far more with abstract speculation for which the Hasid as such had little use. There is, however, considerable agreement in the stress on repentance.

'At this time, when the Temple no longer exists, and we have no atoning altar, there remains nothing but repentance. Repentance is resisting a temptation previously succumbed to, not from fear or from lack of ability. Even if he has been a sinner all his life and repents on the day of his death, so that he dies in a state of repentance, all his sins are pardoned. It is of the essence of repentance that the penitent should cry unremittingly before God, with weeping and supplication, and should practise charity according to his means, keeping himself free from the object of his sin. He should alter his name—as though to say "I am a different person, and not the same man who committed those actions." He must amend his whole conduct and turn towards the right path. Another thing he should do is to leave the place of his domicile, because exile atones for iniquity, since it causes a man to be humbled, and thus to become meek and lowly of spirit.' [111]

The general teachings of Maimonides have been clearly arranged and summarized by Cohen but for the special purpose of this study isolated quotations do not appear to take us further.

A figure of more practical potency in his effect upon the period is that of Abraham ben Samuel Abulafia (1240–91). He is an attractive person, but restless and eclectic to a degree that may seem to take him far from the simple ways of the Hasidim. He was clearly fascinated by the doctrines of Maimonides, but the same can be said of Meister Eckhardt, with whom interesting parallels can be found. After this principal education in Spain, there was a long period of wandering in the near East, and later in south-eastern Europe before he finally returned to Barcelona. His teaching there was characterized by a profound certainty and assurance regarding his own knowledge of the true nature of God. He gives the grounds for this certainty in precise and detailed instructions to his disciples, who are counselled to a severe form of *via negativa,* though this is confused by elements of magically-infused knowledge derived from a symbolical interpretation of the Names of God. His counsel is still plain, but is not encouraging for our purpose. 'The less understandable the Names are, the higher is their order, until you arrive at the activity of a force which is no longer in your control.' It is natural that in this quest he strayed into practices which appear very dubious, but his own records still show evidence of sincerity and conviction, and even of a strange plainness of speech, as if in some distorted paraphrase of the pseudo-Dionysian writings. It is even possible to imagine (though without apparent direct literary evidence) that he had found in thirteenth century Spain a similar literary scheme to that used far later by Teresa of Avila in the Interior Castle. Abulafia knows of seven stages in the ascent of a mystical ladder, at the summit of which he has been introduced to ineffable mysteries. Even here the goal appears something deliberately conceived. It is described as a 'rationally prepared ecstasy'—more akin to the practices of Yoga than to the awed humility of St. Paul in the mysteries of the third heaven. There is all too little of the authentic note of the Hasidim —too much of the spectre of pride. The prophet has entered, and is prepared to communicate to others, a personal attainment of the un-attainable. He will take from the Torah only that which ministers to his own perfection. Yet Scholem, more alert than any to such dangers, is prepared to conclude 'that Abulafia himself decisively rejected magic, and condemned in advance all attempts to use his doctrine of the holy Names for magical purposes . . . which he condemns as a falsification of true mysticism.' [112] There is further recorded a very interesting work, dating apparently in Palestine at the end of the thirteenth century, in which a disciple of Abulafia describes in detail the threefold path which he has himself followed. He concludes with affirming that 'God is my witness that my intention is *in majorem Dei gloriam.*' For the Christian mind, without doubting this intention, the quest may well appear to have become involved with dangerous and needless complication.

CHAPTER EIGHT

THE COMING OF THE BRIGHT
SPLENDOUR

AND then something happened which on any showing was a remarkable development in Jewish mystical thought. The pressure of life in its daily actuality weighed upon the Ashkenazim, and the first trends towards a more speculative and less realistic emphasis were not sufficient for them, or even for the more relaxed atmosphere of Sefardic Judaism, to divert the popular piety into a new direction. But, with two centuries still to pass before the great dispersion of 1492, any early tendencies toward an esoteric interest were made dominant by the appearance of the BOOK OF SPLENDOUR—the *Zohar*. The term 'appearance' might equally be either discovery, disclosure of the past, or invention *de novo*. Whatever the verdict of history, the book achieved the astonishing status of ranking with the Scriptures of the Old Testament and with the Talmud as a third parallel source of inspiration and authority. It came near for a time to supplementing them in popular estimate and enthusiasm. A young Sefardic Jew in modern times has written with uncritical joy, which needs always to be tempered by the considerations presented by Scholem. The literary controversy cannot concern us. It appears to be established by the present time that the compilation of *Zohar* was a deliberate work of the late thirteenth century, and that its author, Moses de Leon, had reasons of his own for representing it as a discovery, or even as a revelation, given to a famous second century Rabbi—Simeon ben Yochai. There need be no taint of forgery in such a conclusion. The method of pseudepigrapha is a recognized and thus a legitimate literary style. The fact remains, however, that the book of *Zohar*, and the whole spiritual method of which it stands as the supreme example, became the foundation of a spiritual development in Palestine even before, and certainly for long after the Spanish dispersion. It is in this fact—in the great revival of Sefardic life in Safed, and in the lesser centres such as Hebron and Bethel, that the Zohar is able to form a major bridge between early Hasidism and the rise of the Eastern settlements of which such rich evidence now exists. There is also the important fact that these centres prepared a Messianic outlook which was a main inspiration of later Hasidic hopes.

Bension blends an intense family loyalty to his Sefardic forebears

with the zeal of a converted man. It may be noted with interest that
the same spirit of joyous enthusiasm is found in another product of
Sefardic life, this time from a Christian convert, in Miss Levertoff's
moving study *The Wailing Wall*. A modern Christian study—Abbot
Lev Gillet's *Communion in the Messiah*—bears similar marks of true
enthusiasm. The common element between the two latter writings and
Bension's study of the *Zohar* is perhaps that of caring—which is less
noticeable in the more scholarly research of Scholem. Bension finds
the Zohar to be a creative source of Jewish spirituality, and to rekindle
a light from a world of feeling and emotion, by contrast with the more
rational principles of the *Talmud*.

> 'At a time when spiritual creativeness in the rest of the world was at a low
> ebb, three great cultures—Jewish, Christian and Moslem—flowered and
> rose to supreme heights in the Peninsula. In close proximity they influenced
> and stimulated one another.' [113]

A view not really dissimilar comes from Scholem's more cautious and
scholarly account. The purpose in the mind of Moses de Leon was

> 'to stem the growth of the radical rationalistic mood which was widespread
> among his educated contemporaries . . . who had broken in theory as well
> as in practice with large parts of Jewish tradition and religious law. In
> opposition to them he strives to maintain the undefiled Judaism of the
> Torah as he interpreted it in his mystical way. A mystical *Midrash* which
> presented an impressive picture of the profundity of the Divine Word
> appeared to him the best instrument for awakening an understanding of
> the grandeur of true Judaism when it is properly (i.e. mystically) under-
> stood. And since he was a man of genius, he succeeded, over and above the
> immediate purpose which he set himself . . . in giving magnificent expression
> to the spirit of that contemporary world of Spanish Kabbalism which was
> the abode of his own restless mind.' [114]

In introducing his own translation of portions of *Zohar*, Dr. Scholem
characterizes the book as 'a sacred text supplementing the Bible and the
Talmud on a new level of religious consciousness.' And in the passage
quoted above he has spoken of 'true Judaism properly, i.e. mystically,
understood.' It is remarkable that such a judgment can be made by a
scholar in his position—remarkable also that a great Hebrew University
is ready to appoint a Professor of Mysticism—a chair that could hardly
be imagined outside Judaism, and is a tribute to its supremely
religious character. Dr. Scholem is clearly concerned to support the
Zohar in its Jewish purpose. The theme of the present book naturally
must go further. It is important for us to find, as far as is possible, the
continuing trend that has been traced in Judaism from the period
when Judaism and Christianity shared their common origin—the period
as it were of the 'undivided Church.' But Christian contemplative

experience, most notably in the twentieth century, has reason to guard against tendencies which have marked revivals of Eastern mystical thought. Kabbalism was, after all, 'the secret doctrine in Israel,' and under this guise in modern times it has been presented as a so-called Theosophy, as Rosicrucianism and its many derivatives, and by other outcrops of the perennial heresy of the Church. It is therefore important to be clear as to those aspects of *Zohar* in which 'the undefiled Judaism of the Torah' is really preserved. In view of what has been said above, it is useful to note a considered judgment by Professor Abelson in introducing the Soncino English version of large parts of the *Zohar*.

'It mirrors Judaism as an intensely vital religion of the Spirit. More over-poweringly than any other book or code, more even than the Bible, does it pive to the Jew the conviction of an inner, unseen, spiritual universe—an eternal moral order.' [115]

Dr. Buber has already supported and strengthened this view in his stress on the religious life of Judaism, and his own standpoint is so integral both with orthodoxy and with the theme that we are seeking, as to give us confidence. Scholem's comment upon 'the power of contemplative fantasy and creative energy' need not take us astray from the path we have found hitherto. Among the Hasidim of Germany we have seen that the practical simplicity of their way of life was already turning towards a more speculative mood. When it is necessary to find Spanish Kabbalism, and the *Zohar* in particular, marked by theosophical colour, we need not assume the dangers found in neo-Vedantism to-day. *Zohar* deals with the mystery of the hidden God, but insists that the infinite and unknowable has by His own Being and within His own Essence made it possible for man to know Him. 'Something which belongs to the Divine is quickened, and breaks through the closed shell of His hidden Self.' For the *Zohar* every phase of this process goes hand in hand with the words of Scripture, which words are themselves part of God's mercy to men—an impulse of the divine life. To establish this guarantee of orthodoxy, categories of interpretation long used, or misused, by Biblical scholars had to be adopted. There have been undoubted Christian mistakes, notably in the liberal periods of the nineteenth and twentieth centuries : but there have also been undoubted gains. Canons of exegesis which have revived Christian patristic study, and have led especially to the use of typology in modern Biblical theology, cannot look askance at these Jewish types. Yet, in the first Zoharic enthusiasm, 'mysticism' came into some danger of being regarded as an end in itself, which could override Scriptural truth.

The *Sefiroth,* as emanations of the Divine Glory, can confound our purpose by the very subtlety with which they are defined, but can

K

equally show true liturgical insight. From the hidden mystery of the Godhead man was made aware, in an ordered process of self-giving, of the supreme Crown (*Kether*): this was disclosed next in wisdom (*Hokhmah*), Intelligence (*Binah*) and Loving-kindness (*Hesed*). The power (*Din*) in stern judgment is linked with Compassion (*Rahamim*), called more rarely *Tifereth* (Beauty). The physical order of the Creation is displayed by its lasting endurance (*Netsah*), its majesty (*Hod*) and its firm foundation (*Yesod*). The whole sequence and pattern is crowned by Royalty (*Malkuth*). Such is the pattern of the *Sefiroth,* the 'mystical organism—the symbol which supplies the Kabbalist with a ready justification for the anthropomorphic mode of Scriptural expression.' [116] Père Bouyer writes further:

> 'Let us also recall the Sceptre placed in the Ark. Does it not evoke some degree of identification between the Shekinah and *Malkuth*—the last of the Sefiroth, who sums up all the others in the Kabbalistic tradition—that is to say the Reign of Jahweh? To Christians, does not Christ appear also as bearing in Himself the presence of the Kingdom—as being Himself the Kingdom—the *auto-basileia* of Origen?' [117]

This reference seems unquestionable, though we should probably be wise not to read overmuch Christian symbolism into the Sefirotic pattern. Abbot Lev Gillet has spoken of close links with the fourth Gospel in the Zoharic conception of the soul in its vital, moral and rational elements. But this highly mystical pattern is sure evidence of the soul of a people seeking deeply after God in a world of instability and persecution. Scholem speaks of the Sefiroth in such terms:

> 'They are the stages of the inner world through which God descends from the innermost recesses down to His revelation in the Shekinah. They are the garments of divinity, but also the beams of light which it sends forth. . . . The *Zohar* identifies the highest development of God's personality with precisely that stage of His unfolding which is immanent and mysteriously present in every one of us.' [118]

The doctrine is expounded very fully in the sixth chapter of Prof. Scholem's book, to which we are already so deeply indebted, but it can become so complex a subject as to divert from the true values of his book for our purpose. (Even the five volumes of the new Soncino edition of *Zohar* cover only a part of the whole work, which occupies 2,400 closely written folios in its original.) Objective judgment is difficult without accurate knowledge of a text of such prodigious length and complexity. The knowledge, even so, tends to be affected by the personal desires of the critic, as is shown in Bension. *Zohar* has been condemned and praised within Judaism on very similar grounds. It is said to imperil the essential monotheism without which Judaism falls, while others find in it sure support for their faith. It has been charged with gross sexuality in major passages, to which others give quite different interpretations. (This supposed aspect has unfortunately been developed at length by one modern writer, who found in it a main source of curious interest.) Bension makes much of parallels between *Zohar* and the mystical elements in non-Jewish Spain, whether Moslem (as in Isaac ibn-Alatif) or Christian. In the latter case it is not reasonable to suppose that the flowering of Carmelite spirituality in the late sixteenth century could arise *ex nihilo*, or be entirely unaffected by the vivid energies of the earlier mystical periods. Passages which orthodoxy (whether Jewish or Christian) may fear as pantheistic are often capable of a deeper interpretation, though any hasty parallels can colour our judgment. On the charge of erotic interest, it is probably true that Christian mysticism has gained from the Canticles a value which Judaism might wish to avoid. The exegesis of the Fathers, at least since the writings of St. Bernard, did not affect Judaism until after the Spanish Dispersion; for the Ashkenazim, however, the love of the child for the father was already seen as the passion of the lover for his beloved.

In the same connection, as we have partly noted, the *Zohar* lays a new stress upon the Shekinah. The early Hasidim were able to be more direct and even naïve in their view of Creation. The self-revelation of the unknown would raise for them no problem, for both alike are God, and are One. Saadia had described the glory (*Kavod*) as 'the great radiance called *Shekinah*,' and he equates the same glory with the Holy Spirit who speaks the voice and word of God. *Shekinah* is the crown of the emanations which disclose the Being of God. The affiliation is corporate, 'identified with the community of Israel as a sort of invisible church, representing the mystical idea of Israel in its bond with God and in its bliss, but also in its suffering and its exile.' [119]

'The union of Shekinah with the invisible God is complete in the upper world, but in the lower world God suffers the pain of separation. The Shekinah remains for the sake of man's free-will in recovering the effects of the Fall. She is so bound in the world of action that her future union with the King in the Spiritual Marriage is being prepared. The Heavenly Hosts are united in one Body animated by the desire to contemplate the glory of God. In the End of the Days the union will be perfect.' [120]

The same note of the spirtiual destiny of Israel is linked with the Zoharic narrative which tells of the approaching death of Simeon-ben-Yochai. This section is admittedly one of the most beautiful, but is unfortunately not available in a connected English translation.

'I am my beloved's, and his desire draws him towards me. During all the

THE HIDDEN LIFE OF THE BODY OF CHRIST

years in which I have been attached to this world, I have also been attached to God. And now His desire draws Him towards me. He is here with all His holy hosts. . . . All things are in Him, and He is in all things: yet He is separated from all things.'

(It is noteworthy that this passage firmly guards against any charge of Pantheism.) This familiar line of meditation on the approaching union of the faithful soul, which is common in the later periods of Spanish mysticism, suggests a reflection upon the destiny of Israel. There is pictured a dispute between Sammael and Michael (types respectively of the 'left-hand' and the 'right-hand' principles) as to Israel's readiness for the Divine promise. Sammael denies that Israel is ready.

'The Lord turned to Michael and said: "Alas that he should have spoken truth. Yet do I make a vow this day, that so soon as the Community of Israel will open its Heart to me, even so little as the opening of an eye in a needle, then will I open wide to them the doors of salvation." Israel was the foundation of the world: all peoples lived upon her merit. But since the Sanctuary has been destroyed, and the Shekinah is with Israel in exile, the world is accursed. . . . But on the day when the Holy One will send salvation to Israel, there will be joy in all the worlds.' [121]

The material is undoubtedly uneven, but in this particular section there are very apparent links with such a work as *The Interior Castle,* written nearly two centuries later. As one example :

'The guardian of the fifth palace is called "guardian of the Covenant," but his true name is Love. Even the righteous do not come here: but the Hasidim, those who have served God with Love, are allowed to enter. Then were my eyes allowed to gaze upon all the holy spirits who are nourished by the kiss of the eternal.'

Similar quotations could be adduced, but it is not possible in reasonable compass to give any connected picture of the whole book.

The most evident spiritual continuity with early Hasidism, and the most fruitful sign of spiritual growth is, once again, in the heightened emphasis on *Devekuth.* There are undoubted dangers, but there is also much balance and spiritual sanity. An earlier Kabbalist, Moses-ben-Nahman, had thought that true *Devekuth* could be attained through the normal social life of the individual; it was not for him a goal that needed escape from the world. In this connection it is interesting that for the first time such social principles as the religious value of poverty, used in a somewhat Franciscan sense, become an ideal to be sought.

The point of immediate importance for our purpose is more truly a historical one. From being a literary *tour-de-force* disclosed to a somewhat eclectic and established Jewish colony, *Zohar* became 'over-

night' the cherished and closely guarded Bible of a new faith. From
its inspiration we are now able to see something of a life which continued in the too familiar setting of the Wandering Jew, but one in
which a corporate spirituality was developed in the Holy Land itself
on the very sites sacred to Jewish and Christian history. We may find
in due course sectarian developments, but the centre at Safed gained
the earliest and chief prominence, since it marked the burial-place of
Simeon-ben-Jochai, and thus retained the romance attaching to the
legendary hero of *Zohar*. Safed became the directing centre—the
mother-house—for other groups, notably at Tiberias, Hebron and in
Jerusalem itself. Bension speaks from personal knowledge of these
groups to-day when he writes that

> '*Zohar* filled Jewish life so completely that the Zoharistic tradition was
> carried on unbroken by the Dispersion into Hasidic centres both of
> Ashkenazi and Sefardic origin.'

From the book itself it was learned that

> 'Israel must not be turned aside by temporal things when all Eternity is his
> to contemplate. Here we have a key to that extraordinary force which
> sustains the Jewish people.' [122]

It is in these continuing centres, and in the actual life of suffering,
poverty and joy of which there are considerable valid evidences, that
the fruit of *Zohar* must be judged. As we have said, the book has
become the stalking-horse of modern esoteric experimentalists, whose
writing from our standpoint is, at the best, negligible. It has inspired
sects and cults in a way which would have disgusted the purer simplicity of Hasidim, and in the backwash of these movements it has in
places corrupted those who had once known Christian faith. It is
relevant to turn once again to Dr. Martin Buber for our encouragement in following the story further:

> 'Where are the ways of God's working revealed? Exactly at the beginning
> of wandering through the desert: exactly at the height of Job's trial:
> exactly in the midst of the terror of the Other, of the incomprehensible . . .
> exactly from out of the secret. God does not show only mercy and grace to
> us: it is terrible when His hand falls on us, and what then happens to
> us does not somehow find a place beside mercy and grace: it does not
> belong to the same category as these: the ultimate does not belong to the
> attribute of righteousness: it is beyond all attribute. It is indeed the secret,
> and it is not for us to inquire into it. . . . Only when the secret no longer
> stands over our own tabernacle, but has shattered it, do we know . . . God's
> intercourse with us.' [123]

Those words are written most evidently out of actual contemporary experience. Into such a depth of experience and faith the Sefardic exile might have come. But we have to follow as best we can the events which actually met them after the shattering blow of 1492.

From Promise to Disaster

A generation intervened between the actual decree of exile in 1492 and the coherence of the new spiritual energy at Safed in northern Galilee. It was not time lost, but time needed if any recovery were to be made. The storm could not have been wholly unforeseen : some Christian persecution had begun to disturb Spanish Jewry for about a century. But the significance of the final tragedy required even longer to work itself out. Esoteric speculation upon the origins of the Universe were strongly modified by what Scholem feels bound to call 'the pathos of Messianism,' which was pervading the new Kabbalah. In contrast to this rather characteristic note, one is tempted to ask whether this 'pathos' was not in fact a haunting sense of need in the contemporary generation. One does not require to condone either the excesses or the falsity of Sabbatianism to realize that even such developments, lamentable as they are, would be impossible if the Messianic pattern were not rooted in the purpose of God for mankind. One hears at such moments the cry heard first by Hosea—'How can I give thee up? How shall I let thee go? I am God, and not man.' In this case it was undoubtedly part of the sin that factors of ambition and greed on the one hand, and the temptation aroused by popular enthusiasm on the other, entered to pervert what may have been a genuine religious zeal. It cannot be intrinsically tragic that the fruits of the 'Community of the Devout' at Safed bore enduring marks of the tragedy in which the seed was sown.

This point is made forcibly by Scholem in a passage so relevant to the spiritual problems of 'the end of an age' that full quotation may be justified. He speaks of two anonymous contemporary commentaries, one upon the Torah and the other upon the Psalms, which, as in canonical apocalyptic, might appear innocent, but which in fact caused the words of the Psalter to 'stand forth as sharp swords in Israel's hand, and deadly weapons.' The Psalter itself, in a manner which our modern age can fully understand, was envisaged in the double capacity of a book of war-songs, and an arsenal of weapons for the 'last war.' Before the

'final apocalyptic struggle in which these weapons were to be used, the tremendous apocalyptic power latent in the words of the Psalms is to manifest itself in the form of comfort, which is really the glow and crackling of the apocalyptic firse in their depths. Comfort is the classical symbol for delay. Even the delay of the final consummation, undesirable as it is, has a healing force. Comfort paves the way for the apocalyptic struggle. But when once the absolute power of the divine words erupts from beneath the comforting guise of meditation and promise, "all the forces will be transformed." . . . Such deep seated feeling as to the religious significance of catastrophes was bound, after the acute apocalyptic phase had subsided, to be transferred to more solid and substantial regions and there to struggle for expression. This expression was achieved in the far-reaching changes in the outlook on life, and in the new religious conceptions, with which the Kabbalah of Safed laid claim to dominate the Jewish world, and did in fact so dominate it for a long time.' [124]

The outstanding names in the formation and early growth of Safed are those of the poet Cordobero (1522–70) and of Isaac Luria (1534–72). The former is of less relevance for our purpose, though as a learned commentator on the text of *Zohar* he is notable. Luria is more notable as a man of holiness, and it is to his originating leadership that later generations in Safed have looked. The extremists of rationalist orthodoxy naturally revile him, just as they refuse to recognize any validity in the spiritual revival within Judaism. But those less extreme may still fear a danger of conflict between a true Theism and Pantheism. Even to recognize the possibility of conflict is enough to make Luria suspect, but it is not the monopoly of the *Zohar,* or even of Judaism as a whole, to know that any human comment upon the mystery of the Divine Being is bound to be imperfect. Only the constant guarding of humility and due reticence can make the path at all safe. A *jeu-d'esprit* such as Cordobero's saying 'God is all reality, but not all reality is God' can mean more or less what the speculating mind desires to find in it. He is less elusive in direct reference to the meaning of the Sefiroth. 'His substance is present in His Sefiroth, and He Himself is everything, and nothing exists outside Him.' His output of writing was remarkable, a fact which puts him in strong contrast to his immediate contemporary.

Though the undoubted spiritual leader of the Sefardim after the exile, Isaac Luria was himself of an Ashkenazi family, and came to Safed after a period of solitude in Egypt. More is known of him from his *alter ego* Hayyam Vital, who did not share Luria's unwillingness to teach by writing. Yet the hiddenness of the master so impressed the pupil that his own writings were circulated unwillingly, and mainly by the stealth of others. Scholem pays a striking tribute to Luria, more especially considering his own caution in the matter : 'Luria himself was the living example of an outspoken Theistic mystic. He gave to the *Zohar,* for all its intrinsic Pantheism, a strictly Theistic interpretation.' [125]

From a complex theosophical network appears the strange but central doctrine of a withdrawal of God within Himself, to be followed by a re-emergence or renewal. This is represented by the disclosures culminating in the redemptive revelation of the *Shekinah*. The term 'followed by' must not be interpreted in a normal sense of sequence. Men may perceive an apparent succession of events, but the concept of *Tsimtsum* implied rather an overriding aspect covering the visible events. It in no way suggests a divine 'reculer pour mieux sauter.' The work of 're-emergence'—of restoration or restitution—(*Tikkun*) is shared also by the fidelity of Israel. At this point we approach what is for our purpose the most significant aspect of the *Zohar*.

> 'It is man who completes the enthronement of God, the King and mystical creator of all things. . . . The historical process and its innermost soul, the religious act of the Jew, prepare the way for the final restitution of all the scattered and exiled lights. . . . The Jew who is in close contact with the divine life through the Torah, the fulfilment of the Commandments, and through prayer, has it in his power to accelerate or to hinder this process (*sc.* Tikkun). Every act of man is related to the final task which God has set for His creatures. . . . It follows from this that for Luria the appearance of the Messiah is nothing but the consummation of the continuous process of restoration (*Tikkun*). The true nature of redemption is therefore mystical, and its historic and natural aspects are merely ancillary symptoms which constitute a visible symbol of its consummation. The redemption of Israel concludes the Redemption of all things.' [126]

We have already noted with great respect, though agreement is impossible for a Christian, the strength of Scholem's conviction regarding Jewish Messianism. It may be that he, and even Dr. Buber, are as it were haunted by the spectre of Sabbatai Zevi, but before we reach that historical tragedy the question must be further examined, and an important distinction must be noted.

In the Old Testament, and chiefly in Deutero-Isaiah the Messiah is engaged in a process of redemption : in the Kabbalistic doctrine he crowns the achievement of others—call them persons or agencies as you will. Since the world is manifestly in a state of sin, it is natural that the Jew cannot accept the Messiahship of Jesus. The Advent of Messiah must await the end of history—not cause it. In this view Judaism is in fact refusing the redeeming Advent, and clinging to the impending doom of judgment. This conflict of theme is of the greatest importance in the light of certain Christian conviction that the Parousia could begin in compassion before it ended in the appointed judgment. The Jewish outlook is well expressed in one of the later Hasidic legends :

> 'When R. Menahem was living in the land of Israel, a foolish man climbed the Mount of Olives unobserved. When he got to the top he blew the ram's horn. The people were startled, and soon a rumour sprang up that this was the blowing of the ram's horn that was to precede redemption. When this

was reported to R. Menahem, he opened his window, looked out into the world, and said: "This is no renewal." ' [127]

The final reintegration of what has been disjointed (let us say plainly the Redemption of the World) is thus presented as a retraction or contraction of the Divine power, as though to throw upon Man the final responsibility for completing the Divine purpose. This is far from the truth so tragically rejected, but it cannot be ignored unsympathetically. Luria and his school seem to have begun to express a new phase of the greatest importance. They cannot *from their present position* realize the rejected truth, but are they not still crying out for what God had intended from the beginning? When the fullness of time came (not from a hopeful readiness but rather from a desperate unreadiness in the popular mind) the Word was made flesh—He was made Man. The final act in the Restoration (*Tikkun*) was indeed an act framed in human terms. There was a withdrawal—as though God the Hidden Mystery had to disclose Himself by a supreme act of *Kenosis*. The tragedy of all self-willed Messianism is precisely its self-will. The Humanity in which the Incarnation was actually wrought is the unique Humanity conceived by the Holy Ghost upon the humanity of the Blessed Virgin. But we have already realized the need—in discerning the marks of the hidden Body of Christ so to assert the Divine Nature as not to detract from the consequent mystery of such a human nature. Even for us by whom the perfect gift was acknowledged—still more for the chosen people of God for whom it was paramountly intended—there is a true searching for our own true human part in the restoration. The restoration is in fact a restitution—a reparation. It cannot be the fruit of a human effort until that fruit has sprung from the true Seed of the Redeeming Life.

More clearly than at any period since the parting of the ways we can realize the immense nearness to the truth for which Luria was groping. His confusion, his risk of truth, even his Gnosticism in part, may lead an orthodox Jew to set up every barrier and safeguard. But to those who have been brought into the hidden life of the Body, the task of reparation stands out at this juncture more dominantly than ever before. The earlier Hasidim were exhibiting that life in an attractive way, which calls for sympathy and for a sense of comradeship with them. Here is a moment of Truth, and the right estimation of Luria and his companions at Safed may seem to us of greater importance than Scholem is prepared to concede. For he himself says : 'The world of *Tikkun* is therefore the world of Messianic action. The coming of Messiah means that this world of *Tikkun* has received its final shape.' [128]

In the prayer-life of Safed, or at least in the teaching upon which Luria desired to found it, this task is clearly central. The old 'tension' between individual spirituality and the liturgical task of the community seems no longer acute. The purpose of the whole activity of prayer has again possessed the field. Perhaps chiefly in corporate liturgy, but also in private, the act and intention guides the Hasid in his ascent through the cloud and in his adherence to God. Even more, and of more immediate relevance, the spiritual intention (*Kawwanah*) is an effective agent. 'The true worshipper, in short, exercises a tremendous power over the inner worlds, just as he bears a correspondingly great responsibility for the fulfilment of his Messianic task.' [129] The vocation of the contemplative intercessor could hardly be put more plainly, but that vocation is closely bound in Christian experience with the principles both on *Kawwanah* and of *Devekuth*, and has in fact brought many contemplative saints to what would be termed '*unio mystica*,' if St. Teresa had unfortunately talked formal theology. An aspect of the same sense of corporate vocation is in a reparatory use of the dominant tragedy of *Galuth* (Exile). 'This is the secret why Israel is fated to be enslaved by all the Gentiles in the world : in order that it may uplift those sparks which have also fallen among them. . . . And therefore it was necessary that Israel should be scattered to the four winds in order to lift everything up.' [130] Père Louis Bouyer confirms the same point when he writes :

> 'In the normal Protestant conception, the religion of the prophets, tending as it does toward an action which is to transform the real world, ignores the desire for union with God. This is because it is entirely moved by an initiative of God's coming to man without his having sought for it. . . . It must be made clear that this unmerited and wholly unmeritable "grace" is very far from being the granting of any natural desire. . . . It was not in order to satisfy contemplative piety egotistically that God came down of His own accord to man in the religion of the Bible. It was to make man His servant, the servant of the Word by which God wishes to impose His Holy Will upon the world.' [131]

The true *theologia mystica* of Judaism is still condemned for its eschatological mood. It developed a clear doctrine of penitence, following in this the old Hasidic practices of Germany, of which Luria may well have heard. But, despite all his hesitation, Scholem brings his final tribute to Lurianic Kabbalism in describing it as 'the last movement in the history of Rabbinic Judaism which gave expression to a world of religious reality common to the whole people.' [132] One might add that it seems further, to recover for all influenced by it some of the spiritual perceptions which we shall later study in Eastern Hasidism, and which are a living fact to-day.

As we now pass, however briefly, to consider a dark period of mystical aberration, it may be well to recall the passage quoted above

(p. 152f. *supra,* ref. 126) which must continue to pierce the densest fog of Kabbalistic groping. It is notably true that where the scholarly Jewish mind—even the saintly mind of a Martin Buber, finds an element of warning in the Messianic hopes that have stirred Judaism, and which we have just noted in Luria and at Safed, the whole concept of *Tikkun* shows how impossible it is to separate the consummation of Judaism from the Christian hope. The one cardinal division in the Body of Christ is really that between Judaism and Christianity as a whole. But the Jewish fidelity to the pattern of Law and Liturgy means that this supreme fact can only truly be appreciated by the Cathloic mind, in East and West alike. The task of understanding must rest upon those who can bear it. But we should recall as a corrective the essentially undogmatic structure of Judaism. 'No one really wanted to know what God was, or what the Shekinah and the Holy Spirit were, in their absolute and essential nature. The reality of their existence was experienced in the practical life. This was all, and this was enough.' [133]

The Tragedy of Sabbatai-Zezi

'A people which had suffered from all the tribulations which exile and persecution could bring, and which at the same time had developed an extremely sensitive consciousness of life actually lived between the poles of Exile and Redemption, needed little to take the final step to Messianism. The appearance of Sabbatai-Zevi and Nathan of Gaza precipitated this step by liberating the latent energies and potentialities which had gradually accumulated during the generations immediately preceding them. The eruption of the volcano, when it came, was terrific.' So far we seem to be repeating the most sombre judgment of Scholem. Yet he goes on—'For an entire year men lived a new life which for many years remained their first glimpse of deeper spiritual reality.' [134] The crucial year was 1665 to 1666, close to the actual time when, in England, the uprising and influential Quaker movement had to face the shock of the defection of James Nayler and his worshippers. Nayler was won back to a spirit of deep humility and repentance. Sabbatai-Zevi ended in tragedy, and dragged tragedy after him in the following of Jacob Frank.

Scholem's final sentence really presents the core of the matter. The concept of *Tikkun* (restoration) may be seen, in the theme of this study, as one which could call forth a true spiritual sacrifice. But the same conception presented to an exhausted popular mind could, and did, become almost hysterical excitement, and little more. It seems to have fascinated the strange temperament of Sabbatai-Zevi, of whom it has recently been suggested on careful evidence that he was a victim of manic-depression. The concept presented to him, or to one part of his divided self, an illumination and a personal destiny. The temptation for a younger enthusiast, Nathan of Gaza, must have been very great. He could find 'a quasi-sacramental character in antinomian action,' and it apparently took little for him to persuade himself of a dramatic revelation which he had to hold secret. Sabbatai, in a seclusion in Egypt, heard from a third associate of a prophet who could speak to his condition, and at a critical moment in his sickness he became persuaded that his supposed illusions were reality. (From certain hints in the *Zohar* there was a Gnostic sect available which was closely relevant to these delusions, and may have sponsored them.) The historical facts are uncertain, being rarely recorded save in scorn. Sabbatai's Messianic mission was apparently proclaimed more than once, in terms which rightly gave unforgivable offence to any serious Jew. Strange antinomian doctrines, fathered upon the *Zohar* and upon Luria himself, gave rise to a widespread sectarian movement in Europe. Sabbatai-Zevi ultimately reached Byzantium, where he was betrayed to the Moslem authorities—less disposed even than the Jews to tolerate Messianic pretensions. To save his life he embraced Islam. In some quarters disillusionment and confusion resulted. In many others the apostasy was woven into a pseudo-mysticism. A perverted antinomian formula, based on a play upon a *Midrash* sentence, became a kind of password in Salonica, and was attributed to Sabbatai-Zevi himself: 'Praise be to Thee, O Lord, who permittest the forbidden.' [135]

Such a dismal and unsavoury phase might well seem best forgotten. But it does not invalidate the primary point emphasized above. Even more widespread, although confused by evil notions and by self-will, there had grown from Safed a concept of Redemption which we cannot ignore. No longer was the symbolic history of the Exile all important: it had taken on cosmic significance as the restitution of a fallen race—a task in which even humanity must take part along with the eternal hidden purpose of God. Even the hopes, once more terribly shattered, of the return of a personal Messiah could not cloud altogether this burden laid upon the devout.

> 'The significance (*sc.* of Redemption) is seen to be not so much the end of that Exile which began with the destruction of the Temple, as rather the end of that inner exile of all creatures which began when the father of mankind was driven out of Paradise. . . . Lurianic Kabbalism had as its main purpose the preparation of men's hearts for that renaissance the scene of which is the human soul.' [136]

There is a danger in overstress upon the weight of darkness. The wisest intercessors have constantly to guard against such an assault upon their faith, since it can only cause them to centre upon self, instead of upon God. This danger was even enhanced, as may be understood in the secret warfare of the soul, by a pessimism that could not be patient in a purely spiritual redemption. Another primal lie arose in one of the tributary sects—'Evil must be fought with evil.' Scholem speaks wisely of 'the deeply fascinating doctrine of the holiness of sin.' The final perversion associated with Jacob Frank, who had, unfortunately, some association with Eastern Catholicism, is found in the modern Communist heresy of 'double-think' (one's heart and one's mouth must not be one). The familiar Gnostic dualism of the demi-urge is a natural concomitant, and Scholem justly concludes : 'It is not surprising that their God, no less than their Messiah, bears the mark of self-contradiction and disintegration.'

CHAPTER NINE

THE NEW HASIDISM

HOWEVER necessary this hard judgment may be, the task of the Hasidim remains. This following of the hidden life in its intercession and its reparation had to be carried on, but the setting was largely new. The continuity of an ancient name cannot in itself ensure any close historical links. The mediaeval Hasidim of Germany had not, save in a much later age, to assimilate and accommodate themselves to the heady wine of the *Zohar*, to its theological development after the Spanish exile, or to the confusion and moral chaos left by Sabbatai-Zevi.

None the less, we venture to suggest that Jewish scholarship has felt itself unduly compelled to undervalue, and even to deny at times, the continuing task which rested on the new Hasidim. They entered into the inheritance of the great concept of *Tikkun*—no mere cosmological or religious notion, but a task to challenge human endeavour. That task had to evoke a humility which the prophets at least would have demanded from God in fervent prayer, knowing their own incapacity to attain it. Here is a race newly charged to share the Divine Redemption, and to live out their own spiritual task. As we shall see in watching that task, they are not legalists or philosophers, but holy and humble men of heart. They are poor, wandering, and insecure, save for their living consciousness of the Divine Presence, and of the society of the people of God.

But there may well be a more vivid continuity, since for the first time we are in a contemporary age. We may study the legends of the Polish and Ukrainian settlements, and may find in them some of the naïveté and directness of spiritual children. But the descendants of those children live on in the same tradition to-day.

What, then, confronts us as the curtain rises again after the dark scene of a false Messianism? The scene has shifted to Eastern Europe. However close the links with Sefardim or Ashkenazim, we are meeting a new Jewry in a new environment, driven out and concentrated in large settlements in Russian Poland and the Ukraine. The agelong piety of the country will certainly have affected the spiritual atmosphere, quite apart from direct Christian influence in doctrine and worship. One may recall the writings of Mme. Iulia de Beausobre, both in her personal recollections and in the history of St. Serafim, when she speaks of vast areas of land in which latent forces both of good and evil are obvious to this day. Similarly the Spanish climate has already begun to ripen the fruit of Spanish Mysticism, and must unquestionably have affected the very different world of *Zohar*.

But the new Hasidim brought with them a legacy of their own. If in fact they sought to leave much of it aside, taking only what they felt they could use, they added the governing conviction that the Messianic burden now lay upon all men—not merely on an esoteric few. This major innovation was not made in ignorance of the values of Safed, and of the hidden groups which that centre had fostered. By now the most potent of these was probably the house of Prayer at Bethel—a retreat-house if not in fact a monastery. Bension speaks with his accustomed enthusiasm of this place where his own father had made his home :

> 'Bethel was a community resolved to live in unity and sanctity. Of those who thought to enter its portals it demanded the attainment of the scholar and the self-abnegation of the ascetic. . . . It demanded a pure life, based on a sense of personal responsibility for the discord in the universe, coupled with the use of *Kawwanah* for its redemption. . . . To the poor and to the exalted : to the down-trodden and the illustrious, Bethel restored the mystical tradition in which the Creator and the created thing—man and a grain of sand—meet together and are essential to each other.' [137]

Scholem also throws light upon the new life :

> 'As mystical moralists the Hasidim found the way to social organization. Again we see the ancient paradox of solitude and communion. He who has attained to the highest degree of spiritual solitude, who is capable of being alone with God, is the true centre of the community, because he has reached the stage at which true communion becomes possible. . . . To live among ordinary men and yet be alone with God : to speak profane language and yet draw the strength to live from . . . the upper root of the soul—that is a paradox which only the mystical devotee is able to realize in his life, and which makes him the centre of the community of men.' [138]

In this sense the Hasidim used, and transcended, the necessary power-house at Bethel. Such power-houses of the spirit were probably known but to a few of those who led the widespread Hasidic groups. This leadership tended to become dynastic, though in a new form. For Rabbinical Jewry, particularly in those centuries,

> 'the ideal type recognized as the leader of the community is the scholar, the student of Torah, the learned Rabbi. Of him no inner revival is demanded : what he needs is deeper knowledge of the sources of holy Law, in order that he may be able to show the right path to the community, and to interpret for it the eternal and immutable word of God. In the place of these leaders of the Law, the new movement gave birth to a new type of leader,

the illuminate, the man whose heart has been touched and changed by God, in a word—the prophet. . . . When, as happened more than once, both types were combined in one person, that was all the better, but it was not considered essential.' [139]

But the evidence is far too compelling to allow a picture of the enthusiast, the ecstatic, or the Dervish. If the concept of prayer is a prayer born in the world, and not sheltered in the Beth-El, it was none the less in prayer that the whole life was founded. The values of *Devekuth* and of *Kawwanah* became more firmly established. It is fair, also, to define Hasidism not only by what it was, but by what it was not. It was not Sabbatai, and it was not Jacob Frank. Of the latter even Dr. Buber will say: 'This man is not a liar—he is the Lie. . . . He populates the nothing with divine forms, the spawn of late gnostic feeling.'

> 'Historically, Hasidism is the reply to the crisis in Messianism. The way to Hasidism, to the concentrated attempt to preserve the reality of God for the Jew, was paved by the extreme antinomian development of the Sabbatian movement. . . . Jacob Frank's enterprise, which ran grotesquely amok and took the final leap into a kind of nihilism draped in mythology, had shown wakeful souls that the whole community was on the edge of the abyss, and this realization had led the most valuable forces into Haisdism.' [140]

More nearly its type may be found in R. Nahman of Bratislava. He was a formidable leader—a dominating authority—though one senses the obvious concern of the spiritual aspects of Zaddikism. But the test of leadership is in the following, and from countless Hasidim known only through the mass of legend faithfully handed down, the real quality of the hidden life may be discerned. These legends are not inspired by curiosity or boasting. They became a religious act in the nation of supreme story-tellers. 'By telling the traditions of the Zaddikim one draws the light of the Messiah into the world, and expels much of the darkness.' In a well-known legend this general quality is illustrated. The founder Baal-Shem-Tobh (*Besht*) used to go to a place in the woods and meditate before a fire, and his prayer was granted. In the next generation they could not identify the place, but the words of the prayers were known. A successor found the place, but the prayers had been forgotten. Finally, both place and the forms of prayer were unknown, but the faithful telling of the legend was rewarded by the fulfilment of the *Kawwanah*.

Much could be said of the tensions raised within orthodox Judaism, of jealousy, pride and other too-human mistakes. But the hidden life is its own testimony. For those who seek that life, the name of Dr. Martin Buber stands as an example. He has said that the discovery of one saying of the founder Baal-Shem-Tobh so forcibly impressed him that he dedicated himself as a disciple of that long-dead leader. During five years of intensive study, he began the work of shaping, re-telling and interpreting the chaotic literary material, a work which he describes as a form of stewardship. From this work the Christian in his remote, non-Jewish setting, may discern the effect in character and the power in life of 'the hallowing of every day'—what he knows from de Caussade as 'the sacrament of the present moment.'

'Among all movements . . . none more greatly than Hasidism has proclaimed the infinite ethos of the moment.' As we come to find in Hasidic legend the clear marks of the hidden life, this existentialism will be seen to go hand in hand with the prayer in which their lives were rooted. It is a deeply religious existentialism, and one which closely reflects Christian endurance and Christian hope. For this endurance is no Stoicism—no putting up with what cannot be changed. It is a conscious participation in a living task, which rests not upon a human dream but upon a divine vocation—even a Divine partnership. The mysterious conceptions which we have noted in the Kabbalah concerning the 'standing-back' (*Tsimtsum*) of the Creator and the drawing forward of the created being into his redeeming task (*Tikkun*) have become for a great body of simple folk the life to which they were born.

> 'A teaching which sets the winged HOW of an act high above the codified WHAT is not able to hand down its substance in writing: it is transmitted by life from master to disciple . . . the substance of its truth is only open to him who verifies it by his life.' [141]

One of R. Moshe's Hasidim was extremely poor. He complained to the Zaddik that his wretched circumstances were an obstacle to learning and praying. 'In this day and age,' said R. Moshe, 'the greatest devotion, greater than learning or praying, consists in accepting the world exactly as it happens to be.' [142]

'Soon after the death of R. Moshe, R. Mendel asked one of his disciples : "What was most important to your teacher?" The disciple thought, and then replied, "Whatever he happened to be doing at the moment." ' [143]

This 'infinite ethos of the moment' took striking forms : R. Burman was once walking outside the city with some of his disciples. He bent down, picked up a speck of sand, looked at it, and put it back exactly where he had found it. 'He who does not believe,' he said, 'that God wants this bit of sand to be in this particular place, does not believe at all.' [144] Dr. Buber comments in the first introduction : 'The Hasidic movement did not weaken the hope in a Messiah, but it kindled both simple and intellectual followers to joy in the world as it is, in life as it is, in every hour of life in that world as that hour is.' [145]

L

But in any study of Hasidism which seeks to find an increasing spiritual fulfilment of the task of the hidden life, the Christian student must face firmly and continually that the new sense of a Messianic task is built on a very strange hope, however deep its conviction and tenacity. Buber insists in many of his teachings on a blunt fact, in which we can find no modification : 'For Judaism redemption is not a historic fact, but pure futurity.' There are wide differences between his spiritual horizon and that of Scholem, but on this fact they insist firmly and repeatedly.

> 'Before the glowing plenitude of fate given by the *here and now,* even the horizon of *the last things* is apparently drained of its colour before our eyes. The kingdom of God . . . appears on the horizon of the absolute future, where heaven and earth meet: but timelessly it reveals itself ever and again where truly human beings act with the whole of their nature, and thus unite God and His Shekinah.' [146]

And yet the task goes on. It is undertaken successively by the Zaddik, 'who is more intent than other men in putting his hand to the task of salvation, which is common to all human beings and all times whose powers, purified and united, are turned to the one duty.' [147] It would be easy for orthodox Judaism, and likewise for any rigid and externalized Catholicism, to underrate the Hasidic contribution because it so clearly uplifts spiritual meaning and intention above the correctness of ritual obedience. But the impression made by the collected legends of the early Hasidism, from which we can quote only a few, does not justify such criticism. They are dealing with the little daily events of poor and simple folk. The close relation between the Hasid and the Zaddik—between disciple and spiritual master—is something far more adapted to an Eastern life than anything which Western spirituality either achieves or desires. In this respect there are obvious parallels in Hinduism or Buddhism, but there are virtually no hints throughout these legends of the typical neo-Vedantism of the modern world. References to the *Zohar* and to other Kabbalistic writings can be found, but for the purpose of our own study the material is unspoiled, and of infinite value.

The external structure of the Hasidic settlements did not differ greatly from other Eastern religious communities. It was, in fact, the same structure as is disclosed in the Gospels. The Zaddik will probably be centred in a given place, whether as great as a Beth-El or as small as a Polish hamlet. His spiritual fame will have gone far, and many come on special holy days to stay in the neighbourhood, and to take the chance of bringing smaller or greater problems, whether of body, mind or spirit, for spiritual counsel. Others live more permanently in the

neighbourhood. He has to live with them rather than they with him.
But within this natural social or official grouping there will be an
inner community of choice sharing the Zaddik's life. It is the normal
situation of the Church and the remnant—the situation of contemplatives in the world. If the sin of exclusiveness and pride is avoided,
there is a common unity of prayer. But at the centre is the inner group
of chosen Hasidim, to whom and by whom the tradition is handed
down. Within this group prayer is closely shared, but even so it does
not cut them off from their fellows.

> 'The Hasidic world is the concrete world as it is in this moment of a person's
> life—a world ready to be a sacrament, ready to carry a real act of redemp-
> tion. The complete unity of the God who is transcendent to the world,
> and who yet dwells within it, restates the undivided wholeness of human
> life in its full meaning: there is an acceptance of the world from God's
> hand, and an acting on the world to make it exist for God's sake. From
> the meeting of God and man there issues no mere event in the life of the
> soul: but from out of this meeting vital events come upon the world.' [148]

It is with the Hasidim of Eastern Europe that we see most clearly
the hiddenness of the life which we are studying. This could appear
paradoxical. The life does not hide itself in esoteric rites behind closed
doors; nor do we find in it any exaggerated or self-conscious abasement.
The life is unknown to men, in the sense that it is unnoticed, commonplace, even ordinary. It is very well known to God, in the sense that
the whole is directed toward Him in a concentrated intention. The
intention may be explicit, either in liturgy or in private prayer, but it
has seized upon the whole life. It is hidden from men because it is in
no sense their business. Hence, so far from self-awareness, there is a
deep self-forgetting.

There are many legends concerning Baal-Shem-Tobh (d. 1760) but
the purity of the general tradition is shared with other leading Zaddikim.

> He was in prayer, and reflected on the words of the Canticle: 'At our
> door are all manner of precious fruits, new and old, which I have laid up
> for thee, O my Beloved.' And he added: 'Whatever is in me, everything,
> new and old, for you alone. . . . When I weld my spirit to God, I let my
> mouth say what it will, for then all my words are bound to their root in
> Heaven.' [149]

> The Rabbi Baer (The Great Maggid: d. 1772) said to his disciples: 'I
> shall teach you the best way to say Torah. You must cease to be aware of
> yourselves. You must be nothing but an ear which hears what the universe
> of the Word is constantly saying within you. The moment you start hearing
> what you yourself are saying, you must stop.' [150]

> Another said of the learned rabbis: 'What does it amount to—that they

expound the Torah! A man should see to it that all his actions are a
Torah and that he himself becomes so entirely a Torah that one can learn
from his habits and his motions and his motionless clinging to God, that
he has become like Heaven itself, of which it is said, "There is no speech
nor language, and their voice cannot be heard." ' 151

The self-forgetting is a constant note. R. Nahman of Bratzlav has
handed down these words of his great-grandfather, the Baal-Shem-
Tobh :

'Alas! the world is full of enormous lights and mysteries, and man shuts
them from himself with one small hand.'

This metaphor is interestingly reflected in the Bengal village tradition
quoted above (p. 91 *supra*) : 'One small candle in your own window
can shut out from you the splendour of the stars.'

R. Zahman once interrupted his prayer with the words : 'I do not want
your paradise : I do not want your coming world. I want You and You
only.' 152

Such a self-forgetting was seen in the Great Maggid when a young disciple
came to him for his first visit. 'When I came before the Maggid I saw
him on his bed : something was lying there which was nothing but simple
Will, the Will of the Most High.' 153

The work of these leaders was so far identified with the needs of their
time that any withdrawal from the world would tend to be regarded
as self-seeking. But in themselves they longed for hiddenness.

'When the Maggid realized that he had become known to the world, he
begged God to tell him what sin of his had brought this guilt upon him.' 154

'On one of the days of heart-searching . . . R. Zusya sat in his chair, and his
Hasidim stood around him from morning until evening. He had lifted his
eyes and his heart to Heaven, and loosed himself from all bodily bonds.
While looking at him, one of his Hasidim was overcome with the desire
to turn to God, and the tears streamed over his face. And just as a burning
coal kindles those beside it, so man by man was lit with the flame of
turning. Then the Zaddik looked around and fixed him with his gaze.
Again he lifted his eyes and said to God—"Lord of the world, this is
indeed the right time for turning. But you know that I have not the
strength to do penance; so accept as penance my love and my shame." ' 155

The same humility and dedication to the need of others is shown in a
question from a learned Rabbi to the Zaddik R. Yitzhah.

'How is it that so many flock about you? I am much more learned than
you, and yet they do not throng to me.'

The Zaddik answered :

'I too am astonished that so many should come to one so insignificant as myself to hear God's word, instead of looking for it to you whose learning moves mountains. Perhaps this is the reason: they come to me because I am astonished that they should come: and they do not come to you because you are astonished that they do not come.' [156]

While we find in the existential quality of Hasidism the characteristic that best expresses the spirit of the hidden life, there are among the legends valuable insights into the prayer we have come to expect as its concomitant. If most of these extracts are concerned with intercession, this fact expresses the dominant spiritual quality that was developed in the movement.

'Some disciples once asked R. Pinhas why, when he prayed, they could hear no sound and see no movement, so that he seemed to lack the fervour which shook the Zaddikim from head to foot. "Brothers," he answered, "to pray means to cling to God, and to cling to God means to loose oneself from all substance, as if the soul left the body. Our sages say that there is a death which is as hard as drawing a rope through the ring on the mast: and there is a death as easy as drawing a hair out of milk; This is called the death in the kiss. This is the one which was granted to my prayer." ' [157]

'Someone asked R. Shelomo of Karlin to promise to visit him the next day. "How can you ask me to make such a promise?" said the Zaddik. "This evening I must pray and recite 'Hear O Israel.' While I say these words my soul goes out to the utmost rim of life. Then comes the darkness of sleep. And when it is day, the great morning prayer is apacing through all worlds, and finally, when I fall upon my face, my soul leans out over the rim of life. Perhaps I shall not die this time either, but how can I now promise to do something at a time after the prayer?" ' [158]

One of the legends preserves an unusual and very effective comment on the question of Aridity in prayer, which has the advantage of diverting attention from the mood of the subject to the purpose for which his prayer is being undertaken:

'Several disciples of R. Nahum came to him and wept, and complained that they had fallen prey to darkness and depression, and could not lift up their heads in prayer. The Zaddik saw the state of their heart, and that they sincerely yearned for the nearness of the living God. He said to them: "My dear sons, do not be distressed at this seeming death which has come upon you. For everything that is in the world is also in men. And just as life ceases in all the stars, and they sleep and are strengthened, and awake with a new power of shining; so those who truly desire to come close to God must pass through the state of cessation of spiritual life: the falling is for the sake of the rising." ' [159]

The intercessory motive is clearly stressed at a time when the corporate prayer of the community was falling short of its true intention.

R. Shelmo of Karlin intervened with those who would abandon the duty of intercession. 'He shook the world with the storm of his prayer and said: "I am prayer. I take it on myself to pray in lieu of all Israel." ' [160]

'At a time of great anguish for Israel, R. Elimelech brooded more and more upon his griefs. The Maggid appeared to him. R. Elimelelch cried out: "Why are you silent in such dreadful need"? The Maggid answered: "In Heaven we see that all that seems evil to you is a work of mercy." ' [161]

'Another Rabbi said to God. "Lord of the world, I beg of you to redeem Israel; but if you do not want to do that, then redeem the *goyim* (Gentiles)." ' [162]

'Whenever the Rabbi of Sarov saw any one's suffering, either of spirit or body, he shared it so earnestly that it became his own. Once someone expressed his astonishment at this capacity to share in another's trouble. "What do you mean—share? said the Rabbi. It is my own sorrow; how can I help but suffer it?" ' [163]

R. Mendel used to say that during the time he was silently reciting the Eighteen Benedictions, all the people who had asked him to pray to God on their behalf would pass through his mind. Someone asked him how this was possible, since there was surely not enough time. R. Mendel replied: 'The need of every single one leaves a trace in my heart. In the hour of prayer I open my heart and say: "Lord of the world, read what is written here." ' [164]

Soon after the death of R. Mendel's wife, his daughter also died. He finished the Prayer of the Benedictions and said: 'Lord of the world, you took my wife from me. But I still had my daughter and could rejoice in her. Now you have taken her from me too. I have no one left to rejoice in except you alone, so I shall rejoice in you.' [165]

A Rabbi was asked, 'How are we to interpret the message in the Talmud where R. Simeon ben Yochai says to his son "My son, you and I are enough for the world?" He replied, "In the Tosefta we read, 'The meaning which underlies the creation of the world is that the creature says "You are our God" and the Holy One (Blessed be He) says "I am the Lord your God." This YOU and this I are enough for the world.' " ' [166]

Such a centring upon God alone implies the corresponding recognition of the place of the creature in His sight. The interpretation of that truth in daily life is the true mission of the Hasidic way. It is embodied, for our modern Western thinkers, in Dr. Martin Buber's book—*Ich und Du.*

Another aspect of this relation is told of R. Bunam, who said: 'When I look at the world, it sometimes seems to me that every man is a tree in the

wilderness, and that God has no one in His world but him, and that he
has no one to turn to save only God.' [167]

The foregoing extracts from the Hasidic legends are but a few
quotations which seem specially relevant to our theme. In closing this
second part of our study, it appears evident beyond doubt that a well-
spring of true spirituality arose from what would in any normal judgment have been considered a barren historical desert. There is ample
sign of external hardship and poverty, of persecution and loss. And yet
at every stage of this crowded and limited history there appears an
understanding of spiritual living which must give profound cause
for Christian reflection. It is needless to minimize the depth of the
gulf which still separates the families that should be one. The fact is
indelible that the Christian hope is already and completely fulfilled
in the Incarnate Word of God—the anointed King—however long
be the time of waiting for His return in judgment and in glory. But
it is equally indelible, from the evidence adduced by those Jewish
scholars whom Christians must hold in respect and in trust, that the
Jewish hope is a pure futurity. The nearest point of contact—and a
significant one—is the concept of *Tikkun,* the purpose of God in
a redemptive reparation which fills the thought of the religious Jewish
mind, unable to listen to His clear and final answer in Him who came
as Messiah and was rejected by His own.

The more that this cruel contrast asserts itself in cumulative evidence,
the more must we find that, in the spirit of Hasidim, the hand of God
is at work holding in one Truth what our partial understanding cannot
at present conceive. It may seem to our minds that there can be no
meeting. The Jew cannot approach the Christian fact and still preserve
his own integrity. He cannot look again at Jesus in a wistful mood
which could say 'Perhaps after all there is a sense in which. . . .' The
Christian may, indeed, approach the Jewish position as it has matured
in Hasidism, but in so doing he cannot look back at Jesus in a mood
of revision. For us He is TRUTH, not merely *our* truth, even as He is the
Way which leads to the Life that is Himself. Short of that absolute
conviction there is no Christian standing ground, and compromises
between liberal theology and a liberal Judaism are only harmful and
misleading. Yet in that conviction, with all its granite strength, the
Church must repent much of her past uncharity. The clauses in the
Litanies of the Good Friday Rite, as they were at times thoughtlessly
muttered, had become impossible as the language of the Body of Christ.
One cannot look at Hasidism and speak of 'the faithless Jews.' Our own
Christian living often proves our own lack of such triumphant cer-
tainties.

Though the medieval period admittedly yields but little conclusive evidence of the emergence of the hidden life as it was clearly evident in pre-Christian Judaism, the story of later Hasidism makes it essential that we should find in the parallel Christian period a living tradition of the same authentic quality. *'Something was lying there which was nothing but simple Will—the Will of the Host High.'* The offering of love in which the hidden life supremely rests must show the same marks.

PART III

CHAPTER TEN

THE EARLY CHRISTIAN DEVELOPMENTS

THE conviction that has emerged from our study of the hidden life in medieval and later Jewish history must not obscure the bitterness of the parting of the ways. Yet, as we now turn back to trace the Christian development in the same period, it is impossible to regard that history as a total divergence, which can be swept aside. Rather is it a measure of the tragedy—a cause of deep penitence and regret for any share of blame which rests upon the Church. It is a constant reminder of personal and corporate loss which needs the mercy of God upon us all if it is to be made good on behalf of the whole Body. More than a reminder, it is a challenge from the best Jewish insights to those of their Christian contemporaries. Generations have been living upon the Eucharistic mystery which has brought to them, if by faith alone, His continual presence. We have eaten His flesh and have drunk His blood. Have we known the fullness of His life within us? Or shall we say that the Jewish saints, whose lives we have watched as they have spoken and lived under the continual shadow of the rejection, were left unnourished and unsustained in their worship of our common Father in Heaven?

In the light of such questions we dare not return to the specifically Christian insights without keeping in mind the prayer of the Publican. We have learned from the Hasidim, both in their earlier and later periods, a depth of penitence which, alike in its nature and its expression, is characteristic of their Christian contemporaries. This penitence, as we have seen, was the environment of the whole life, going far beyond awareness or confession of some specific act of sin in the given moment.[168] 'Against thee, thee only have I sinned, and done this evil in thy sight: that thou mightest be justified in thy saying . . .' (Ps. 51 : 4). An essential link has been broken : the life is disturbed and thrown out of balance. There is no remedy save in the contrite renewal of a humble obedience and total dependence. This threefold emphasis needs no justification : it is manifest in any true estimate of Christian spirituality, the formative pattern of the contemplative way for Jew and Christian alike.

The period of Christian development from the end of the Apostolic

Age none the less needs separate treatment. The Biblical material presented in the earlier chapters has indicated the sources upon which the whole Christian Church has been able to draw, and the ground need not be traversed again. Yet in this later period there is a major difference. In its best spiritual energies Judaism looks forward to an unrealized future. This futurity, as we have seen, has acquired an almost polemic quality. As the centuries have passed, leading Judaism to dramatic developments in its secular hopes, a sense of exhaustion is surely evident. 'How long, O Lord, how long?'

The Christian hope, it is true, has still its own futurity, but the difference of mood cannot be overstated. From the glorious fulfilment of the Resurrection it has been vindicated by the Ascension and sealed at Pentecost. There is no need or excuse for the impatience of an 'interim-ethic,' if indeed there ever was such a thing outside the imagination of liberal New Testament critics. The present life of the Church is empowered by the Holy Spirit with all that she needs. 'He shall teach you all things, and bring to your remembrance all that I said unto you' (John 14: 26). She has received the abiding of the Paraclete in her life and with her life, and her members may be renewed and revitalized every day by the new Manna of her Eucharist. The one paramount difference separating this Christian course from its Jewish counterpart is the choice between rejection and acceptance. We do not reject the *Shekinah,* nor fail to respect the faithfulness of the Jewish hope. Yet the veil of the Temple has been torn aside, and the Glory of the Presence continues, and shall continue until for us Time gives place to Eternity. Almost any mistakes can be atoned in the faith of the Living Christ. The only irrecoverable failure is the rejection of His Truth.

We have seen the contemplative pattern as it worked itself out in three formative periods of post-Christian Jewish history. The earliest carried the Rabbinic tradition into the simple and not markedly intellectual period of the Dispersion in Northern Europe. This was followed by the more brilliant phase in the development of Spanish Judaism, and the dangerous intellectual extremes of the Cabbalists. The final period, persisting as we have seen to the present day in some parts of Eastern Europe, showed a spiritual maturity which would appear to ensure its continuing influence, even amid the paganism which has supervened.

This threefold division may prove convenient also in presenting its Christian counterpart, though we cannot follow a strict chronological parallel, and a large element of selection will be needed. The corresponding periods may be summarized briefly as follows :

1. After the first consolidation of the Desert Solitaries, and the

THE EARLY CHRISTIAN DEVELOPMENTS

discipline placed upon them by Pachomius, and later by St. Basil's ascetical guidance, the main interest is centred in the Western Church. St. Benedict, himself a solitary drawn unwillingly into the cenobitic pattern, designs his Rule for normal Christian living rather than for any extreme demands. St. Gregory the Great and St. Bernard show their knowledge of the hidden life which lay behind its genius, and it is mainly from these that the life is first formed in the West, and reaches out alike in its Benedictine, Cistercian, Franciscan or Dominican expression. Great names appear as outstanding within their ordered seclusion. In Germany, Gertrude and his sister St. Mechtild, followed by Mechtild of Magdeburg and St. Gertrude the Great, preserve it in the Benedictine Order. St. Bernard himself and many disciples, with seventy Cistercian foundations in four countries : St. Bonaventura, with Jacopone and the Blessed Angela of Foligno : the German Dominicans, who must have had contact with Ashkenazic Judaism : Blessed Jan Ruysbroeck, so close to these but surely greater than all in his insight, and the remarkable tradition of the English Solitaries, together with the Cloud of Unknowing and the *De Imitatione Christi* : such sources among many others suffice to show the wealth of evidence in this first period.

2. As in the Jewish story, so in its slightly later Christian parallels, the fertile soil of Spain, having given birth to the *Zohar* and the later Kabbalists, produced in the Carmelite Reform its spiritual fruit in the work and teaching of St. Teresa of Avila, and of her colleague and master St. John of the Cross.

The power of the second period is full evidence that the contemplative tradition of spirituality sustained the energy of the Church in her life of adoration, intercession and reparation, and so continues in our present day.

3. The third and final period must include two very diverse elements, each of which, however, relates closely to what we have learned in the later periods of Hasidism. One of these is a representative of one aspect of the later French School—Père de Caussade, s.j. (d. 1751). His doctrine of 'Abandon à la Providence Divine' (inevitably rendered in English as 'Abandonment') shows as its dominant theme the sacrament of the present moment. Here is a Christian existentialism closely parallel to the Jewish outlook which we have learned from Dr. Martin Buber. The other strand, a constant theme of Eastern mysticism, may be traced in two examples in two of the greatest *Startsy*—St. Serafim of Sarov (1759–1833) and the Staretz Silouan of the Monastery of St. Pantel-eimon on Mount Athos (1866–1938). This Eastern aspect, both in its

hiddenness and in the perfection of its dedication to the pure will of God, brings us likewise into the authentic quality of Hasidism. For St. Serafim the link became very close, and his contact with the Rabbi of Sarov, whom we have met earlier (p. 331), is important.

The stories of the Desert Fathers may introduce the first phase. Their record begins with the life of St. Anthony by St. Athanasius, which reached through Western Europe in its Latin versions, and drew upon it the admiration of the whole Church, as well as the scorn of Victorian rationalism. The charges of exaggerated asceticism need not detain us. If there is truth in them, it is an index of the need which pressed upon the Church to turn back the sin of the world in a life of reparation. The large collections of the 'Sayings of the Fathers,' brought together by the Church with the same intention which moved the recording of the *Pirqe Aboth* in Rabbinic times, will seem familiar from our earlier study. They may be judged remote from the modern world: they show in fact some of the timeless necessities of the hidden life.

The silence of the solitaries in the Egyptian Desert belongs to those who have passed through deep spiritual discipline. The life could not be endured on any other terms. A contemporary account says of them:

> One by one they abide in their cells, a mighty silence and a great quiet among them: only on the Saturday and the Sunday do they come together in Church, and there they see each other face to face as folk restored in Heaven. . . . Many of them go three and four miles to Church, and the distance dividing one cell from another is no less great: but so great is the love that is in them and by so strong affection are they bound towards one another and towards all brethren that they be an example and a wonder to all.[169]

Such an expression had no need to begin in the Apostolic Age. The sense of the immediacy of the end would forbid any such life. But here is that note of coinherence, and its consequence in the true bearing of one another's burdens and so fulfilling the Law of Christ. Under the stress of fierce temptation in the Unseen Warfare, a solitary would undertake his penance 'not for himself but for his brother, as if he himself had sinned. And God, seeing his love and his labour, revealed . . . that for the great love of this brother who had not sinned He had forgiven the brother who had. And verily this is to lay down one's soul for one's brother.' [170] We have already observed this practice of substituted love as a true mark of the hidden life.

The hiddenness is marked in many stories of the Desert. 'A treasure that is known is quickly spent. . . . Even as wax is melted before the face of fire, so is the soul enfeebled by praise, and loses the toughness of its virtues.' [171] The vast Christian energy that was generated in the

Desert from the fourth century onwards has naturally evoked violent reaction in the modern West. Yet it is not the degree of asceticism—target of the scorn of Gibbon and Lecky—which is the deepest source of its strength. The hidden life is marked by the complete abandonment which we have seen repeatedly in another setting. 'Unless a man shall say in his heart—'I alone and God are in this world—he shall not find peace.' [172] Such abandonment cannot rightly be condemned as treason to the *civitas dei*. If it was not the way of St. Augustine, it was still not anti-social. The life was marked by a depth of charity, of which there are countless examples :

> 'The abbot Silvanus with Zachary his disciple came to a certain monastery, and before they took their leave the monks made them eat a little. But after they had gone out his disciple came on water, and would fain have drunk. Then said Silvanus, "Zachary, to-day is a fast." He said, "But, father, did we not eat to-day?" The old man said, "That was love's bread, my son : but for us, let us keep our fast." ' [173]

This age of solitude gave birth to the more formalized monastic age. Its demands were so great that the necessary maturity of training could not be dispensed. Later on, the problem of compromise with the activity of the world came to be solved in varying stages of reform. But St. Augustine had already discerned what the Church has since come to learn as her choicest pattern : the mixed life is not a mitigation or a compromise, but a deeper understanding of one whole, 'wherein the love of truth doth ask a holy quiet, and the necessity of love doth accept a righteous business.' [174] From this day, until the *Summa* and beyond, the pattern of the mixed life has become more clear. The blessed Ruysbroeck shows its true quality :

> 'Furthermore between action and rest live love and fruition. Love would ever be at work, since it is an everlasting inter-action with God : but fruition must ever be at rest, above all will or desire, in the embracing of the well-beloved in the well-beloved, in a love pure and without images. . . . Our active life consists of loving God : our passive life of receiving the embrace of His love. . . . And the spirit of God Himself drives us out by His breath to works, love and virtue, and draws us back into Himself for quiet and fruition. . . . And so, to enter into a restful fruition and go forth again to good works, but ever remain united to the Spirit of God : this is the life of which I wish to tell you. . . . So we are to go out into the activity of the life of sense, then go in again by love and cleave to God, and remain ever motionless in community with Him.' [175]

The balance of this judgment anticipates a later growth. We shall return to Ruysbroeck in due course. At first, however, the growth of monasticism was marked by violent oscillation. While St. Pachomius is named as the first to bring order into the desert, St. Basil found a vast congregation marked by noise, activity, and a grave loss of charity and coinherence. Discipline had given place to a hard, impersonal and even proud dictatorship. By the middle of the sixth century St. Benedict 'shifted the whole impact of asceticism to the interior—from the flesh to the will.' Mortification is not an end in itself. It is given 'to open our eyes to the deifying Light'—so reads the Prologue to the *Regula Sancti Benedicti*. Later reforms often cost too dear, and various attempts were made not only to withstand abuses in the Church, but also to seek the greater perfection of solitude. The work of St. Romauld combined solitude and enclosure in a form which has often been emulated, and which appeared notably in later Eastern use. The Grande Chartreuse guarded the purity of solitude, binding the adoration of each separate soul around the kernel of the monastic Church.

Coming in a period of marked decline and laxity, the Cistercian Reform, starting from the Benedictine Abbey of Molesmes, seemed a drastic revolution, but 'was attempting nothing new. . . . The monks simply wanted to return to the Rule of St. Benedict in all its simplicity.' When St. Bernard of Clairvaux laid down the foundations of Cistercian spirituality he was still working in Benedictine terms. 'St. Bernard's humility, like that of St. Benedict . . . is an experimental knowledge, a deep-seated sense not of mere shame, not of mere confusion, but also . . . of love and peace at the recognition of the human weakness and insufficiency that are in us all. . . . He calls it the *spiritus lenitatis,* a tenderness born of the experience of suffering, which expands and reaches out to embrace all other men.' [176] Once again we are listening to the voice of St. John the Apostle : 'Let us love one another, for love is of God, and every one that loveth is begotten of God and knoweth God' (1 John 4 : 7–8). For St. Bernard, even this command of humility and charity is but 'the means to a more perfect end : mystical contemplation and union of the soul with God.' In this discovery, says M. Gilson, 'St. Bernard came to add a mystical renaissance to all the others that adorned the century.' But the mysticism has a purity and simplicity, as it sets itself to be brought to this desired haven by humility and charity—'the rectification of a nature in revolt.' As we have already noted (p. 51 *supra*) St. Bernard knows well the varied motives which can bring us to the love of God. They must be known and acknowledged in true humility, lest by clinging to the least part of self-love, we should fall short of the perfection of God's intention for our souls.

The vital importance of Cistercian life in this period of its first flowering separates it from much that is of undoubted value elsewhere. It is possible to find, in the Kabbalists, speculations and suggestions similar to much in medieval Christian teaching. But the Cistercian movement is defined by more than this. The degrees of humility through which St. Bernard sought to recover the purity of the Benedictine Rule are needed because the centre of the life—the charity through which we are made one with God—is the very love of God for man made manifest in the Incarnate Lord. 'Bernard and his Cistercians rediscovered that love of the Saviour which had put such fire into the Gospel of St. John and the epistles of St. Paul.' The quest of Jewish spirituality also bore the marks of humility and charity, and in the love of God for His chosen people the Holy Spirit did surely reach to them in that quest. In the veiling of the Truth from their eyes (Luke 19 : 42), we must realize that the very means by which St. Bernard learned and taught were always in their hands. The common Scriptures of the Old Testament were as fully known to them as to the Christian twelfth century. The Scriptures became their own interpreter to the Church, as they constantly were to the faithful of the Old Covenant. As the *Opus Dei* and the adoration of God went on throughout the Church's year, it was the old Covenant that continually spoke of Christ. In the vivid phrase of Thomas Merton, 'the Cistercians transfigured the Old Testament with their one great obsession, the love of Christ.' That love was the daily food of their souls as well as of their minds, and it brought many even in this life to the fulfilment of their longing in the vision of God.

In this same period, however, the hidden life was not free from danger. A speculative spirituality appeared with the School of St. Victor, reminiscent in some respects of the Christian Platonists of Alexandria. We have seen that Judaism at the same time, and likewise in Western Europe, came under speculative influence which it was perhaps less able to control. It is one thing to aim, by a humble contemplation of God, at a union of will with His Will. We shall find this desire recurring continually. A notable passage in the *De Imitatione Christi* (III : 15) may again be anticipated as illustration.

> 'Let Your will be mine, and let my will ever . . . be conformed wholly to Your own. Let me ever will and not will in union with Yourself, and be unable to will otherwise than as You will or do not will.'

But even fervent prayer is not abiding accomplishment of this request : still less is it such an identity with God as could be made to imply the impossibility of sin against Him (cf. p. 71). As often with the speculative mind, it is too easy to pass from truth into imaginative creation, easier still to suppose that the imagined idea is operative fact.

> 'The unity of the mind with God, in the man who keeps his heart raised to heaven, is the state of perfection of the will which tends towards God. It is realized when not only does he no longer will other than God wills,

177

but is so advanced in love (*in affectu perfectus*) that he is not able to will other than God wills. For to will what God wills is to be like Him: and to will only what God wills is to be already what God is.' [177]

The mystical union of which St. Bernard speaks would never so confuse the will of God with that of men, but rather see the longing for a perfect accord of the two wills—the human with the Divine. St. Bernard will speak freely of 'deification,' but he will never fall into confusing this greater gift of Love with the union which subsists between the Divine Persons.[178] This speculative trend was somewhat modified by the later Dominicans, basing their thought—with St. Thomas Aquinas —on Aristotle rather than on Plato.

While St. Bernard is still living, a very different aspect of the contemplative way appears in Germany among a remarkable group of Benedictine women. There is an extravagance of poetic imagery, of which only one or two examples must suffice.

> 'The beatings of the heart of God sounded like so many invitations which thus spake: Come and do penance, come and be reconciled, come and be consoled, come and be blessed. Come, My Love, and receive all that the Beloved can give to His beloved. . . . Come, My Bride, and enjoy thy Godhead.' [179]

This phase of piety, as distinct from later examples in Germany, has little place for speculation. It is entirely affective. It is not surprising that it also follows St. Francis in a devotion to God displayed in his natural creation. The quality of St. Gertrude the Great is shown in her Revelation of an experience of union with the Child Jesus, who said to her:

> 'As I am the figure of the substance of God the Father in the Divinity, thus shalt thou be the figure of My substance in the humanity; and thou shalt receive in thy soul the emissions of My Divinity, even as the air receives the rays of the sun. Penetrate therefore into the innermost of that ray that must unite us, and thou shalt become capable of a more familiar union.' [180]

The early form of the Devotion to the Sacred Heart, fully developed by St. Margaret-Mary Alacocque towards the end of the seventeenth century, seems to have begun at this time.

A contemporary in Italy, Blessed Angela of Foligno, shows a different sense of the same sure Presence.

> 'One day I was in prayer, uplifted in mind: God spoke to me in peace and in love. I looked and saw. . . . It was Himself, and I can say nothing more. It was a fullness, it was an inward and overflowing light for which neither word nor comparison is worth anything. I saw nothing corporeal. That day was like heaven on earth; a beauty which closes the lips, the supreme beauty that contains the supreme Good.' [181]

In St. Catherine of Siena there is combined a far more profound mystical insight with a deep practical impact on the world. She shaped history by fearless intervention in public affairs, but all that she did rested on a passionate intercession. Her Dialogue defeats our customary suspicion of ecstasy and visions by its realism and its humble desire for truth. Her service of the Church and of the world when she restored the exiled Papacy to Rome, and played a large part in healing the Great Schism, led her clear and forceful mind to see the essential action. Yet the mood of this action is a penitent and deeply charitable intercession. 'In her hunger she spread her prayer over the whole world, as if the world itself caused her to pray' (Dial. 16). Her keen sense of human sin leads her to contemplate the wonder of the Redemption and yet to be able to pass judgment. 'Another thing is necessary for thee to arrive at this union and purity, namely that thou shouldst never judge the will of man in anything thou mayst see said and done by any creature whatsoever, either to thyself or to others. My Will alone shalt thou consider both in them and in thyself' (Dial. 100). How could she do otherwise? Her deep compassion reaches to the Lord Himself in the redeeming task into which she has been called. 'In the height of heaven Thy mercy shines. . . . If I turn to the earth it abounds with Thy mercy. In the darkness of Hell Thy mercy shines. . . . By Mercy thou hast washed us in Thy Blood, and by mercy Thou wishest to converse with Thy creatures. O Loving Madman! Was it not enough for Thee to become Incarnate that Thou must also die?' (Dial. 30).

A life which brought her into such notoriety was still rooted in hiddenness and seclusion. She was committed, by the demands of Christ upon her from childhood, to a complete self-emptying through the sheer humility of her estimate of herself. 'In self-knowledge, then, thou wilt humble thyself, seeing that in thyself thou dost not even exist : for thy very being . . . is derived from Me, since I have loved both thee and others before you were in existence; and that through the ineffable love that I had for you, wishing to recreate you to grace, I have washed you, and recreated you in the blood of my only begotten Son, spilt with so great a fire of love' (Dial. 4).

St. Catherine was indeed burned by that fire of love, and not without a constant sharing of its pain. She accepted it 'as Thou wilt, and when Thou wilt, and as long as Thou wilt.' On one occasion, and perhaps often, she was driven to cry, 'Where wast Thou in that time of being overwhelmed?' She had her answer, 'I was in your heart, otherwise you would not have been able to bear it.'

The speculative trend noted in the Victorines was not wholly checked. The mental climate of Germany was perhaps accountable, but the sober learning of St. Thomas Aquinas did not mark all his fellow-Dominicans, and the influences which we have noted among the Ashkenazim were not absent from their Christian neighbours. Our purpose will be better served in what follows by letting them help us as far as may be, rather than by searching out the heresies in Meister Eckhardt, Tauler, Suso, and the rest.

> 'The man who comes to God is, indeed, still present in the world with his body, but he is outside the world with his spirit and his desire.' [182]

Eckhardt adopts the now classic threefold way of the mystical life, but man's real progress is by the way of perfect abandonment (*gelassenheit*). We shall meet this truth in another form in the final chapter of this study. If St. Bernard and Ruysbroeck (the greatest neighbour of the German School) are prepared for the figure of the mystical marriage, Eckhardt is more austere.

> 'The man who loves God does not love Him because of His wisdom and His Eternity. . . . He loves *these* because they are God.' [183]

As so many before him, he seeks to understand the fact of the human capacity for God. The Victorines found this power to rest in the highest part of the mind. Eckhardt anticipates St. Teresa of Avila in seeking it in the centre of the soul, but he appears to mean the same thing. (The thought occurs too frequently to assemble a catena of references, but a modern English writer may be quoted for a very valuable comment. Dr. Austin Farrer writes:

> 'We pray with the apex of the mind, with the intelligent will.') [184]

In the soul which has renounced itself, sanctifying Grace brings to birth the Divine Word, and this Grace makes men one with God. 'I live, yet no longer I, but Christ liveth in me' (Gal. 2 : 10). Eckhardt links this mystery of Christ in us with the mystical Body of Christ in the Church, of which we are members.

The abandonment, the total detachment from all creatures, is the goal of the will which would be perfect.

> 'The friends of God are never without consolation; for their greatest consolation is what God wills, be it consolation or lack of it. . . . However, as God wants to give us Himself and all things for our possession, He will take away from us all property (*sc.* power of possession—*proprietas*). . . . The more we have of our own, the less we have of Him: the less we have of our own, the more we have Him with all that He can give. When, therefore, our Lord wanted to speak of all the Beatitudes, He placed poverty of spirit at the head of them all.' [185]

The fine intellectual distinctions which later brought Eckhardt, and others of this school, under suspicion of Pantheism, and drew from the Pope the rebuke that 'Eckhardt wished to know more than he should,' were partly modified by Blessed Henry Suso in a more ardent and affective mood. But abandonment and renunciation are the notes which sound through all the Rhineland mystics, and the great value of this teaching is weakened by intellectual exaggeration. They will speak of the ultimate goal of union between the soul and God—as we have seen—as taking place in the essence of the soul, direct and immediate. Finally there remains no difference between God and the soul. Here is the crucial danger for over-ambitious speculation. The blessed Jan van Ruysbroeck, first Prior of Groenendal, and an Augustinian canon, seems to be held safe from its dangers by his devotion to the person of our Lord. 'What I wish to say is true, and Christ the everlasting Truth has said it.' The Spiritual Espousals are so authenticated. In the well-known *Seven steps of the ladder of spiritual love* he writes :

> 'This living unity with God is our essence, and we have no power to understand, attain to, or grasp it. It baffles our powers, asking us to become one with God without medium, which indeed we have no power to grant. Therefore we follow it with the repose of our being, and in this repose the Spirit of God rests and dwells with all His gifts, infusing both grace and gifts into our faculties, and calls on us to rest and be one with Him above all virtues.' [186]

The final steps of this ascent need full preparation.

> 'If any one would experience this, he must offer to God all his virtues and good works, without thought of any reward. . . . His inner life must be full of grace and charity. . . . His memory, freed from care and solicitude, should be free and empty, delivered from all images. His heart should be free, open, and raised above all the heavens; his intellect free from reflections and naked in God. . . . This purity is the dwelling-place of God within us, nor can any but God alone act upon it. It is eternal, and in it is neither time nor place, neither before nor after : but it is ever present. . . . In it we are all one, living in God and God in us. . . . Our Heavenly Father is the beginning and end of all that is. In Him we begin every good thing with mind bared in imageless contemplation. In His Son we contemplate every truth in the Divine Light with an illumined understanding. In the Holy Spirit we bring to perfection all our works, and when in naked love we go forth from ourselves in the presence of God, then are we made free and void of every happening and every dream. . . . Finally the Holy Spirit works in us . . . all our good works. He cries within us with a loud voice, yet without words, 'Pay your debt. Love the love that ever loves you.' [187]

It is certainly possible to find in Ruysbroeck signs of undue speculation, but he is still the outstanding master of that age and place. The true reaction from speculative mysticism comes in the *Devotio Moderna*, and is well illustrated in his fellow Augustinian Thomas à Kempis. For him the task is far simpler. He might wonder why his neighbours, and even the revived 'Dionysian' school in the Cloud of Unknowing, troubled to be so nebulous. He prefers to be an ordinary monk, pledged to the teaching of Holy Church, and especially to the Scriptures which the Church has given to the world. The life of Grace, which is the Christian's share in the Church, is a life of virtue leading to a life of Union, nourished and sustained in the Mass. Ruysbroeck would agree, but even he would want to say so much beside. For Thomas the theme is essentially practical and ascetic. It begins with counsels of perfection which govern the spiritual way, setting out the character and practice of the hidden life, and ends with a doctrinal and practical treatise on the Holy Eucharist. He spent his life in Holy Religion, and the *De Imitatione Christi* belongs to its earlier years.

However simply he may wish to begin, we reach almost at once the ultimate cry of the contemplative—'God who art Truth, make me one with Thee in everlasting love' (I : 3). This is ultimate, but its attainment brings us down to commonplace demands. The hidden life must be hidden in fact.

> 'No man can live in the public eye without risk to his soul, unless he who would prefer to remain obscure. No man can safely speak, unless he who would gladly remain silent. . . . Leave empty matters to the empty-headed, and give your attention to those things that God commands you. Shut your door upon you, and call upon Jesus the Beloved. . . . Remember your avowed purpose, and keep ever before you the likeness of Christ crucified' (I : 20, 25).

This last counsel appears perhaps for the first time, but it marks the teaching of the coming age. St. Teresa stresses it at a very advanced stage of the spiritual journey, for it is often conveniently forgotten by those who aspire to spiritual attainment in self-will.

> 'No good deed will prove an obstacle if you are inwardly free from uncontrolled desire. . . . If not set a great value on any worldly things, it will prove a great obstacle. Let nothing be great, pleasant or desirable to you save God alone. . . . You are none the holier for being praised, and none the worse for being blamed. You remain what you are. . . . When comfort is withdrawn, do not immediately despair, but humbly and patiently await the Will of Heaven; for God is able to restore to you a consolation even richer than before. This is nothing new or strange to those who know the ways of God' (II : 5, 6, 9).

The third Book, in the form of a dialogue between Christ and the soul, deserves the closest study. Two passages must suffice. The first is a prayer we have already quoted repeatedly:

'Give me always to will and desire whatever is most pleasing and acceptable to You. Let your Will be mine, and let my will ever follow and be conformed wholly to Your own. Let me ever will or not will in union with Yourself, and be unable to will otherwise than You will or do not will' (III: 15).

The second is a striking foretaste of the most extreme ascetic teaching of St. John of the Cross (Ascent, I : 13) which will arise later. The Imitation reads : 'Always choose to possess less rather than more. Always take the lowest place and regard yourself as less than others.' But the desire which springs even from the last remnants of self-will is treated in a well-known chapter which seems to hold the secret of the hidden life. The speaker is Christ :

'I have often said to you, and I now say once more : Renounce yourself, surrender yourself, and you shall enjoy great inner peace. Give all for All, look for nothing and ask nothing in return. Rest purely and trustingly in Me and you shall possess Me. Then you will be free in heart, and no darkness will oppress your soul. Strive for this, pray for this, desire this one thing, that you may be stripped clean of all selfishness, and may follow Jesus in complete self-abandonment (lit.: being naked mayest follow the naked Jesus) dying to self that you may live to Me for ever. Then will all vain fantasies be put to flight, and all evil disorders and groundless fears vanish. Then will all fear and dread depart, and all disordered love die in you' (III : 37).

The truth in the former part of this counsel is proved repeatedly in the hidden life. The naked prayer which goes into the will of God, and waits there with no presupposition, must give all for All, asking for nothing and refusing nothing. But so easily the passing of an actual crisis can lead to the relaxing of its laws. Hence there follows the stern demand that we may be polished clean from all claim to ownership of our life (*ut ab omni propietate possis exspoliari*). So only will all disordered love be destroyed. The operative word is *inordinatus*. It is not so much a moral judgment as a theological canon. Until love has been reborn as Charity it is to that extent 'out of order.'

Finally Thomas à Kempis anchors his teaching to the fundamental action of the Church. The soul has prayed for union with the God who is Truth. The Truth Himself answers unequivocally : 'Whosoever eateth My Flesh and drinketh My Blood dwelleth in Me, and I in Him. . . . Take and eat. . . .' For all its gracious consequences, the Eucharist is not the reward of saints, but the daily food of those who labour and are heavy laden, and who will come to the Giver to receive the gift that is Himself. The task is defined precisely :

'Naked I hung upon the Cross with arms outstretched, offering Myself freely to God the Father for your sins, My whole Person a sacrifice of Divine propitiation : you, too, must willingly offer yourself daily to me in the

Eucharist with all your powers and affections. . . . I require nothing less of you . . . what you offer to Me beside yourself, I account as nothing: I seek not your gift but yourself' (IV: 8).

The Lord echoes the prayer which His Spirit has inspired in the Liturgy. At every Offertory the priest prays 'Offero tibi, Deo meo, vivo et vero' (I make offering to Thee, my God, the living and true). Even as was our Lord's, this offering is 'for their sakes.' It is not only personal, but intercessory.

The responding gift is mercifully veiled, though not thereby diminished.

'I could not endure to gaze on You in the full glory of Your Divinity, nor could the whole world bear the splendour and glory of Your Majesty. Therefore You bear with my frailty and conceal Yourself in this most holy sacrament' (IV: 11).

So also St. Thomas Aquinas speaks in the *Adoro te devote* :

'I cannot touch, I cannot taste, I cannot see,
All sense is cheated of Thee but the ear.
The Son of God hath spoken: I believe;
For naught hath truth beyond the Word I hear.'

So in faith Word and Sacrament fulfil each other. But the act of faith may either bring the grace of devotion, or may remain in dryness of soul. 'You have need of Me: I have no need of you' (IV: 15).[188]

The Cloud of Unknowing

The English contemplatives may be introduced by an unknown writer, who is prepared to use, and even to popularize, one of the extreme traditions of medieval mysticism. Yet, if his background is intellectual and philosophical, the work is essentially practical. The theory is familiar from Maimonides, but as he was largely saved from the errors of early Kabbalism, so the writer of the *Cloud* leans over further than his European predecessors, and offers a safer and saner Christian path. The teaching would seem to come from a contemplative cloister, perhaps a Charterhouse, and shows a penetrating though kindly criticism of many religious quirks.

God is ever the hidden God, veiled in a Cloud of Unknowing impenetrable to man. So also the hidden life needs the protection of

'a Cloud of forgetting betwixt thee and all the creatures that ever be made. . . . For though it be good to think upon the kindness of God and to love Him and praise Him for it, yet it is far better to think upon the naked being of Him and to love Him and praise Him for Himself. . . . There-fore I would leave all that thing that I can think, and choose to my love that thing that I cannot think. For why? . . . By love He may be gotten and holden; but by thought never. . . . Smite upon that thick cloud of unknowing with a sharp dart of longing love' (Chaps. 4–6).

The classical interrelation between active and contemplative are set out. This book is for the contemplative. Yet

'a man may not be fully active, but if he be in part contemplative; nor yet fully contemplative . . . but if he be in part active. The condition of active life is such that it is both begun and ended in this life; but not so of contemplative life. For it is begun in this life, and shall last without end' (Chap. 8).

The example of Mary of Bethany illustrates the writer's own intention.

'She hung up her love and her loving desire in this Cloud of Unknowing, and learned her to love a thing which she might not see clearly in this life by a light of understanding in her reason, nor yet verily feel in sweetness of love in her affection' (Chap. 16).

The work is not 'without full great travail,' but the travail is on man's side, in his effort to remember, not on God's side, in the constant stirring of love.

'And therefore do on thy work, and surely He shall not fail in His.'

But there will come times when

'God will work all by Himself, and then thou wilt think it merry to let Him alone' (Chap. 26).

There is due stress upon Penance.

'Thy foredone special deeds will always press in thy remembrance betwixt thee and thy God. . . . Try and look as it were over their shoulders, seeking another thing; the which is God, enclosed in a cloud of unknowing. . . . When thou feelest that thou mayest in no wise put them down, cower thou down under them as a coward overcome in battle, and think it is but folly to strive any longer with them, and therefore thou yieldest thyself to God in the hands of thine enemies. And then feel thyself as thou wert foredone for ever.'

The two aspects of this counsel turn first upon charity and secondly upon meekness.

'This meekness obtaineth to have God Himself mightily descending, to venge thee of thine enemies, for to take thee up . . . as the father doth the child that is in point to perish under the mouths of wild swine or wode biting bears' (Chap. 32).

To these brief extracts we may add one passage from the *Epistle of Privy Counsel,* another of the group that brought the Dionysian mysticism to English readers.

> 'When thou comest by thyself, think not before what thou shalt do after, but forsake as well good thought as evil thoughts . . . and look that nothing live in thy working mind but a naked intent stretching into God, not clothed in any special thought of God in Himself . . . as if thou saidest then unto God. . . . "That what I am, Lord, I offer unto Thee, without looking to any quality of Thy being, but only that Thou art as Thou art, without any more." That meek darkness be thy mirror and thy whole remembrance.' [189]

The *Cloud of Unknowing,* as we have said, is still connected with the more esoteric mysticism of the Continent of Europe. There is, however, a plainness of speech in the English school as a whole that is more congenial even than the teaching of Ruysbroeck, still more so than that of Eckhardt. The next point of contact may be with Walter Hilton, a native Yorkshireman with the plain speech of his forebears, who was also an Augustinian Canon-Regular. His main work, *The Scale of Perfection,* is eminently the work of a Spiritual Director. His thought is so closely reflected in the *Revelations of Divine Love,* which we shall next consider, that he is thought to have been the Confessor and Director of the solitaries among whom Dame Julian is outstanding.

Hilton teaches the now classical structure of the Spiritual Life, and the stages in its Ascent, but he is not writing merely 'another book on prayer.' He is concerned with the recognition and destruction of the image of sin in the soul, and the control of impulses of pride. For this the life of Jesus must be formed within the soul. Therefore

> 'when thou shalt rise against the ground of sin in general or else in any special sin . . . set the point of thy thought more upon God whom thou desirest than upon the sin which thou reprovest. For if thou do so then God fighteth for thee, and He shall destroy sin in thee. Thou shalt much sooner come to thy purpose if thou do so, than if thou leave thy meek desire to God principally, and will set thine heart only against the stirring of sin, as though thou wouldest destroy it by mastery. . . . Thou shalt never so bring it about' (I: 91).

The dark night of the later spiritual journey, so fully treated a century and a half later by the Spanish mystics, is real enough to Hilton, though perhaps without the anguish revealed by St. John of the Cross in his more detailed exposition.

> 'This is a good night and a light darkness. . . . Soothly the darker the night is, the nearer is the true day of the love of Jesus.'

There is much wise teaching with which we are already familiar, though Hilton's bluntness of speech makes it seem new. He does not expect the spiritual course to be smooth or easy.

> 'He that perceiveth no changeability in feeling of his grace, but is ever alike whole and stable, unbroken and unhurt as he thinketh, he is either full perfect or full blind.' [190]

The Revelations of Divine Love

This well-known work, from the greatest of the English woman solitaries, will further illustrate the teaching of Hilton. She has given to the Church the record of one astounding day—the eighth day of May 1373. The record is marked by a calm and reflective character. She does not make us anxious regarding visions and locations, nor is her record distorted by any self-awareness. During a vivid meditation on the Passion of Christ,

> 'suddenly the Trinity filled my heart with utmost joy. And so I understood it shall be in heaven without end to all that shall come there. . . . The Trinity is our everlasting love. . . . And I said: *Benedicite Domine!* . . . for wonder and marvel . . . that He that is so reverend and dreadful will be so homely with a sinful creature living in wretched flesh' (Chap. 4).

She realized, as we have constantly sought to do in this study, the paramount place of the Mother of God in the life that we seek.

> 'She is more than all that God hath made beneath her in worthiness and grace; for above her is nothing that is made but the blessed Manhood of Christ' (Chap. 4).

She had a sense of the wholeness of God's Creation, as

> 'a little thing . . . in the palm of my hand. . . . What may this be? It is all that is made. . . . It lasteth and ever shall last, for that God loveth it' (Chap. 4).

At once she knows her supreme desire :

> 'God, of Thy Goodness, give me Thyself: for Thou art enough to me, and I may nothing ask that is less that may be full worship to Thee; and if I ask anything less, ever me wanteth—but only in Thee I have all' (Chap. 5).

As the ground of this complete trust in God she was told :

> 'See! I am God: see! I am in all thing: see! I do all thing: see! I lift never my hands off my works, nor ever shall, without end: see! I lead all thing to the end I ordained it to from without beginning, by the same Might, Wisdom and Love whereby I made it. How should anything be amiss?' (Chap. 11).

187

As she ponders more and more upon the nearness of our Lord and the depth of His Redeeming, she is led to an understanding that is essential to the hidden life. It has been mistaken for gloom. It is in fact penetrating truth.

> 'Our Lord God showed that a deed should be done and He Himself shall do it, and I shall do nothing but sin, and my sin shall not hinder His goodness working. And I saw that the beholding of this is a heavenly joy in a fearing soul which evermore kindly by grace desireth God's Will. . . . Let be all thy love, my dearworthy child: turn thee to Me—I am enough to thee—and for My Love enjoy thou in Me: for of all things therewith mightest thou please Me most' (Chap. 36).

There is a long and searching study of the meaning of Prayer (Chaps. 41–3) which may be omitted in view of the further study to be made of St. Teresa of Avila on this subject. Finally, we may note from her Revelations a stress upon the coinherence of all things in Christ (Col. 1 : 15–17).

> 'What man or woman with firm will chooseth God in this life, for love, he may be sure that he is loved without end. . . . It is God's Will that I see myself as much bound to Him in love as if he had done for me all that He hath done; and thus should every soul think inwardly of its Lover. that is to say, the Charity of God maketh in us such a unity that, when it is truly seen, no man can part himself from other. And thus ought our soul to think that God hath done for it all that He hath done' (Chap. 65).[191]

The Revelations bring to us an affirmation of an infused Contemplation which, by the Grace of God, may be for us even in this life a foretaste of the Beatific Vision. There is no hint in Mother Julian that such Grace may be achieved or wrought by any virtue of man. But it is well to know, as we close this first period, that the giving of the Grace is understood and acknowledged. For by such Grace the hidden life exists and is sustained.

CHAPTER ELEVEN

THE SPANISH RENAISSANCE

THE flowering of Jewish spirituality in Spain, according to Bension, shows direct parallels with the writings of the Carmelite Reformers. A major question of dating is raised by this judgment, since the *Zohar* could not have been used under Jewish influence after 1492 at the latest. A recent study of the Mediaeval Tradition in its relation to St. John of the Cross judges that Mediaeval Spain produced no writers of the calibre of the Victorines, no 'school' such as that of the Rhineland and the Low Countries; and when eventually we do have native Spanish writers their works are ascetical.[192] The decline of the Carmelite Order, which Teresa of Avila discovered by experience, would not in itself suggest any great spiritual power in Spain at the time when Jewish mysticism was reaching a somewhat dizzy height. But even the extremes of Kabbalism, however dangerous in method and in philosophical theory, claim to be rooted in the basic religious character of Judaism. If we add the witness of Islam and Christianity, Spain must have acquired a tangible spiritual heritage, and the *Zohar* would not have been an entirely lonely voice.

But the atmosphere of the century following the Jewish expulsion is beyond question. The volume of material makes any full summary impossible in a reasonable space, but the attempt is fortunately needless. We are concerned with two masters of the hidden life of whom full and accurate knowledge is now available. Teresa of Avila (St. Teresa of Jesus), after struggling under the Carmelite Rule until well on in middle age, emerges as a new person, casting off the hindrances that had fettered her spiritual growth. She becomes the main human agent in the total Reform of her Order. The story begins with fantastic opposition against one tenuous Foundation on the doorstep of her own convent, and goes on to the firm establishment of no less than sixteen other Foundations. The whole story, and the teaching upon which it rests, is now assembled in the *Collected Edition* of her Works, to which general reference may here be made, and detailed references appended in the text.[193]

The chief figure in her story is the Friar who became her colleague in 1568, and later her close spiritual friend. The works of St. John of the Cross are likewise available in a *Collected Edition*.[194]

St. Teresa gave to the Church the *Way of Perfection* and *The Interior Castle*: important spiritual teaching is also included in the *Life*. St. John of the Cross left a major theological work in the form of commentary upon a spiritual poem 'Wherein the soul sings of the happy chance it had in passing through the Dark Night of Faith, in detachment and purgation of itself, to Union with the Beloved.' Of this poem only two of the eight stanzas are actually reached in two long uncompleted works—the *Ascent of Mount Carmel* and the *Dark Night of the Soul*. Two other poems, *The Living Flame of Love*—'Songs of the Soul in intimate communication and union with the Love of God'; and *The Spiritual Canticle*—'Songs between the Soul and the Bridegroom' based on the Song of Songs, are fully treated by exposition. A further collection of his *Poems*, though included in the Collected Edition, has also been translated separately.[195]

St. John sets out in a formal preface what is implied also by his older companion.

> 'I shall trust neither to experience or to knowledge, since both may fail and deceive; but . . . I shall avail myself . . . of Divine Scripture; for if we guide ourselves by this we shall be unable to stray, since he who speaks is the Holy Spirit. . . . It is not my intention to depart from . . . the doctrine of our Holy Mother the Catholic Church. . . . I submit and resign myself wholly . . . to whatever judgment she may pronounce concerning it.'

In the event, the Church's judgment rests not only in his Canonization, but in his unique title of Doctor of the Universal Church.

The Way of Perfection

This work contains the main substance of St. Teresa's novitiate teaching on Prayer. Prayer is the purpose of the Carmelite life, and their life is set in detachment so that they may learn to pray. In our study of our Lord's prayer-teaching we suggested that the Dominical Prayer for disciples was a way of learning, rather than a picture of our Lord's hidden life of prayer (p. 166 *supra*). St. Teresa writes, however:

> 'In the Paternoster the Lord has taught us the whole method of Prayer and of high contemplation, from the very beginnings of mental prayer to Quiet and Union' (Chap. 37).

Her commentary clause by clause in the last fifteen chapters of the *Way of Perfection* therefore demands very careful study.

OUR FATHER, WHICH ART IN THE HEAVENS

The invocation is from 'the Son of such a Father' to 'the Father of such a Son.' 'Wherever God is, there is Heaven.' . . . 'However quietly we speak, He is so near that He will hear us : we . . . have only to find a place where we can be alone, and look upon Him present within us' (Chap. 27f.). St Teresa needs no excuse for digressions, and from this point she teaches in the next two chapters the prayer of Recollection. We are in the atmosphere of the Jewish *Kawwanah,* the continual, loving attention that prayer needs.

HALLOWED BE THY NAME. THY KINGDOM COME

The approach to such a Father must be in full reverence. How can we know what to ask? 'Couldst not thou, O Lord, have ended this prayer . . . by saying "Give us, Father, whatever is good for us" . . . But thou knowest us, my Lord, and Thou knowest that we are not as resigned as wert Thou to the Will of the Father.' But 'in Heaven we shall have . . . a joy in the rejoicings of all . . . when we see that all are hallowing . . . and blessing His Name, and that none is offending Him.'

From this point she speaks of the 'beginning of true contemplation' . . . the Prayer of Quiet.

> 'The Lord begins to give us His kingdom on earth so that we may truly praise Him and hallow His Name. This is a supernatural state . . . and we cannot reach it for ourselves. . . . The soul sees that it is in the Kingdom and it feels such reverence that it dares to ask nothing. . . . There seems nothing left for it to desire. The faculties are stilled and have no wish to move, for any movement they may make appears to hinder the soul from loving God. They are not completely lost, however, since, two of them being free, they can realize in whose Presence they are. It is the Will that is in captivity now . . . The mind tries to occupy itself with one thing, and the memory has no desire to busy itself with more: they both see that this is the one thing needful. . . . Sometimes tears come into their eyes, and they weep very gently, and quite without distress: their whole desire is in the hallowing of this Name. . . . When the Will finds itself in this state of Quiet, it must take no more notice of the understanding than it would do of a madman. . . . Thoughts will come and go, but the Will is mistress, and will recall them without having to trouble about it. . . . It would seem that the eternal Father has already granted its (the soul's) petition that He will give it His Kingdom on earth. . . . You are doing much more by occasionally repeating a single petition of the Paternoster than by repeating the whole of it many times in a hurry . . .' (Ch. 31).

THY WILL BE DONE, AS IN HEAVEN SO ON EARTH

> 'Since my earth has now become heaven, it will be possible for Thy Will to be done in me. . . . Realize . . . what Jesus offers on your behalf to the Father, and what you are doing when you pray that His Will may be done in you. . . . Would you like to see how He treats those who make this prayer from their hearts? Ask His glorious Son, who made it thus in the Garden. . . . . You must say *Fiat voluntas tua* . . .' (Chap. 32).

GIVE US THIS DAY OUR DAILY BREAD

'But as for that other bread, have no anxiety about it if you have truly resigned yourselves to God's Will. . . . At these times of prayer you are dealing with more important matters' (Chap. 32ff.).

FORGIVE US OUR DEBTS AS WE FORGIVE THEM TO OUR DEBTORS

'He does not say "As we shall forgive." Any one who asks for so great a gift must have done this already. . . . His Majesty knows that if our actions and our words are one, the Lord will unfailingly fulfil our petitions, give us His kingdom, and help us by means of supernatural gifts such as the Prayer of Quiet, perfect contemplation, and all the other favours which the Lord bestows on our trifling efforts. . . . These two things—surrendering our will to God, and forgiving others, apply to all. Some practise them more, and some less. . . . So, lest we should fail to realize our danger and suffer deception, He offers these petitions so necessary to us all while we live in this exile' (Chap. 36).

AND LEAD US NOT INTO TEMPTATION

'The soldiers in Christ—those who experience contemplation and practise prayer—are always ready for the hour of conflict. They are never much afraid of their open enemies. . . . Those whom they fear, and rightly, are the enemies who are treacherous, devils who come to visit them in the guise of angels of light. . . . Show us, then, O our good Master, some way in which we may live through this most dangerous warfare without frequent surprise. The best way we can do this is to use the love and fear given us by His Majesty. For love will quicken our steps, while fear will make us look where we are setting our feet, so that we shall not fall on a road where there are so many obstacles' (Chap. 40).

BUT DELIVER US FROM EVIL. AMEN

'By the word AMEN I understand that the Lord is begging that we may be delivered from all evil for ever. . . . I cannot pay what I owe, and may run further into debt each day. And the hardest thing to bear, Lord, is that I cannot know with any certainty if I love Thee. O my God and Lord, deliver me from all evil for ever. . . . May His Name be ever hallowed in the Heavens and on the earth, and may His Will ever be done in me. AMEN. (Chap. 42.)

Even from a brief synopsis of fifteen chapters, St. Teresa's treatment of the Lord's Prayer deserves careful study, and is at certain points unusual. In training her young communities in the Life of Prayer, she placed great stress on the Paternoster as a teaching source. She does not raise the question which we have considered in our fourth chapter—the important question as to the relation of our Lord's own prayer-life on earth to the teaching which He gave to the disciples as recorded in the Gospels. Her own answer is suggested by the fact that she finds

in the Paternoster 'the whole method of prayer and of high contemplation.' The contemplative of to-day would hardly imitate her humility
by questioning that estimate, and still less could any one question the
fact that the Lord Himself gave to the Church those oft-repeated and
unvarying words as their first lesson in prayer. Yet we have also to bear
in mind the incomparable mystery of our Lord's inner life, and the
depth of his constant communion with the Father while on earth.
Beyond these facts, we have before us St. Teresa's own insights as they
are disclosed in her writings, more specially in the latter parts of the
Interior Castle. Even when certain theologians differ from the sense in
which she uses the term 'contemplation,' she evidences a far greater
knowledge of those heights than she gives, or could have given, to
novices. Her later teaching, as well as that of St. John of the Cross in
the *Spiritual Canticle* and the *Living Flame of Love,* goes further than
anything in the *Way of Perfection.* Whatever she knew at that stage,
she came to know a great deal more. There is no doubt that she found
the Paternoster of great teaching value, and that she saw in it much
that our hasty life misses. But in her teaching she is drawing upon
her own knowledge. We must question, in that sense only, whether
'the whole method of prayer and of high contemplation' were ever
the original purpose of our Lord in framing His first clear teaching in
the words of the Paternoster. We have seen already (pp. 87-9) that
those words would take the disciples at once into country with which
as Jews they would be at home, and thus enable them to accept the
further lessons that the Master would bring. But He could not have
desired to present to the untrained minds of the Twelve what He later
gave to the Church through the mature mind of St. John, nor the gifts
which He gave to St. Teresa when He raised her to so high a union
with Himself. On these grounds our comments in Chapter Four of
this book may stand alongside those of St. Teresa in the *Way of
Perfection* without raising any invidious comparison.

The Similitude of the Waters

St. Teresa has inserted into her autobiography (*Life,* Chaps. 11-22)
some further consistent teaching on prayer under a 'similitude' in which
she likens the nurture of the soul to the watering of a garden, in which
the Lord is to take His delight. Those who lived in the fierce sun-
shine of Spain would better realize the relevance of the parable. There
are four methods : the gardener may draw laboriously by hand from a
well. Secondly he may fit the well with a mechanical chain of buckets.
Thirdly, he may arrange for a stream to flow through his garden, thus
keeping the soil moist. Fourthly, and best of all, 'with no labour of
ours,' is the gift of heavy rainfall. The garden must be watered some-

N

how, and we are bound to desire the best method since the garden is not our own but the Lord's freehold.

The First Water corresponds to our striving for recollection, and to the practice of Meditation. But the well may run dry. The beginnings (and also the later stages) of spiritual growth may be beset by

> 'aridity, dislike, distaste, and so little desire to go and draw water that he would give it up entirely if he did not remember that he is serving the Lord in His garden. . . . Let him not wish to have his kingdom on earth, or even cease from prayer; and let him resolve, even if this aridity should persist his whole life long, never to let Christ fall beneath the Cross.'

She continues to speak also of those more advanced.

> 'When the understanding ceases to work, they cannot bear it, though perhaps even then the will is increasing in power, and putting on new strength without their knowing it. . . . The understanding may lose its power of working because God suspends it. What we must not do is to presume or think that we can suspend it for ourselves, nor must we allow it to cease working: if we do, we shall remain stupid and cold, and shall achieve nothing whatever' (Chap. 12).

The Second Water suggests the Prayer of Quiet.

> 'The water is nearer, for grace reveals itself to the soul more clearly. This state is a recollecting of the faculties within the soul . . . they are not lost, neither do they sleep. The will alone is occupied, in such a way that, not knowing how, it becomes captive.'

As the Prayer of Quiet is a gift unmerited, so it is impossible to keep hold of it beyond due time. Its beginning is

> 'a spark given to the soul as a sign or pledge that He is already choosing it for great things if it will prepare itself to receive them. It is a great gift. . . . I know many souls who attain thus far: and I know too that those who go further are so few that I am ashamed to confess it.'

St. John of the Cross (*Dark Night*, I, ix, 9) agrees

> 'Not all those who consciously walk in the way of the Spirit are brought by God to contemplation, nor even half of them: why, He best knows.'

The Prayer of Quiet must learn to *be* quiet.

> 'What the soul has to do is to go softly and make no noise.'

St. Teresa interposes a vivid simile of the folly of piling great logs on a fire that is only beginning to burn.

194

'A few little straws laid down with humility . . . are more to the point here, and of more use for kindling the fire than any amount of wood— that is, of the most learned reasoning—which . . . will put it out in a moment.'

She leaves the simile, for the aridity that comes through such a mistake may in fact come from the devil. If so,

'it leaves neither light in the understanding nor steadfastness in the will' (Chap. 15).

The Third Water

'The state is a sleep of the faculties, which are neither wholly lost, nor yet can understand how they work. . . . The faculties retain only the power of occupying themselves wholly with God . . . this holy, heavenly madness. . . . The will has only to consent to the favours which it is enjoying' (Chap. 16).

'Those in this state are not wholly masters of themselves and they know very well that the better part of the soul is elsewhere! It is as if we were speaking to one person while someone else was speaking to us: we cannot be absorbed in either one conversation or the other.'

An important variation upon this matter is seen when

'God constrains the will, and also . . . the understanding. But the memory remains free—both it and the imagination must be so—and when they find themselves alone one would never believe what a turmoil they make, and how they try to upset everything. . . . This makes me realize what harm is done to us by sin, which has bound us in this way so that we cannot do as we would—namely be always occupied in God' (Chap. 17).

The Fourth Water

'In this state of prayer . . . there is no feeling, but only rejoicing, unaccompanied by any understanding of the things in which the soul is rejoicing. . . . All the senses are occupied, so that none of them is free to act in any way, either outwardly or inwardly . . .'

'This rain from heaven often comes when the gardener is least expecting it . . . the soul becomes conscious that it is fainting almost completely away. . . . He can apprehend nothing wtih the senses, which only hindre the soul's joy. It is futile for him to attempt to speak. . . . If the period were to last for half-an-hour, that would be a long time. . . . It is the will that maintains the contact with God.'

The simile ends by returning to her constant insistence on the need for humility. It is possible for some foolishly to imagine that meditation upon the Humanity of Christ could be a hindrance to exalted prayer. This is utterly false.

195

'Who can there be (like myself) so miserably proud that . . . he does not count himself . . . abundantly rewarded if the Lord allows him to stand with St. John at the foot of the Cross. . . . We are not angels and we have bodies. . . . We must not show ourselves to be striving after spiritual consolations: come what may, the great thing for us to do is to embrace the Cross. . . . Love begets love. May His Majesty give us this Love . . . for the sake of the Love which He bore us, and through His glorious Son who revealed it to us at such great cost to Himself. AMEN.' (Chap. 22.)

The Interior Castle

At a time when the *Life* was in the hands of the Inquisition, Gracian laid upon St. Teresa the obligation of recalling and writing the teaching on the spiritual life which was then in danger of being destroyed. She did this under the metaphor of a Castle, having many rooms. 'In the centre . . . is the chiefest mansion, where the most secret things pass between God and the soul. . . . The door of entry is prayer and meditation.' In the second and third 'Mansions' she deals with the craving for consolations. In the Fourth mansions she makes clear the difference between a measure of spiritual sweetness that may be granted at times, and the true Prayer of Quiet, which she has already described as the beginning of contemplation. (It should be noted that one of the major ascetical controversies turns upon this point. The long essay entitled 'Afterthoughts' in Dom Cuthbert Butler's *second* edition of his *Western Mysticism* may be consulted.)

The Fifth Mansions goes beyond what we have hitherto discussed in this chapter. From this point St. Teresa seems to be writing from an even more deeply established maturity in her spiritual life. She speaks next of the *Prayer of Union*.

'If you are to gain this, He would have you keep back back nothing: whether it be little or much, He will have it all for Himself. . . . Do not think this is a state like the last, in which we dream. . . . Here we are all asleep, and fast asleep to the things of the world: the soul is without consciousness, and has no power to think. . . . Even in loving, if it is able to love, it cannot understand who or what it loves, nor what it would desire. . . . God implants Himself in the interior of the soul in such a way that, when it returns to itself, it cannot possibly doubt that God has been in it, and it has been in God . . .' (5: 1).

'This union has not yet reached the point of spiritual betrothal. . . . The contract is already drawn up, and the soul . . . is determined to do the will of her Spouse' (5: 4).

The Sixth Mansions. There are many trials, from slander and abuse, and the worse trial of insincere praise. There are bodily infirmities, and unwise advice due to misunderstanding by superiors.

'Before the soul is wholly one with Him, He fills it with fervent desire . . .
a person . . . is not even thinking of God, and He is awakened by His
Majesty as though by a rushing comet or a thunder-clap. Although no sound
is heard, the soul is very well aware that it has been called by God.'

There is a great increase of the sense of total unworthiness, St. Teresa
tells how on one occasion

'she was looking at a Crucifix and thinking she never had anything to offer
to God or to give up for His sake. The Crucified Himself comforted her
by saying that He was giving her all the pains and trials which He had
suffered in His passion, so that she should have them for her own to offer
to the Father.'

There is great detail in this chapter that cannot rightly be summarized
here, but is of very great importance. In a final discussion of suffering
she exclaims :

'Ah! God help me! Lord, how thou dost afflict thy lovers. Yet . . . it is
well that great things should cost a great deal. . . . And in the end He
repays for everything at once.'

The Seventh Mansions. Here we are in a totally different situation.

'The Spiritual Marriage takes place in the deepest centre of the soul, which
must be where God Himself dwells, and I do not think there is any need
of a door by which to enter it. . . . He has been pleased to unite Himself
with His creature in such a way that they have become like two who
cannot be separated from one another. The Spiritual betrothal is different:
here the two persons are frequently separated, as is the case with Union.
. . . Union is as if the ends of two wax candles were joined so that the
light they give is one: the wicks and the wax and the light are all one:
yet afterwards one candle can be separated from the other, and the candles
become two again. . . . When our Lord brings the soul into this Mansion,
which is the centre of the soul itself . . . it seems, on entering, to be subject to none of the usual movements of the faculties and the imagination,
which injure it and take away its peace. . . . The soul seems to be in
safety . . . for so long as the Divine Majesty holds it by the hand and
it does not offend Him. . . .
    'Sometimes the Lord leaves such souls to their own nature . . . and all
poisonous things . . . seem to come together to avenge themselves. . . . Fix
your eyes on the Crucified, and nothing else will be of much importance
to you. . . . The devil sometimes puts ambitious ideas into our hearts, so
that, instead of setting our hands to the work which lies nearest . . . we
rest content with having desired the impossible. Apart from praying for
people, by which you can do a great deal, do not try to help everybody.
. . . We must not build towers without foundations, and the Lord does not
look so much at the magnitude of anything we do as at the love with which
we do it.'

The Interior Castle is dated from the Convent of St. Joseph of Avila
on November 29th, 1577. Thirteen years earlier a young friar, after

Jesuit training, was professed in Carmel at the age of twenty-two. He was ordained priest in 1567, intending to return to his studies. But 'the light of Spain and Christendom' was aware of a strange call from God—'Thou shalt serve Me in an Order whose perfection thou shalt help to restore.' By that time Teresa had spent thirty years in the lax discipline of the *Incarnation* at Avila, and had at last received permission to found the first Convent of the Discalced Reform. A second followed at Medina, but her hopes of further growth seemed blocked by a total lack of sympathetic priests to serve her flock. Beyond her hopes, the Prior of the neighbouring monastery pledged his support in her new Rule, and brought her into touch with his young subject Fray Juan of Matthias. Now the way seemed clear, with 'a friar and a half' to begin with. St. John's call was perhaps explained. The first Community Mass was said at Duruelo on Advent Eve, 1568.

Five years was enough to accumulate tension between the Discalced and the Mitigated Observances. St. Teresa was scorned by the Provincial : St. John was actually captured and imprisoned. Experience of long persecution could not move him. 'He who seeks not the Cross of Christ seeks not the glory of Christ.' From his prison cell there came poems in which his spiritual vision was disclosed, and on which he began to base the theological commentaries of his major writings.

In the end he escaped, somewhat in the manner of the first Apostles, and resumed his work with the new Foundations. By 1580, the Discalced were an independent Province, free for a time from the old hindrances. But before ten years had passed, while St. John was depressed with the burden of unwelcome administrative work, his own Order added to his suffering. A final illness, relieved only by complete reconciliation with the Prior of Ubeda, ended with a peaceful death at midnight on December 14th, 1591.

The Ascent of Mount Carmel

Out of a life blended of suffering and triumph, the Church has gained an incomparable presentation of the Spiritual way. In three books of the *Ascent,* left unfinished, and in the likewise unfinished *Dark Night of the Soul* he shows the 'rapture of the soul which has reached the height of perfection in union with God by the way of Negation.'

'Upon that lucky night
In secrecy, inscrutable to sight,
I went without discerning,
And with no other light
Except for that which in my heart was burning.

'It lit and led me through,
More certain than the night of noonday clear,

To where One waited near
Whose presence well I knew,
There where no other presence might appear.' [195]

Even these third and fourth stanzas of the principal poem are not reached in either volume. They may serve as a prologue to our study. Yet we are dealing with cold prose, and with no poetic fancies or romantic piety.

Early in the first book (I, xiii, 6) he writes :

'Strive always to prefer, not that which is easiest but that which is most difficult;
Not that which is most delectable, but that which is most unpleasing;
Not that which gives most pleasure, but rather that which gives least;
Not that which is restful, but rather that which is wearisome;
Not that which gives consolation, but rather that which makes disconsolate;
Not that which is greatest, but that which is least;
Not that which is loftiest and most precious, but that which is lowest and most despised;
Not that which is a desire for anything, but that which is a desire for nothing;
Strive not to go about seeking the best of temporal things, but the worst.
Strive thus to desire to enter into complete detachment and emptiness and poverty, with respect to that which is in the world, for Christ's sake.'

If such darkness can be sustained, the *purgation of faith* now begins. The virtues infused by the Holy Spirit—those of Faith, Hope and Charity, are now at work in the soul.

Faith brings the understanding into darkness
Sensual purgation is only a beginning.

'To seek oneself in God is to seek the favours and refreshment of God: but to seek God in oneself is not only to desire to be without both of these for God's sake, but to incline oneself to choose for Christ's sake all that is most distasteful, *and this is love of God.*'

(The comment is staggering, but that is what we shall learn to expect from St. John of the Cross.) All the supposed spiritual achievements, visions, revelations of truths and mysteries, spiritual locutions and feelings—all alike must be distrusted or even disregarded, by being brought under subjection. 'Learn to abide attentively and wait lovingly upon God . . . and pay no heed to imagination or its working' (II, xii, 8).

'The soul must pass from the work of meditation to a more interior prayer, but it is meet for him to lay them (*sc.* imagination) aside . . . neither sooner nor later than when the Spirit bids him. The first sign is the realization that he can no longer meditate or reason with his imagination, neither can take pleasure therein . . . the second sign is that he has no desire to fix his meditation upon . . . particular objects. . . . The third and surest sign is that the soul takes pleasure in being alone, and waits with loving attentiveness upon God, in inward peace and quietness and rest. . . . These three signs . . . the spiritual person must see in himself, all together, before he can venture with security to abandon the state of meditation and sense, and to enter that of contemplation and spirit. . . . The less they understand, the farther they penetrate into the night of the Spirit' (II, xiii, 4; xiv, 4).

Hope brings the memory into darkness

'The more nearly the memory attains to union with God, the more do definite kinds of knowledge become perfected within it, until it loses them entirely, when in perfection it attains to the state of union. Thus at the beginning . . . the soul cannot but fall into great oblivion . . . it is guilty of many omissions . . . through the absorption of the memory into God. But when once it attains to the habit of union . . . actions which are seemly and necessary it performs rather in a greater degree of perfection' (III, ii, 8).

Charity brings the will into darkness

The passions of the soul and the affections of the will are shown as joy, hope, grief and fear. ('These are the four lingering burdens which he laughingly designates elsewhere as 'four silly sheep' which persist with the soul.)

'If a man desire to have a certain degree of joy in creatures, he must of necessity have an equal degree of disquietude and grief. . . . But he that is detached is untroubled by anxieties, whether in prayer or apart from it. . . . The other man loses everything, running to and fro upon the chain by which his heart is attached and bound' (III, xx, 3).

After discussion of the varying attachments that fetter us, the *Ascent of Mount Carmel* is curtailed, short of its intended scope. *The Dark Night of the Soul,* properly the fourth part of the total work, and not a separate book, deals with the passive purgations of sense and spirit.

The Dark Night of the Soul

Souls enter this passive night 'when God draws them forth from the state of beginners, which is the state of those that meditate on the spiritual road, and begins to set them in the state of progressives, which is that of those who are already contemplatives, to the end that . . . they may arrive at the state of the perfect, which is that of the Divine union of the soul with God' (I, i, 1).

The imperfections of the early stage are grouped systematically to accord with the seven deadly sins, pride, avarice, *luxuria,* wrath, spiritual gluttony, envy, sloth. In them all the teaching is summed up in the 'reality of interior perfection, which is to give pleasure to God, and in naught to give pleasure to ourselves' (I, iii, 2). The signs of the passage to contemplation are again developed (I, i, 9) and the soul may be assumed to have entered the Prayer of Quiet, in accordance with St. Teresa's treatment of the life of prayer. This night of sense, the theme of the first book, gives a purging self-knowledge, a deeper reverence towards God, and a spiritual humility, tempered by momentary graces of illumination. The devil brings great affliction through the spirit of impurity, the spirit of blasphemy, and the spirit of giddiness (Isa. 19 : 14) which darkens the senses, brings scruple and perplexity, and cannot be helped by the counsel of others.

The passive night of the Spirit is more terrible, but is sometimes delayed to allow the soul some respite after the night of sense. St. John, however, gives ample evidence that these two passive stages cannot be finally determined in any given case. They overlap and interact, so that no hard lines may be drawn. In the first onset of the 'second night' the soul is aware as never before of its own impurity, and feels itself set against God (Job 7 : 20). Its sense of weakness brings pain, and also the knowledge of the gulf between what it is and what it should be.

But the dark contemplation that brings such pain is also purifying the soul, though the soul is unable to believe this, and thinks its advisers are blind guides. No degree of possession of the theological virtues can bring consolation. The soul has a great love for God, but cannot realize His love for itself : in any case it could never feel to deserve His Love.

The darkness goes on, proportionately to the habits of natural affections which the soul formerly had.

'In order to attain the . . . union to which this dark night is disposing and leading it, the soul must be filled with a certain glorious magnificence in its communion with God' (II, ix, 4).

Yet it longs for its former peace, though this was in reality no peace at all. 'Such is the work wrought in the soul by this night that hides the hopes of the light of day.'

'Therefore, O spiritual soul, when thou seest thy desire obscured, thy affections arid and constrained, and thy faculties bereft of their capacity . . . be not afflicted, but rather consider it a great happiness, since God is freeing thee from thyself and taking the work out of thy hands' (II, xvi, 7).

'This dark contemplation . . . is mystical theology . . . secret wisdom which . . . is communicated and infused into the soul through love' (II, xvii, 2).

There follows St. John's exposition of the Ten Steps of the Ladder of Divine Love. We have met this metaphor in Ruysbroeck, but here the teaching follows rather that of St. Bernard and St. Thomas Aquinas.

'The first step of love causes the soul to languish, and this is to its advantage.

The second step causes the soul to seek God without ceasing.

The third step . . . causes the soul to work, and gives it fervour so that it fails not.

The fourth step . . . causes . . . an habitual suffering because of the Beloved, yet without weariness.

The fifth step . . . makes the soul to desire and long for God impatiently.

(On) the sixth step the soul runs swiftly to God and touches Him again and again.

The seventh step . . . makes the soul to become vehement in its boldness.

The eighth step . . . causes the soul to seize Him and hold Him fast.

The ninth step . . . makes the soul to burn with sweetnses.

The tenth step . . . belongs not to this life. . . . It causes the soul to become wholly assimilated to God . . . wherefore our Saviour says "In that day ye shall ask me nothing" ' (II, xx, xxi).

Beyond this major but uncompleted work, St. John of the Cross left the *Spiritual Canticle* (Songs between the soul and the Bridegroom) and also the *Living Flame of Love* (Songs of the soul in intimate communication and union with the love of God).

We have in these works an ordered and fully theological exposition of the hidden life. We may recall two further stanzas of the poem upon which its truth rests :

'O night that was my guide!
O darkness dearer than the morning's pride!
O night that joined the lover
To the beloved bride,
Transfiguring them each into the other.

'Lost to myself, I stayed
My face upon my Lover having laid
From all endeavour ceasing:
And all my cares releasing
Threw them among the lilies there to fade.' [195]

CHAPTER TWELVE

'A PASSION OF PATIENCE'

THE wealth of spiritual energy shown in the last two chapters makes it certain that the course of the hidden life will certainly go forward into continuing history. It might seem, moreover, that the essential pattern has been shown to the Church in the period we have already covered. The Spanish Renaissance was not only reforming the decadence of the Carmelite Order. It was disclosing the principles of Christian Contemplation in a more complete way than had been previously possible.

In developing in the first instance the Jewish insights, we wished by this means to avoid partial comparisons. Whatever it was necessary to say in opening the Christian period, it has not been necessary to search for isolated examples in Judaism bearing some resemblance to Christian insights. Rather have we found gladly, and with no strained search, that the Holy Spirit had in fact guided the people of God's predilection, and we can know with certainty that this guidance must still be active in His Love.

We move now into a later and markedly different period. The flame of Carmelite spirituality was at its height in Spain when a new phase had begun in France. The first foundations were possibly due directly to St. Teresa, since her writings, and a Carmelite group which she had personally trained, became established in Paris. If this link is as close as it appears to be, she would certainly not have desired the later developments. When such figures as St. Francis de Sales, St. Jane Frances de Chantal, or the Carmelite Friar Brother Lawrence are considered, it might seem possible to overlook the infection of Quietism which poisoned the next two centuries, and endangered the inner life of the Church, quite apart from the diversion of numbers of Protestant sects. The passionate devotion to our Lord in His Divine Humanity, so notable in the Carmelites and in many of their immediate successors, makes the best 'Theocentric mysticism' seem insipid. It had tempered and controlled the influence of extreme Dionysian thought, but in France ascetic discipline had become weakened. Even at its best the tendency to relaxation and calm passivity was dangerous, though the best was still very good indeed. Yet the *Introduction to the Devout Life* could hardly content those who needed what St. John of the Cross had lived and taught. Wherever the decline began, Recollection changed to Introversion, and it meant too often a turning inwards to a strangely unprofitable self-centre, rather than centring all the powers of the soul on God. The Prayer of Quiet, the very gateway to true contemplation, as St. Teresa and St. John have determined, was in time perverted to a dream of passivity and spiritual self-indulgence. It is easier and less exacting to sink into a dream of 'undifferentiated Godhead' than to strive daily for the Imitation of Christ. And the added tragedy, as we have noted, is that the Quietist approach is deemed 'more spiritual.' Dr. Evelyn Underhill, in her major study of Mysticism, wisely writes :

> 'The great teachers of Quietism, having arrived at and experienced the psychological state of quiet, having known the ineffable peace and certainty, the bliss which follows in its act of complete surrender, its utter and speechless resting in the Absolute Life, believed themselves to have discovered in this half-way house the goal of the mystic quest. Therefore, while much of their teaching remains true, as the real description of a real and valid state experienced by almost all contemplatives in the course of their development, the inference which they draw from it, that in this mere blank abiding in the deeps, the soul had reached the end of her course, was untrue and bad for life. . . . The true contemplative does not desire "extraordinary favours and visitations" but the privilege of breathing for a littls while the atmosphere of Love. He is about that which St. Bernard called "the business of all businesses" : he goes, in perfect simplicity, to the encounter of Perfection, not to the development of himself.' [196]

For this wisdom we may be grateful, but also realize that in her own later writing the author might have spoken even more firmly. The present generation can spare no time for this. We have become too clear that the downward slope that begins from Molinos, Benet Canfield, and Madame Guyon is continuous to Aldous Huxley and the Vedantist revival. We do not forget the finest periods of the Quaker movement, but must still remember that Jakob Boehme and the modern Rosicrucians are not out of sight.

The necessity of this digression is not to deal harshly with the dross, which can well be laid aside, but rather to put the gold into its true setting. The third period of the Jewish story, for which we have foreshadowed historical parallels, can now be placed alongside a teacher and spiritual director who stands as a great Catholic figure, though he was living very near to the frontiers of Quietism.

Père de Caussade, s.j., in his *Abandon à la Providence Divine*, is really as far removed from the inactivity of the Quietists as true Christian resignation is distinct from Muslim fatalism. To de Caussade, as Dom Arnold, o.s.b., has written, 'the *Ita Pater* of our Divine Lord, or the *Fiat mihi* of our Blessed Lady, is the shortest, surest, and easiest way to holiness.' The opening phrases of the book support that judgment :

'In former times . . . all spirituality was comprised in fidelity to the designs of God, for there was no regular system of guidance in the spiritual life. . . . For those who led a spiritual life, each moment brought some duty to be faithfully accomplished. Their whole attention was thus concentrated consecutively like a hand that marks the hours. Their minds, incessantly animated by the impulsion of Divine Grace, turned imperceptibly to each new duty that presented itself by the permission of God. . . . Such were the hidden springs by which the conduct of Mary was actuated. Mary was the most simple of all creatures, and the most closely united to God. Her answer to the angel when she said "Fiat mihi secundum verbum tuum" contained all the mystical theology of her ancestors, to whom everything was reduced as now to the purest, simplest submission of the soul to the Will of God under whatever form it presents itself.' [197]

From these opening words the spiritual climate in which the hidden life of the Body has been nourished, is shown as being an alert contemplation, reflecting more closely the concept of the mixed life from Blessed Ruysbroeck than from St. Gregory. 'The duties of each moment are the shadows beneath which hides the Divine operation' (I, i, 2). He is careful to show that the spiritual principle is the same alike for Religious and Secular. French mysticism had been notably an age of laity. We have, for the time, left aside the monastic assumptions of the last two chapters, but may in the process have lost too much of their implied ascesis.

'The active practice of fidelity consists in accomplishing the duties which devolve upon us. . . . Its passive exercise consists in the loving acceptance of all that God sends us at each moment. . . . When one thirsts after sanctity, the desire to know about it only drives it farther away . . for those things which happen at each moment by the Divine command or permission are always the most holy, the best, and the most Divine for us . . . our moments are made fruitful by our fulfilment of the will of God' (I, i, 3–5).

The hidden life, at least in one of its aspects, can be discerned by faith alone. God's sacrament is presented under forms that we find hard to recognize, whether owing to adverse circumstances, or from a disordered desire for spiritual sweetness.

'To adore Jesus on Thabor, to accept the will of God in extraordinary circumstances, does not indicate a life animated by such great faith as to love the will of God in ordinary things, and to adore Jesus on the Cross. For faith cannot be said to be real, living faith unless it is tried, and has triumphed over every effort for its destruction' (I, ii, 2).

To speak so confidently of the will of God needs a discernment of what it is.

'There could be nothing more reasonable, more perfect, more divine than the Will of God. Could any change of time, place or circumstance alter or increase its infinite value? . . . The present is ever filled with infinite treasure; it contains more than you have capacity to hold. Faith is the measure. . . . The Divine Will is a deep abyss of which the present moment is the entrance' (I, ii, 3).

In the complex revelation of God in Holy Scripture, in the action of Jesus in the souls of men, that Will is spoken. But when the disclosure in the events of history seems to offend our infidelity, we cannot understand, and appear to think that we can induce God to act within the limits of our reason.

The value of this doctrine is at times weakened by overstress upon its 'easiness.' French spirituality tended to value the easy path, as has been suggested in the comparison between St. John of the Cross and St. Francois de Sales. One passage may suffice as warning.

'I will make perfection so easy for you that you will find it everywhere and in everything. I will unite you to God, and make you walk hand in hand with Him from the moment you begin practising what I will teach you.'

Such a statement might cause us to question the firm judgment quoted from Dom Arnold, O.S.B. De Caussade was, if only historically, very near to the frontiers of Quietism, and he can also come too near to the fruits of Quietism. We need only refer to Malaval's widely read but dangerous dialogue on a *'Simple method of raising the soul to Contemplation'*—a title that has proved a snare for the unwise. The real core of de Caussade's teaching is, however, far from such dangers. It is by the Divine action alone that we can be sanctified—by the conformity of the stone to the hand of the sculptor.

The Second Book opens with an important distinction between two spiritual 'states,' which requires careful examination.

'There is a time when the soul lives in God, and a time when God lives within the soul. What is appropriate to one state is inconsistent with the other. When God lives within the soul it ought to abandon itself entirely to Divine Providence. When the soul lives in God, it is obliged to procure for itself, carefully and very regularly, every means it can devise by which to arrive at the Divine Union' (II, i, 1).

It is not our purpose to discuss the quality or methods of spiritual direction, but it is clear that in this passage de Caussade is deliberately separating the two states as alternatives, and indicating strong preference for the first. Yet, in the similitude of the Vine and the Branches our Lord clearly treats this essential relationship without any contrast. 'Abide in me and I in you. As the branch cannot bear fruit of itself except it abode in the Vine, no more can ye except ye abide in me' (John

15 : 4). There is no contrast of the kind suggested : if in fact we look for contrast we might say (wrongly) that our Lord in this and in much other teaching points the Church to its now established teaching on the Unitive Way as being (from the human understanding) the gift of entry (though never absorption) into the Divine Life. But, in fact, the contrast is false. The abiding is in Him by virtue of His abiding in us. It is mutual—an ineffable coinherence. There is further the consideration that, in the period in which de Caussade was teaching, the thought of the indwelling of the Holy Spirit in every soul had become dangerously perverted, to the virtual exaltation of the human spirit as the arbiter of its own life, and the norm of its own spiritual judgments. We do not weaken the truth of the Divine Indwelling by desiring its consummation in Divine Union. We thereby acknowledge the fact that the acceptance of the 'infinite joy of the finite soul' can be only by a correspondence of Will in all things. Knowing how fully this fact is supported in the ascetic teaching of earlier ages, it will be well to recall the Rabbinic counsel quoted in an earlier chapter (cf. p. 65) : 'Do His Will as if it were thy will; that He may do thy will as if it were His Will.' Not only does it show the harmony of two distant periods, but may also suggest a closer approach to the truth which de Caussade may be intending. The substantial Divine indwelling in the human soul is an indwelling of submission—a Divine humiltiy— even the indwelling of a Guest whose presence might not be desired. Before the soul can reach the full blessing of that presence, the guest must be made to rejoice in His abiding. This can only come about by the growth within the soul of a truly formed will-in-love. Thus can the desire of the Bridegroom be satisfied, and the true union between the soul and God made possible. An obscure saying of Nicholas de Cuso is here made relevant : 'God dwells beyond the contradiction of opposites.' St. John of the Cross in the *Ascent* (II, v, 3) deals clearly with this distinction :

'God dwells, and is present substantially, in every soul, even in that of the greatest sinner in the world. And this kind of union is ever wrought between God and His creatures, for in it He is preserving their being: so that if union of this kind were to fail them, they would at once become annihilated and would cease to be. And so, when we speak of the union of the soul with God, we speak not of this substantial union which is continually being wrought, but only when there exists that likeness that comes from love: we shall therefore term this the union of likeness, even as that other union is called substantial or essential. The former is natural, the latter is supernatural. And the latter comes to pass when the two wills—namely that of the soul and that of God—are conformed together in one, and there is nought in the one that is repugnant to the other. And thus, when the soul rids itself totally of that which is repugnant to the Divine Will, and conforms not with it, it is transformed in God through love.' [198]

St. John of the Cross is here developing part of our Lord's teaching upon the Holy Spirit which precedes the simile of the Vine : 'If a man love me, he will keep my word, and my Father will love him, and we will come unto him and make our abode with him' (John 14 : 23).

Though it has been necessary to clarify this important doctrine, de Caussade fully understands the condition of the soul in this 'divine darkness,' and that its response is solely one of faith.

'It is with these souls like the changes of the wind. The direction is known only in the present moment, and the effects follow their causes by the Will of God, which is only explained by these effects because it acts in their souls, and makes them act either by hidden, undoubted instincts, or by the duties of their state. This is all the spirituality they know' (II, i, 2).

The abandonment to Divine Providence is a great and universal act. Its precondition as a way of life is that purity of heart which is the virtue of the Beatific vision and the fruit of the single mind. 'Purity of heart,' said Kierkegaard, 'is to will one thing.' That 'one thing' is never the tenacity of self-willed ambition, but the flexibility of which the Epistle of Privy Counsel speaks—'as a roan glove upon the hand of a man.' 'In the state of faith, as in that of glory, God and His Will is the eternal object that captivates the heart, and will one day form its true happiness' (II, ii, 1).

The soul set upon this course may show many defects, which are sometimes those permitted by God in the course of its spiritual growth. If a soul is unable to govern its outward life by obvious method and plan, it may be hard to believe that God may wish it to be in that state. But the demand of faith stretches into far deeper places than this.

'For a soul that desires nothing else but the will of God, what could be more miserable than the impossibility of being certain of loving Him?'

It beholds, perhaps in others, 'a brilliant sanctity' which leads only to discouragement.

'It is from this sad trial that the principal merit of the state of abandonment is gained' (II, iii, 4).

Here the teaching accords closely with that of St. John of the Cross, and answers to the experience of many who seek to follow the hidden life. For it is, even more clearly than before, a way of faith. It demands the conviction that 'all things work together for good to them that love God, even to those who according to His purpose are called to be saints' (Rom. 8 : 28). The essence here is the working together. There is a completeness of pattern which the soul is not allowed to realize, save after a long time of trial, and after living painfully through apparent failure and frustration, when in fact God's hand has never let go its hold.

'The effects of grace . . . are nothing short of marvellous. Without method, yet most exact: without rule, yet most orderly: without reflection, yet most profound: without effort, yet everything accomplished: without foresight, yet nothing better suited to unexpected events' (II, iv, 4).

This is pattern. It is profound design and superb achievement. But this the soul may be unable to discern : it rests only in the belief beyond all reason, in the hope beyond all hope, that here are God and itself, bound in His perfect Will.

'Love can refuse nothing that Love desires, nor desire anything that Love refuses' (II, iv, 10).

We are again close to past insights, and almost to the words of the *De Imitatione Christi* : 'Let me ever will and not will in union with Yourself, and be unable to will otherwise than You will or do not will.' The crux is in the apparently negative clause. To stand still in peace of soul when all human judgment cries out for some decisive action need not be Quietism. It is in fact the cardinal point of the Hidden Life. It is, in the words of the late Charles Williams in his Arthurian poems *'A passion of patience.'*

Much of the teaching here examined, though it follows closely upon earlier periods, also brings us into the spiritual climate of the later Hasidism. No charge of heresy lies against de Caussade, and yet the doctrine tends towards a more spontaneous and personal spirituality. There are signs of the temper of mind notably evident in the Quaker movement. It is a spirituality that has freed itself—even at some risk— from rigid and legalistic elements in medieval Catholicism in the West. It will always temper the dogmatic with the experimental. Père de Caussade did not escape, in serving the Visitation Nuns, from his surrounding environment, and the influence of Mme. Acarie and Mme. Guyon was widespread. Even at its best, however, the Gallican tradition will find itself more congenial to the Eastern mind than are other aspects of Latin Christendom. The Hasidic developments which are almost contemporary with de Caussade in their early period draw significantly in their best spiritual character from their Eastern environment. The affiliations with the twelfth and thirteenth centuries have been rightly sought, but in another sense it is not the Judaism of the Rhineland or of Spain. It was Judaism with a difference, and the difference sufficed to bring it very close to the 'Sacrament of the present moment.' Eastern Catholicism likewise shows a certain freedom in the same direction, however doctrinally certain and definite its Orthodoxy.

O

The Western student may be struck, in the closer understanding of Orthodoxy which ecumenical fellowship has brought him, with the notable and even unexpected sympathies in Orthodox circles with a tradition that has continued from France into modern times. It may fall short by dogmatic standards, but it seems to be understood in Byzantium more readily than in Rome.

It is therefore noteworthy that, contemporary with Eastern Hasidism in Russian Poland and the Ukraine, Russian Christianity had known such a figure as Serafim of Sarov (1759–1833). In her brief portrait of him as a *Flame in the Snow*, Mme. Iulia de Beausobre writes :

> 'The part of every human being (in the universal praise of God) is unique. Only God knows a man's part before the man himself has learnt it through facing and overcoming his temptations. In prayer . . . every one can learn from God the interpretation of his own part : but God's purpose often appears incredible to all except the person concerned. Therefore every one must be left spiritually free : free to follow God's inscrutable intentions. No one may interfere, few dare interpret. But if, through contemplation, a man attains to a particular kind of nearness to God, and comes to hear God's own interpretation of His Word, and to perceive God's purpose for every one of His creatures, that man becomes a *staretz*, a spiritual director. . . . Love, kindled in them by their nearness to God, leads them back to man. They can no longer dwell in unbroken beatitude. But once love is Christ's, and Christlike action renders present the Comforter who is Joy, those who for the love of their brethren, leave the delights of Contemplation, attain to joy in the Holy Ghost. The outward sign of this grace is a great simplicity, chief mark of the Russian *staretz*.' [199]

With this interpretation we are able to meet another, and a different pattern of the hidden life of the Body of Christ, for which, none the less, we have been prepared both in the Jewish and the Christian study. It is clear, for example, that in some of the Hasidic *Zaddikim* we have already met the *Staretz*. In the last part of our study we have already met the freedom of which Mme. de Beausobre speaks, and the momentary absorption in the Divine Will, which was then termed the Sacrament of the present moment. The parallel must not be strained. The Orthodox *Staretz* was usually a monk, enclosed save for the ministry that was laid upon him (or granted to him) under obedience. His spiritual children came to him from the world into his privileged seclusion, and returned with his counsel and his blessing to the world where the life had to be worked out. The Jewish *Zaddik* would certainly be one of the local Rabbis, and the Hasidim who formed his inner circle of disciples were working in close physical and spiritual contact with him. They were colleagues as well as pupils, and the whole group would form a spiritual coinherence, through which the work of healing, of teaching or of intercession would be done.

At times this parallel became specially evident, and the Staretz Serafim (St. Serafim of Sarov) is a notable instance. His monastic obedience was as perfect as that recorded also of other hesychasts, whose spiritual tradition was built upon the *Philokalia*. After a long period he sought, and finally obtained a complete retirement from all contacts with the world, to a degree which his brethren could not pretend to understand or willingly accept. He was outstanding in his devotion to the Holy Spirit, and offered the ancient teaching to a generation that seemed to have lost it entirely.

The strict enclosure had marked a time of inner warfare which he had to fight alone, so far was it beyond any comprehension or sympathy from those on whose behalf he was carrying the burden. But there came, almost suddenly, a moment when he was ordered to return, by a clear intervention of the Queen of Heaven. He had felt himself too far separated from the common needs, and seemed hesitant at her words : He was answered 'You who have looked into the face of My Son, have you not read the burden of His love? Open your ears and listen. Listen to their endless, weaving tales of woe' (p. 113).

From that moment, whether or no he wanted it, the door stood open. The first impact of the change upon his neighbourhood is reminiscent of the daily life of St. Jean Vianney—the Curé d'Ars. The cell was still a cherished shelter, but the new-found joy overflowed its limits. The legend tells that :

'All through these years of return manward, the Queen of Heaven watched over him. . . . She visited him in his sleep and said : "You can now openly do My Son's Will. Come out of your enclosure. Roam the forest, visit the hut, renew your . . . interchange of wisdom with nature. True Will can now express itself through your words and actions : true love can now shine unhampered out of the dwelling that you have become" ' (p. 127).

Early in this new phase of his life, the governor of the province had brought to him news of a great spiritual awakening at the Court of the Tsar Alexander, which the Holy Alliance was intended to implement in practical terms. At this point it appears that St. Serafim made his first spiritual contact with the Hasidim, who had clearly implanted in Poland the Messianic interpretation which had been laid upon them. 'Here on earth,' he was told by the Governor, 'God's kingdom must be brought about in the thick of life . . . goodness will manifest itself everywhere, in the empty spaces between men. That is the Messiah, according to them.' The governor apologized for what he feared was heresy : 'You see, this is really what our Tsar is striving after, this congregation of all men, with God binding, cementing all. And the Jews understand it—the Jews! But our fellow-Christians! they mock!'

Between these apparent extremes, and underlying all his later work, was his spiritual direction of the Convent of Divei. When he resumed that charge after the period of strict enclosure, he had to build again the spirit of our Lady of Tenderness, who in solitude had been his 'joy of all joys.' 'It was in the guidance and instruction of the sisters . . . that Serafim's paternal love found its deepest expression, and they were his confidantes concerning the most mystical of his visions and prophecies.' The stories of this spiritual linking, and of its frequent miraculous elements, offer a parallel with that of the inner group of Hasidim with their *Zaddik*. The hidden life is being expressed in a new way. The conception of Blessed Ruysbroeck is being demonstrated.

'St. Serafim was the prophet of the expected revelation of the Holy Spirit, and the forerunner of the new form of spirituality which should succeed merely ascetical monasticism: in symbolic terms, the white, spirit-bearing flame of mystical prayer, embracing the hearts of all men in the unity of the Love of God, which should succeed the black night of austerity.' [200]

The term 'succeed,' in this modern Orthodox comment, must not be overlooked. The time may now have been reached in that one period of the hidden life, even in that one place, if anything so vast as Russia may be termed 'one place.' But this period does not, and must not, be thought to supersede what has gone before. In the Christian understanding the Carmelite austerity is not a 'black night,' but the Divine darkness through which many must pass—in which, indeed, many may live their whole lives on earth when once they have been brought within it. But beyond it there is a way, too easily imitated, but still rarely realized in truth. It is, at present, still mainly in the understanding of Eastern Orthodoxy, but in these last days the East is drawing nearer to the West, and it is not for nothing that the East is 'unchanging': we may look to the Holy Spirit, and to the intercession of our Lady, to implant that new character within the restless materialism and fear of the modern West. It is a way that may appear to 'supersede,' yet St. Serafim himself would deal diversely with one person and another—sending one from the world to strict enclosure, and refusing an identical desire in others, for whom he discerned God's Will as contrary to their own. The life of prayer was open to all, rich or poor, great or humble. Not only those who can bestow lavish charity, and benefit many by such means, but all those who will, may receive the Spirit.

'Once He has come, the Comforter, our prayer is a pure rejoicing. And where those who rejoice come together, there is the Church.' The coinherence fuses into one the separate joy of each. 'Whenever we consciously do His Will we stand within it (the shining glory). We have grown blind to it, but it is there all right' (p. 196f.).

Yet he would lead others, by a commanding love, into an austerity of reparation and sacrifice that goes back to the Desert for its outward form, and reaches far beyond the limited understanding of the Desert in its depth of tenderness.

Near to the end, a mighty task of intercession for one sinner brought upon Serafim a diabolic onslaught. In the ensuing weakness he felt drawn back to solitude and prayer, but the demands of his unique apostolate forbade him. Before long, however, the earthly work was closed by death; but the impact of his prayer is known in Russia even to-day. The thought of the past glory, and of the system which has overrun it since his death, may often tempt the Church to despair. We should recall a blessing he once gave to some younger monks of Sarov.

'Fill my heart with joy, St. Mary, conqueror of sin and sorrow, vessel gladly bearing joy'—so he prayed: and then, taking hold of their hands he called out, 'Away with despondency. There is nothing that Christ has not conquered—nothing' (p. 155).

We have not stressed the evidently miraculous elements in the life of St. Serafim. The Western mind can hardly distinguish, for the whole is so foreign and wistfully fascinating. The proved element of miracle was never for its own sake : it was woven inseparably with his task of intercession, and with his discernment of souls. The demands that followed from his spiritual direction are thus explained. It was in pure humility, and in his full share of the task of reparation that he could require, as her oblation to God, the death of a nun, whom he had already named against her will as Abbess of Divei. He laid this new obedience on her as a freely-willed act of substituted love for the life of another of his children, whose help he needed in following out his own work for the Community. Such commands are even an offence to the Western outlook. They are misrepresented as gross violations of human personality. But to Serafim they were simple fulfilment. There was never coercion. The way must be seen and followed freely. He simply knew what the way should be, and himself bore the pain if it were refused.

Such examples, which filled his later life, and were the harvest of its early dedication, can show to us the spiritual goal of the hidden life, though they could never be claimed to represent our own achieved course. They do, however, make clear that in Eastern Orthodoxy there is a spiritual link with the Hasidim which might begin to bridge the gulf of rejection. Such a bridge is no compromise task : it is simply a depth of charity which the Russian soul has been able, more perfectly than the saints of the West, to interpret to the Church. The hidden life so displayed is closely akin to that of the *Philokalia*. In it, the true demands of a mystical perception, and a constantly sustained 'acquisition of the Holy Spirit,' are the inspiration of the daily moment. Such a concept is still unfamiliar, and yet these demands and counsels were offered to all Christians as their natural right. We may perhaps learn more from St. Serafim and those in his tradition than from other great figures of the Russian Church. One final example may be chosen to complete this study.

In the life and teaching of the Staretz Silouan of the Monastery of St. Panteleimon on Mount Athos, we may see a contemporary figure. Legend and romance have their own value, but the actual record of living disciples, and of the Staretz' own writings leave less room for mistaken judgment. At the age of twenty-six a man of no apparent education reached the Monastery where he was to remain for nearly fifty years.

> 'Until I was seven and twenty I simply believed that God was, but I did not know Him; but when my soul knew Him by the Holy Spirit I was consumed with longing for Him, and now day and night I seek Him with burning heart.' '. . . When a man fears God lest he grieve Him in some way—that is the first degree of love. He who keeps his mind pure of intrusive thoughts knows the second degree of love, which is greater than the first. The third and still greater kind of love is when a man is sensible of grace in the soul. The fourth and perfect kind of love for God exists when a man possesses the grace of the Holy Spirit both in soul and body . . .' 201 (p. 164).

The Staretz was precise and definite in his teaching on Prayer, but it was never a system or a theory. His prayer was essentially to be proved in life.

> 'If you are forgetful of the Lord you will not pray, and without prayer the soul will not dwell in the love of God, for the grace of the Holy Spirit comes through prayer' (p. 166).

Beginners will need personal direction, but (as St. Teresa also taught) if an experienced director is not given, the grace of obedience in the confessional will do much—far more than theoretical teaching. Prayer will easily be lost if the spirit of charity is lost—the one is the Lord's grace in return for the other.

> 'The man who loves his enemies soon comes to know the Lord in the Holy Spirit. . . . The soul that loves the Lord is unable not to pray. . . . The man who loves God is able to keep Him in mind day and night, since no form of activity interferes with loving God' (pp.168ff.).

Again, as in many earlier teachings, we are brought back to the central place of humility. The amazing grace given to the Staretz during his novitiate, to which he alludes repeatedly in simple gratitude, gave sure knowledge of our Lord in His perfect Humanity and in His Godhead, and gave him an experience of the abiding presence of the Holy Spirit. But this must give no false confidence. Even then, the power of sin did not leave his thoughts free from the unwanted suggestions of passion. There came to him from the Lord, in answer to petition in this distress, the searching counsel on humility: 'Keep thy mind in Hell, and despair not' (p. 172). He was shown that even in his cell, and in the height of his striving after prayer, a subtle and powerful spirit of pride still beset him. This is a more extreme emphasis than we have yet found in the medieval or the renaissance Church. We are reminded rather of St. Anthony in the terms of the Desert. It is a call to self-abasement of a kind that we might hardly conceive, were it not for the actual evidence of the Staretz.

> 'During his lifetime he actually descended into the darkness and torments of Hell, not once but over and over again, until his heart was so permeated that he was able to repeat the movement at will.'

This is a level of asceticism that we can only accept with wonder. The Staretz was aware that the real danger was not in the failure of ascetic resolution, but in the darkness of despair that might follow it. He was so convinced of the love of God as the sole mover of his action, that he could stand unafraid on the very brink of despair.

> 'When the burning torment has destroyed the passionate thought or feeling, he would stay the all-consuming fires by the saving action of the Love of Christ, which he also knew and bore within him' (p. 105).

One may recall, as a parallel in spiritual counsel for souls less gifted, the teaching of the *Cloud of Unknowing*. 'Cower down under them (assaults of temptation) as a coward overcome in battle, and think it is but folly to thee to strive any longer with them, and therefore thou yieldest thyself to God in the hands of thine enemies, and feel thyself as thou wert foredone for ever.' The same spiritual principle of humility —the same ultimate trust in the intervention of God in the last extremity—may help us to interpret the one counsel in the light of the other, and not to presume beyond what God may lay upon us. But there is always one abiding fact in our human life :

> 'The humility of the Mother of God is greater than any, wherefore all generations on earth exalt her, and all the heavenly hosts serve her; and this His Mother hath the Lord given us to intercede for us and be our help' (p. 180).

As in the spiritual counsels of St. Serafim, the Staretz Silouan returns constantly to the special gift of the Holy Spirit in bringing to the soul all the truth concerning the Lord Christ.

'He who has known the sweetness of the Holy Spirit knows that it is beyond compare, and there is nothing on earth can captivate him, for he is held in thrall by the love of the Lord alone, anl finds rest in God and rejoices, and weeps with pity for mankind because all men have not come to know the Lord' (p. 189).

The Staretz was trained, as were many of his Order, in the spiritual warfare taught by the Eastern Fathers. For him it was a constant repetition of recovery.

'Our battle rages every day and every hour.' In countless detailed ways, through passing failure, the soul loses grace, and endangers its pure love for God. So often the assault comes by loss of charity: as often the studied forgiveness of injury, and the disciplined refusal to take offence, will bring restoration. 'Make trial with yourself: ask God one day for brotherly love, and the next day live without love, and you will see the difference' (p. 198). 'Were I to be asked what would I have of God, what gifts, I should answer, The spirit of humility in which the Lord rejoices above all things. . . . According to the measure of your humility you will be sensible of grace within you: and when your soul finally humbles herself, then will you attain perfect rest. And this is the war man wages his life long' (p. 202).

Near to the time of his death the Staretz left a testimony which may serve to sum up the quality of all his teaching.

'The soul from love of the Lord has lost her wits: she sits in silence, with no wish to speak, and looks upon the world with mazed eyes, having no desire for it, and seeing it not. And people do not know that she is contemplating her beloved Lord, that the world has been left behind and is forgotten, for there is no sweetness therein. Thus it is with the soul that has come to know the sweetness of the Holy Spirit.

'O Lord, give us this Love throughout Thine whole Universe. O Holy Spirit, live in our souls, that with one accord we may all glorify the Creator, Father, Son, and Holy Ghost. AMEN.' (p. 207.)

With this brief reference to one who is known, already in the present day, as 'The Undistorted Image,' our study may rest. It is of more than passing interest that such profound examples of Eastern Spirituality, which make demands upon our best understanding of the hidden life in Christ, should find subtle but definite response from Judaism in the same period and in part under the same conditions of life. The coincidence demands careful evaluation. Social and political environment have undoubtedly played their part. We have seen St. Serafim actually confronted, by a penitent, with the fact that the neighbouring Jewish Hasidism, who had doubtless suffered there as elsewhere from Christian persecution, were able to show that deep spirit of charity upon which the Christian Tsar had built such hopes, only to be disappointed by the cynicism of the Western powers, who could not understand 'this congregation of all men, with God binding, cementing, all.'

Yet environment cannot account for the gulf between Jew and Christian in that age of common suffering. The rejection of the Son of God by the people of God is cruel fact. None the less, the Russian Church had received through St. Serafim, as well as through his predecessors and his followers, a lesson of charity which could reach to an understanding, though never a condoning of the deepest sin, by the knowledge of its own grievous fault. And there is another factor, closely joined to that charity, and in fact enabling it. The spirit of humility can so form the hearts and minds of those who truly seek it, as to bring them into a true acceptance of all their lives at the hands of God. They no longer entertain their own imperfect desires : no longer do they look wistfully after the forbidden good, or weigh their own hopes and fears. God is all, and in all, and in that knowledge they can rest. Here we are returning to the path shown by the Carmelite saints : here we find the understanding given to the Lady Julian : 'See! I am in all thing : how can anything be amiss?' Here, above all, we are allowed to watch the Mother of God in her miraculous acceptance of the Glory which was her Son, and to hear again her calm response to the Announcer : 'Be it unto me according to thy word.'

We have sought the course of the hidden life in those whom God has chosen for His own. It is a life in which too many of His children fall far short of His meaning for them. It is a life that we who are in Christ can never hope to live unless in His abiding Presence, in the enabling power of the Holy Spirit, and at last—if such may be even for us—in the grace of union with Himself and the Vision of His Beauty. And yet it is a life in which many who are separated from us, because from Him, have clearly understood and interpreted to us much of its expression and its discipline. That discipline remains to be learned in every place and age. The expression of the Sacrament of the present moment must be seen in us who would will one Will with Him; but it must also be evident and compelling to those vast numbers who seek to reshape the world He has given them, and to conform it to their own desires. For their sakes, above all, we are bidden to the suffering of intercession. For their sakes we must be consecrated in His Truth. And yet—'How can I come to Thee without these others?' Are we who have been brought by the only mercy of Christ, and called His own, likely to find that hidden life save in constant caring for these other children of the Father's Love? Silouan has told that 'I was consumed with longing for Him, and now day and night I seek Him with burning heart.'

St. John of the Cross expressed that same longing of the soul which suffers with impatience to see God. In one of his poems he chose words which echo so closely the mood of a Hasidic poem (T.H. I, 212) that they may stand as an Epilogue to this book, since they express the hidden life alike in its pain and in its joy :

'THIS LIFE I LIVE IN VITAL STRENGTH
IS LOSS OF LIFE UNLESS I WIN YOU :
AND THUS TO DIE I SHALL CONTINUE
UNTIL IN YOU I LIVE AT LENGTH.
LISTEN, MY GOD! MY LIFE IS IN YOU
THIS LIFE I DO NOT WANT, FOR I
AM DYING THAT I DO NOT DIE.' 202

NOTES

Ref. Page

1   11   H. L. Goudge: *The mind of St. Paul*, p. 120f.

CHAPTER ONE

2   17   James Stephens: *Cairbre's Harp* (from *The Bell-Branch*).
3   19   Thomas Merton: *Seeds of Contemplation*, p. 199f.
4   20   Charles Williams: *He came down from Heaven*, p. 19 (Faber, 1950).
5   21   Charles Williams: *Descent into Hell* (Faber, 1937).
6   21   C. S. Lewis: *That hideous strength*, p. 178f. (John Lane, 1945).
7   22   St. Teresa of Jesus: *The Interior Castle*, IV, 2.
8   22   ibid., VII, 4.

CHAPTER TWO

9   23   Duns Scotus: *Opus Oxoniense iii, 19*, tr. Westcott.
10   23   St. Thomas Aquinas: *Summa*, Ia, xliii, 1.
11   24   St. Irenaeus: *Adversus Haereses*, IV, 20, 7.
12   27   Guitton: *The Blessed Virgin*, p. 61f. (Burns, Oates, 1952).
13   28   Ruysbroeck: *The Spiritual Espousals*, II, 41, p. 169f., tr. Colledge (Faber & Faber).
14   28   Guitton: *The Blessed Virgin*, p. 51.
15   28   Pere de Caussade, s.j.: *Abandonment to Divine Providence*, I, Cap. 1, 1.
16   35   Bouyer: *The meaning of sacred Scripture*, pp. 244, 249 (Notre Dame University Press, 1958).
17   36   Hodges: *Christianity and the modern world-view*, p. 28f. (S.C.M. Press, 1949).
18   37   *Midrash Rabbah*, xliv, 17.
19   39   Bouyer: op. cit., p. 150f.
20   43   Pusey: *The minor prophets*, ad. loc.
21   43   St. Augustine: *Sermons on N.T.*, 81, para. 2.
22   45   For this concept cf. Charles Williams: *He came down from Heaven* and his novels, especially *Descent into Hell*.
23   45   cf. also Hooker: *Jesus and the Servant* (Lutterworth Press, 1958).
24   46   Wheeler Robinson: *The Cross of the Servant*, p. 86 (S.C.M. Press).
25   47   cf. Luthi: *The Church to come* (Hodder, 1939).
26   49   Scholem: *Major trends in Jewish Mysticism*, p. 123. (Schocken Books, Inc., New York, 3rd Edn. 1954.) The first reference to this work allows opportunity of sincere gratitude to its author, and of respect for a unique authority upon its subject. Even when one ventures to question some particular judgment, it is impossible for the Christian student to value too highly Prof. Scholem's help in his study.
27   49   Scholem: op. cit., p. 34.
28   49   Loewe and Montefiore: *A Rabbinic Anthology*, 690 (Macmillan).
29   49   Maimonides: *Hilkot Tefilleh*, 4, 16, tr. Cohen (Routledge).
30   49   Scholem, op. cit., 101, 275f.
31   49   Merton: *The Psalms are our Prayer*.
32   49   A. H. Small: *The Psalter and the life of prayer*, p. xvi (Foulis, 1914 (Peter Davies)).
33   50   Mowinckel: *He that cometh*, p. 202f.
34   51   *The Cloud of Unknowing*, Chap 3, ed. McCann (Orchard Books).
35   51   St. Bernard of Clairvaux: *De diligendo Deo*, xii, 34.
36   52   Small: op. cit., p. 30.
37   53   ibid., p. 27.
38   54   Oesterley: *A new approach to the Psalms*, p. 173 on Ps. 27.
39   56   *Revelations of Divine Love*, Chap. 11, ed. Warrack (Methuen).

Ref. Page

CHAPTER THREE
40 59 Mowinckel, op. cit., 202.
41 60 Buber: *Mamre*, pp. 116–18.
42 61 Bouyer: op. cit., p. 168.
43 62 ibid., p. 166.
44 63 Coke: *Ezekiel*, p. vi.
45 63 Scholem: *The Book of Splendour*, II, 63b (Schocken Books, New York).
46 64 Maimonides: *Pirke-ha-Hatslahah*, Responsa, II, 32, c. tr. Cohen.

CHAPTER FOUR
48 69 Moore: *Judaism*, Vol. I, p. 112.
49 71 Augustine: *De correptione et gratia*, Chap. 12 (33).
50 72 St. Teresa: *Interior Castle*, Mansion VI, Chap. 7: 8; cf. *Life*, Chap. 22: 9–11.
51 72 cf. *supra*, p. 65, R.A. 961.
52 75 Maritain: *Redeeming the Time* (Bles, 1944).
53 75 Shaw: *A pilgrim's Book of Prayers*, p. xiii (Mowbray, 1945).
54 77 Hoskyns: *The Fourth Gospel*, p. 255f.
55 77 cf. Davey: *The Jesus of St. John* (Lutterworth Press, 1958).
56 77 ibid., p. 112.
57 78 Hoskyns: op. cit., p. 424 on Jn. 12: 31.
58 78 Graef: *The Light and the Rainbow*, p. 117f. Longman, 1959).
59 84 Bouyer: op. cit., p. 151.
60 86 Abrahams: *Pharisaism and the Gospels*, Vol. II, p. 96 (C.U.P., 1924).
61 92 For the 'Jesus Prayer' reference may be made to *Unseen Warfare*, Chap. 51, tr. Palmer (Faber, 1952). Hayman: *Disciplines of the Spiritual Life*, p. 30f. (S.P.C.K., 1957). *The Invocation of the Holy Name* (St. Alban and St. Sergius, London).
62 95 Davey: op. cit.
63 98 Hoskyns: op. cit., p. 505.
64 103 Westcott: *The Gospel of St. John*, ad. loc.

CHAPTER FIVE
65 104 Hall: *Dogmatic Theology*, Vol. VII, p. 285f.
66 107 Buber: *Two types of faith*, p. 127f. (Routledge, 1951).
67 108 Andrew Young: *Nicodemus*. cit. Nicholson: *An Anthology of Modern Religious Verse* (Penguin Books).
68 113 Arintero: *The Mystical Evolution in the development and Vitality of the Church*, Vol. I, p. 87 (Herder Book Co.).
69 113 Barrett: *Romans*, p. 168 (Black 1957).
70 114 Dante: *Paradiso*, Canto, 14, 88–90.
71 115 Bouyer: op. cit., p. 154f.
72 117 ibid., p. 225.
73 117 Gore: *The Gospel of St. John*, p. 207.
74 117 Buber: op. cit., p. 129.

CHAPTER SIX
75 121 Moore: *Judaism*, Vol. II, 323.
76 122 *Jewish Encyclopaedia*, Vol. VIII, pp. 510ff.
77 123 Maimonides: *Yad-Melachim*, XI: 3f., tr. Cohen.
78 123 ibid., on *Mishnah: Introd. to Helek*.
79 123 Lukyn-Williams: *The Messiah*, p. 307.
80 124 Scholem: *Major Trends in Jewish Mysticism*, p. 330.
81 125 Klausner: *Jesus of Nazareth*, p. 413f. (Allen & Unwin, 1925).
82 125 Klausner: *From Jesus to Paul*, p. 466 (Allen & Unwin, 1939).
83 125 ibid.

NOTES

Ref. Page
84 125 ibid., pp. 297f., 438ff.
85 126 ibid., p. 526.
86 126 ibid., p. 545.
87 127 Buber: *Mamre*: The two centres of the Jewish Soul, p. 31 (O.U.P., Melbourne).

CHAPTER SEVEN
88 129 ibid., pp. 2–9 *passim.*
89 130 Abelson: *The Immanence of God in Rabbinical Literature,* p. 349 (Macmillan).
90 130 Bouyer: op. cit., p. 156f. (cf. also p. 210).
91 131 Abelson, op. cit., p. 286f.
92 132 Buber: *Tales of the Hasidim,* Vols. I and II (cited as TH). Vol. I, 124.
93 132 Mishnah: *Genesis Rabbah Vayetse,* 68, 9.
94 132 Bouyer: op. cit., pp. 106ff.
95 132 Scholem: op. cit., p. 19.
96 132 ibid., p. 31.
97 133 ibid., p. 18.
98 134 ibid., p. 101.
99 134 ibid., p. 81.
100 134 Baer: *Religious and Social Tendency of The Sefer Hasidim.*
101 135 cit. Scholem: op. cit., p. 95f.
102 136 Buber: TH, Vol. I, 4.
103 136 cit. Scholem: op. cit., p. 97f.
104 137 ibid., p. 99.
105 137 ibid., p. 108.
106 137 ibid., p. 116.
107 138 ibid., p. 118.
108 138 ibid., p. 19.
109 139 *Jewish Encyclopaedia,* Vol. II, p. 451f.
110 140 Buber: TH, Vol. II, 257.
111 141 Maimonides: *Yad Teshubah,* I, 1: 3; II, 1: 5, tr. Cohen (Routledge, 1927).
112 142 Scholem, op. cit., p. 144.

CHAPTER EIGHT
113 144 Bension: *The Zohar in Moslem and Christian Spain,* p. 4 (Routledge, 1932).
114 144 Scholem: op. cit., p. 203.
115 145 *Zohar* (Soncino Press, London, 5 vols.).
116 146 Scholem: op. cit., p. 214.
117 146 Bouyer: op. cit., p. 107.
118 146 Scholem: op. cit., pp. 214–17.
119 147 ibid., p. 230.
120 147 Bension: op. cit., p. 125f.
121 148 ibid., p. 180f.
122 149 ibid.
123 149 Buber: *Mamre,* p. 43.
124 151 Scholem: op. cit., p. 248f.
125 151 ibid., p. 262.
126 152 ibid., p. 273f.
127 153 Buber: TH, Vol. I, p. 179.
128 153 Scholem: op. cit., p. 274.
129 154 ibid., p. 276.
130 154 Sefer Halkutim: cit. Scholem, op. cit., p. 284.
131 154 Bouyer: op. cit., p. 138.
132 154 Scholem: op. cit., pp. 284ff.

Ref. Page

133 155 Abelson: *Immanence of God*, p. 366 (Macmillan).
134 155 Scholem: op. cit., p. 287f.
135 156 Midrash: *Tehillim*, tr. Buber.
136 156 Scholem: op. cit., p. 305f.

CHAPTER NINE

137 159 Bension: op. cit.
138 159 Scholem: op. cit, p. 343.
139 160 ibid., p. 334.
140 160 Buber: TH, Vol. II, p. 9.
141 161 Buber: *Mamre*, p. 69.
142 161 Buber: TH, Vol. II, p. 166.
143 161 ibid., p. 173.
144 161 ibid., p. 249.
145 161 Buber: TH, Vol. I, p. 3.
146 162 Buber: *Mamre*, p. 81.
147 162 ibid., p. 82.
148 163 ibid., p. 115.
149 163 Buber: TH, Vol. I, p. 51.
150 163 ibid., p. 107.
151 164 ibid., p. 169.
152 164 ibid., p. 267.
153 164 ibid., p. 17.
154 164 ibid., p. 99.
155 164 ibid., p. 243.
156 165 ibid., p. 312.
157 165 ibid., p. 124.
158 165 ibid., p. 275f.
159 165 ibid., p. 173.
160 166 ibid., p. 285.
161 166 ibid., p. 112.
162 166 ibid., p. 289.
163 166 Buber: TH, Vol. II, p. 86.
164 166 ibid., p. 137.
165 166 ibid., p. 137.
166 166 ibid., p. 205.
167 167 ibid., p. 256.

CHAPTER TEN

168 171 cf. *supra*, p. 86 (ref. 60).
169 174 *History of the Monks of Egypt*: Rufinus of Aquilegia, tr. Helen Waddell—*The Desert Fathers*, p. 76.
170 174 *Sayings of the Fathers*: Pelagius the Deacon, tr. Helen Waddell, op. cit., p. 111f.
171 174 ibid., p. 134.
172 175 ibid., p. 298f.
173 175 *Vitae patrum*, Book III, ibid., p. 196.
174 175 Augustine: *De civitate Dei*, XIX, 19.
175 175 The Blessed Jan van Ruysbroeck: *The seven steps of the ladder of spiritual love*, tr. Sherwood Taylor, pp. 58ff. (Dacre Press).
176 176 Merton: *The Waters of Silence*, pp. 19–21 (Hollis and Carter, 1950).
177 178 *Epistola ad fratres de Monte Dei*, II, 3: 15.
178 178 cf. *supra*, pp. 79ff. E. Gilson: *The Mystical Theology of Saint Bernard*, p. 123 (Sheed and Ward, 1940–55 ed.).
179 178 St. Mechtild of Hackborn: *Liber Specialis Gratiae*, I, 2: 1.
180 178 St. Gertrude the Great: *Revelations*, 6.
181 178 Blessed Angela of Foligno: *Life and Revelations*, ed. Hello, Chap. 21.

NOTES

Ref.	Page	
182	180	Meister Eckhardt: *In Johannem*, III, 1.
183	180	ibid., Sermones, VIII.
184	180	Farrer: *The Glass of Vision*, p. 28.
185	180	Eckhardt: *Spiritual Instructions*.
186	181	Jan van Ruysbroeck: *The Seven Steps of the Ladder of Spiritual Love*, tr. Sherwood-Taylor, p. 52 (Dacre Press).
187	181	ibid., pp. 55–9.
188	184	Thomas à Kempis: *De Imitatione Christi* (cf. Penguin Classics, L. 27).
189	186	*The Cloud of Unknowing*, ed. Underhill (Watkins, 1934) (cf. Penguin Classics, L. 108).
190	187	Hilton: *The Scale of Perfection* (Burns, Oates) (cf. Penguin Classics, L. 74).
191	188	Julian of Norwich: *Revelations of Divine Love*, ed. Warrack (Methuen (9th edn.), 1927).

CHAPTER ELEVEN

192	189	A Benedictine of Stanbrook Abbey: *Mediaeval mystical tradition and St. John of the Cross*, p. 14 (Newman Press, Westminster, Maryland, 1954).
193	189	*Complete Works of St. Teresa of Jesus*, ed. Allison Peers (Sheed and Ward, 3 vols., 1944–6).
194	189	*Complete Works of St. John of the Cross*, ed. Allison Peers (Burns, Oates, 3 vols., 1934–5).
195	190, 202	St. John of the Cross: *Poems*, tr. Roy Campbell (Penguin Books, L. 101).

CHAPTER TWELVE

196	204	Underhill: *Mysticism*, 15th edn., p. 323f. (Methuen, 1945).
197	205	Pere de Caussade, s.j.: *Abandonment to Divine Providence*, 3rd edn. (Catholic Records Press).
198	207	St. John of the Cross: *Ascent of Mount Carmel*, II, 5: 3, op. cit., Vol. I, p. 79f.
199	210	Iulia de Beausobre: *Flame in the Snow*, p. 13f. (Constable, 1945).
200	212	Fedotov: *A treasury of Russian Spirituality*, p. 245 (Sheed and Ward, 1952).
201	214	Sofrony: *The Undistorted Image*, p. 164 (Faith Press, 1958).
202	218	St. John of the Cross: *Poems*, p. 51 (cf. 195 *supra*).

INDEX

INDEX

PERFECTION
  Creation inherent in Divine, 17
  of Divine Joy, 17
  of Divine Obedience, 21
  of Divine relationships, 16
  of Divine Will, 17f.
  of humanity in Divine Purpose, 16
  of knowledge and contemplation, 18
  of unity, 18
PRAYER
  always in the Body, 52
  Hasidic Stress, 163, 165f.
  of Jesus, 78f, 81, 86, 92–5, 99f.
  Jewish and Christian linked, 65
  Jewish centres of, 34, 151, 153
  longing in, 218
  misconceptions of, 10, 204, 206
  and penitence, 92
  The Psalms as, 48
  Rabbinic counsel on, 62f.
  St. Serafim and, 211–13
  Temple devotion, 30, 32, 65
  St. Teresa on, 190–7
  Unseen Warfare and, 216
  wholeness of, 46–8
  of the will, 100
PSALMS, 48–58
  basis of worship, 48
  elements of, 50
  and history, 53
  Kingship in, 52
  meaning, 49
  protection, 55, 56
  praise, 51
  personal meaning and gospels, 57f.

QUIETISM
  beginnings in France, 203
  fallacies of, 204

RABBINIC TEACHING, ch. III, passim
  centrality of, 130
  immanence in, 131
  modified in Dispersion, 132
  R. Eleazar outstanding, 136f.
  R. Nahman and Hasidim, 160
REDEMPTION
  foreseen, 23, 24
  inherent in Divine Being, 24
  preparation of, ch. II, passim
  uniquely personal, 41
REJECTION OF MESSIAH
  causes, 121f.
  loss to the Church, 121
  respect due to Orthodox Judaism, 124
  relation to Eucharistic act, 123
  Resurrection charge, 124
  suffering of Messiah refused, 123
  and Zionism, 126

RELATIONSHIP
  and Being, 15, 18
  broken by the Adam, 20f.
  in Mystical Body, 16
  Mystery of, 15, 16, 19
  perfection of, 16, 18, 22
  in Trinity and Unity, 16
REVELATION
  and Being, 15
  and Divine prerogatives, 19
  and Unity, 15
RUYSBROECK: Jan Van
  and the Mixed Life, 175, 181

SABBATAI–ZEVI
  Antinomian delusions, 156
  Dr. Buber's judgment, 160
  and Jacob Frank, 157
  Scholem's judgment on, 157
  tragedy of false Messianism, 155–7
SAFARDIM, 134
  expulsion from Spain, 127
  influence of Neo-Platonism, 139
  linked with Ashkenazim in Luria, 151
  origin of name, 138
  revival in Safed, 143
SAFED—'Community of the Devout' at, 34
  and Bethel, 159
  Cordobers and, 151
  Luria and, 151
  danger of false Messianism, 155
  prayer life of, 153f.
  and Zohar, 149f.
SAMUEL
  as contemplative, 61
  parallel to Jesus, 70
  share in suffering, 41f.
SEFIROTH
  emanations of Divine Glory, 145f.
  suggested links with Fourth Gospel, 146
ST. SERAFIM OF SAROV, 210–13
  call to intercession, 211
  direct contact with Hasidim, 211
  prophet of the Holy Spirit, 212
  as Staretz, 210f.
  withdrawal and return, 211f.
SERVANT, 44–6
SHEKINAH, 65, 71, 117
  special Christian emphasis, 146
  transition to immanent thought, 131
  and Transfiguration, 84
  and transcendence, 131
  and Sefiroth, 146
  and Zohar, 147

Scriptural references throughout in Text.